NOT JUST A TOMBOY

D1079746

of related interest

To My Trans Sisters
Edited by Charlie Craggs
ISBN 978 1 78592 343 2
eISBN 978 1 78450 668 1

He's Always Been My Son
A Mother's Story about Raising Her Transgender Son
Janna Barkin
ISBN 978 1 78592 747 8
eISBN 978 1 78450 525 7

Straight Expectations
The Story of a Family in Transition
Peggy Cryden, LMFT
ISBN 978 1 78592 748 5
eISBN 978 1 78450 537 0

Transitioning Together
One Couple's Journey of Gender and Identity Discovery
Wenn B. Lawson and Beatrice M. Lawson
ISBN 978 1 78592 103 2
eISBN 978 1 78450 365 9

Trans Voices
Becoming Who You Are
Declan Henry
Foreword by Professor Stephen Whittle, OBE
Afterword by Jane Fae
ISBN 978 1 78592 240 4
eISBN 978 1 78450 520 2

Can I Tell You About Gender Diversity?
A Guide for Friends, Family and Professionals
CJ Atkinson
Illustrated by Olly Pike
ISBN 978 1 78592 105 6
eISBN 978 1 78450 367 3

The Trans Partner Handbook
A Guide for When Your Partner Transitions
Jo Green
ISBN 978 1 78592 227 5
eISBN 978 1 78450 503 5

Yes, You Are Trans Enough
My Transition from Self-Loathing to Self-Love
Mia Violet
ISBN 978 1 78592 315 9
eISBN 978 1 78450 628

NOT JUST A TOMBOY

A Trans Masculine Memoir

CASPAR J. BALDWIN

Jessica Kingsley *Publishers*
London and Philadelphia

First published in 2019
by Jessica Kingsley Publishers
73 Collier Street
London N1 9BE, UK
and
400 Market Street, Suite 400
Philadelphia, PA 19106, USA

www.jkp.com

Copyright © Caspar J. Baldwin 2019

All rights reserved. No part of this publication may be reproduced in any
material form (including photocopying, storing in any medium by electronic
means or transmitting) without the written permission of the copyright owner
except in accordance with the provisions of the law or under terms of a licence
issued in the UK by the Copyright Licensing Agency Ltd. www.cla.co.uk or in
overseas territories by the relevant reproduction rights organisation, for details
see www.ifrro.org. Applications for the copyright owner's written permission to
reproduce any part of this publication should be addressed to the publisher.

Warning: The doing of an unauthorised act in relation to a copyright work
may result in both a civil claim for damages and criminal prosecution.

Library of Congress Cataloging in Publication Data
A CIP catalog record for this book is available from the Library of Congress

British Library Cataloguing in Publication Data
A CIP catalogue record for this book is available from the British Library

ISBN 978 1 78592 463 7
eISBN 978 1 78450 845 6

Printed and bound in Great Britain

For my family and friends

CONTENTS

PART IV: BECOMING MY OWN MAN

ACKNOWLEDGEMENTS

I'd like to give special thanks to my family for their love, support and for not objecting to the writing of this book. It is not always easy to look back on things you may have said or done, especially if they do not reflect the view you now hold or the person you have grown to become. I would like to give thanks to Kat 'n' Dave, my oldest and greatest friends, with whom I've had and continue to have so many crazy experiences. What a quality childhood we had. Thanks also to the MedGen girls – Katy, Gemma, Kelly, Anne and Jess for getting me through difficult university days and for all the fun and laughter we continue to share. I'd also like to thank all the trans people and activists who suffered in the past so that I was even able to come out at all and complete the steps I needed to take. And, lastly, thanks to Jessica Kingsley Publishers for asking for trans masculine content and taking a chance on me.

PREFACE

I was scrolling idly through Twitter one day in early 2017 when I noticed a retweet by non-binary trans activist, Fox Fisher, from an editor at Jessica Kingsley Publishers giving a shout out for trans masculine content. I too had noticed how literature and public focus with regards to trans people seemed to be skewed towards the trans feminine perspective. Whilst that is certainly an important viewpoint, I had often wished there was more out there detailing the life perspective of trans men like myself. I was immediately intrigued by this open call, but hesitated to answer it, for I'm not exactly a trained writer. I'd taken another fork years ago and ended up with a PhD in medical science. But I'd never given up my love of writing and had seen it rekindled at my Grandma's funeral a few months before where I had given an emotional eulogy. I realised in the writing of that speech that I had walked again through memories of my early life I'd not visited for a long while and inevitably had come across things there about my struggle with my gender assignment that spoke to me anew, now that I could see them for what they really were. But still, I thought, I'm not a famous person, who would be interested in reading a book about my life? However, the more I thought about it the more I realised that a personal story is actually a very powerful thing. To see in another's story things you yourself have experienced is a profound experience and I remembered those days in my early self-awareness where I had trawled desperately through the Internet looking for accounts of life as I had experienced it. I had wanted kinship and the relief that comes with knowing I wasn't the only one. In truth, I had toyed with the idea of writing out my story a few months before, purely for my own self as a way of organising and working through the sometimes painful memories I had experienced that had got me to this point of transition and peace. It might be useful for my friends and family too, I thought, those people who had been unknowing players in this story themselves and who I really wanted to understand the real reasons behind some of the behaviours I had exhibited in days past. But now here was a call for trans masculine content such as personal stories for a wider audience, for people like me who might be casting around, as I had done, for stories in which they could see themselves reflected. I could make a good crack at it, I thought. Maybe this would be something I could do to help the community and contribute in the fight for full equality. It has been scary, exciting, painful and joyful to write out my story and I sincerely hope you, the reader, find it useful.

A WORD ON THE TITLE

It was difficult indeed to come up with a title for this book. In casting around my mind for one I kept coming back to the word I heard above all else in my childhood that was used to explain who I was – tomboy. Though not all trans boys exhibit such masculine associated traits, either as young children or later (I have no wish to erase feminine trans men), it is one of the key purposes of this book to spread further awareness into the world about the damage caused by fobbing off some young trans boys with the use of the tomboy label. It's not a label that I feel really belongs in the modern world, surely a better descriptor is just 'girls'. In the removal of gender stereotypes there is no place for a word that describes girls whose interests align with those regarded as for boys because those interests aren't actually 'for boys', they are for everyone. But I grew up with that label and with the fact it was falsely placed on me to account for who I was, for the deeply held knowledge I had that my body was wrong and that I was not a girl. Even now, where a trans girl who wishes to be outwardly feminine is often subject to distinct parental and societal distress, which can lead to an earlier awareness crisis; a trans boy is more likely to be given free rein to wear whatever clothes they please and play however they want. This phenomenon, of course, is a function of the greater desire and respect given to traditionally masculine traits and pursuits. But this can have the consequence of preventing trans boys from being able to be recognised for what they really are, both for themselves and others. I cannot count how many times in my 1990s childhood I heard, 'You're a tomboy, you're just a tomboy,' in response to my desperate attempts to convey, with the means I had available to me, the profound pain and aching I felt from knowing, however I knew it, that my body was wrong and I was not a girl of any description. But, since I had nothing else to go on, I had to dubiously accept that premise and the consequences were dear. As gender stereotypes are broken down and awareness of trans people grows ever greater, I hope the critical understanding of the difference between girls who like traditionally masculine things, and those who are not actually girls, prevents any more trans boys falling into the trap that held me for so many years.

Part I

TOO YOUNG TO UNDERSTAND

Chapter 1

LITTLE SISTER

IN THE BEGINNING

I was pulled into the world in the maternity wing of Watford General Hospital at 10.06 am on a roasting July day in 1989 in what my father has described as a quick and slick operation rivalled only by a Formula 1 pit stop. Like a particularly ugly brand of spider, I was all long limbs and little body, full term but only big enough for premature clothes that my father rushed off to buy having, this time, valiantly managed not to faint during the second such procedure he'd had to witness.

I am the last of my mother's two children and my father's four, his first two being from his previous marriage and already on their way into adulthood by the time I came screaming into the world. Like my father, my mother was 43 at the time of my birth. She had become a first time mum at 41, an 'elderly primate' as the medical staff had termed her, much to her displeasure. Having suffered pre-eclampsia and an emergency caesarean 22 months previously, she was calmed to find herself first on the list that July morning. My father too, having looked at the epidural needle and been duly revived with hot chocolate in the waiting room on that last occasion in 1987 and having been unwelcome in the delivery room in the 1960s, was determined to savour this, his last experience of the miracle of birth. They had opted not to 'know' before I was born. They wanted me to be a surprise, and a surprise I would be. Nanny's bet was well placed; that tiny pink dress had been the right decision. I was named Katie Roseanne, apparently because I looked like a rose when I was born, which is an achievement when you're covered in vernix. It had been a close call between Katie and Helen, but the latter had lost out after my Christian parents realised a potential shortening would be quite literally 'Hel'.

I can't help feeling that would have been a better choice, a better descriptor at least, for some of the feelings I was to experience in the years to come. 6lb 1oz, 51 cm, female. And that was that. I had been found wanting of the anatomy that would have seen me assigned correctly, kept my mind at peace, given me a blissful, carefree childhood and a confident adolescence. But, like everyone else in this heavily gendered society, I was given my identification bracelet and card, in my case branded with 'Female', and carted off down the pink paved path before I'd even opened my eyes.

Like many a caesarean new-born, my first few days were spent in the hospital and passed by with a veritable procession of visits by family and friends. Among the first were my much older half-brother Neil and his girlfriend Cathy. They have since married and had four children, who comprise four of my six nephews. All four of my already elderly grandparents lived to see the day of my birth, including my mother's parents, who stayed down from North Yorkshire for several weeks as my parents transitioned from the containable chaos of one small child to the total tornado of two. My father's parents, my Nanny and Grandad, lived in Ruislip and were also on hand to help as much as they could and were a presence throughout my early childhood until they died, within a year of each other, at the turn of the millennium. My mother's father would not live long enough for my memory to capture him, leaving him to exist for me only through photos and the many oil paintings he left behind. However, his wife, my fabulous Grandma, would go on for another 26 years until the complications of old age claimed her in 2017 at the age of 96. None ever saw me wholly for who I really am, with my Grandma the only one alive at the time of my transition. But dementia had taken too much from her by then to make it a kind or worthwhile prospect.

It was there on the maternity ward that I met my big brother for the first time. Almost two years older, bright platinum blonde and cherub-like but with brown eyes, not blue; master of penguin-style walking and two-word sentences; that was James. I was to be his playmate, his co-pilot, his rescuer from the life of an effective only child, the life Dad would rather not have had. Little sister, that was me, lying in my hospital basket with my pink cuddly bunny with its pink silky ribbon. I was not yet aware of the level of disdain I would come to attach to this designation and the anger and the yearning that would engulf it. As James stared down at me, I didn't know just how I would come to be both intensely glad and bitterly jealous of his existence. He has been my greatest protector and my greatest rival without really being aware of being either.

I was brought home in my ridiculously impractical classic Silver Cross Princess pram to a small house in Grove Road, Mill End, within the reasonable affluence of South Hertfordshire. This would soon serve as the reception location for my christening, pink cake and all, that photos would show surrounded by my grandparents, godparents and my one and only aunty, Sue. A formidable former matron in a cottage hospital, Aunty Sue lives in Yorkshire with her second husband, Ian, and is the mother of my only cousins, David and Josephine.

We didn't stay long in Grove Road; before I could remember it we had moved a couple of miles up the road to the house where I would spend the whole of my childhood, a nice semi-detached on the corner of a junction within a long and pleasant street. Worth more than perhaps it should have been due to its London commuter belt location, it was three bedrooms, two floors and one pedigree cat of classic English middle-class suburban comfort, wine rack in converted fireplace and all. Whilst we were not off cruising around the Aegean every summer holiday, I was never aware of the sanctity of money or was ever told I couldn't have something because we couldn't afford it.

Dad worked as a human insurance price comparison website before the first wave of the artificial intelligence (AI) revolution and is the sort of dependable and honest person who points out at the checkout that the lamp shade needs to be paid for separately to the lamp base. He is thoughtful and kind, but slightly buttoned-up in that way that makes it hard for him to discuss difficult topics. He hates drama and confrontation and reacts physically to stress, traits he has most definitely passed to me. By the time I came along he was an old hand at parenting and it showed: he seemed always to be in control and was the sort of dad whose presence in any situation meant you just knew everything was going to be fine. Mum on the other hand has a flair for the dramatic and for hosting perfectly planned dinner parties. She is small and huggable and not at all afraid of confrontation and saying what's on her mind. She is a former secretary and keep fit instructor, whose career ambitions were curtailed in her youth both by her terrible first marriage and the cultural misogyny of her schooling. She was a stay-at-home mum during my earliest years but went to college at 49 determined to fulfil her ambition of becoming a beauty and massage therapist. Smarter than her seemingly haphazard nature and lack of filter often makes her appear, she would go on to found and develop several beauty businesses, both alone and with others, and it is my belief that had she been afforded the opportunity to start earlier in life she could easily have developed a very successful spa empire.

So it was within this social and familial background that I came into the world. Classic and comfortable. Those are the words I have used to describe my childhood to the psychiatrists one meets on the quest to access transition-related medical care. Materially, I wanted for nothing (except an extravagant old-fashioned style rocking horse) and emotionally there was only ever love, happiness and stability. My parents never fought (in a manner that has made any lasting memories) and their marriage, as those of both sets of my grandparents, has endured for many happy decades to make the idea of divorce and the loss of love seem alien and strange. To put it another way, I experienced not one single iota of anything that could reasonably be classed as a trauma, not even close. I like to make this clear to those who assume being transgender comes as a result of such things, and there are still many who make this assumption.

CAPTURED

Babies are clean slates; when they are born we know almost nothing about them. I have felt the truth of this for myself recently, at the birth of my youngest nephew, James's son. As I held him in my arms, I couldn't help thinking, *'Who are you?'* There was absolutely everything about him waiting to be discovered and I couldn't wait. I think we assume too much about babies; as a case in point, within minutes of the first photos appearing on my phone, Mum was assigning each feature of his face to which side of the family, which exact relative even, she believed it came from. Although obviously the cutest and the very best that there has ever been, he just looked like a tiny baby to me. After all, I think it's pretty true what is said about Winston Churchill and all babies! The point is it generally takes time for traits to develop and unfold. For example, his hair was brown for the first few months, which had Mum assigning 'hair' to his mother's side of the family and then suddenly it turned a stunning shade of blonde, to make him look a carbon copy of the tiny child that was my brother, who first peered into my baby basket all those years ago.

However, the idea that you can tell what a person's gender identity is by looking at their genitals is the most powerful assumption of them all. Sex is defined as:

> The classification of a person as male or female. At birth, infants are assigned a sex, usually based on the appearance of their external anatomy. (This is what is written on their birth certificate.) A person's sex, however, is actually a combination of bodily characteristics including: chromosomes, hormones, internal and external reproductive organs, and secondary sex characteristics. (GLAAD Media Reference Guide –Transgender 2018)

However, gender identity is defined as:

> A person's internal, deeply held sense of their gender. For transgender people, their identity does not match the sex they were assigned at birth. Most people have a gender identity of man or woman (or boy or girl). For some people, their gender identity does not fit neatly into one of those two choices. (GLAAD Media Reference Guide –Transgender 2018)

Gender itself is defined by the World Health Organization as: 'The socially constructed characteristics of women and men – such as norms, roles and relationships of and between groups of women and men' (World Health Organization 2018). A person's gender identity is expressed through: 'a person's name, pronouns, clothing, haircut, behaviour, voice and/or body characteristics. Society identifies these cues as masculine and feminine, although what is considered masculine and feminine changes over time and varies by culture' (GLAAD Media Reference Guide –Transgender 2018).

The idea that you cannot tell what a person's gender identity is by looking at their genitals seems to be hard for a lot of people to wrap their heads around, but then, as I like to point out, so is quantum physics; this doesn't make it any less true, you might just have to try a little harder. But because the assigned sex = gender identity assumption is most often borne out in people's lived experience and in the general words used to describe both, it is never questioned or considered.

People often ask me, and I have often asked myself, when exactly I knew that my gender identity was not in sync with that which I was assigned at birth. The answer to that is not straightforward and is really best described as 'I always knew but I didn't know I knew' which makes people give me their confused face. It especially confuses people who have witnessed the rise of prominent examples of very young trans children, 'How do they know so young, if you weren't screaming "I am a boy" at age three, why did it take you until you were 25?' The answer to that, I believe, is a sad indictment of the social confusion over what gender really is and the damage this causes.

It is true, for some small trans children, particularly in recent times, the fact of their true gender identity is as clear to them as looking through pure water, where their mind screams it at them with the alarms of DEFCON 1 as soon as their brains have developed enough to process the concepts. These are the children who you may find subject to certain newspaper front pages as part of a hysterical fit about how four-year-olds are having a 'sex change' (they're not). These are the lucky children whose parents were wise enough to listen, to pause, to think and research instead of dismissing their child offhand for having some crazy childish fantasy. Sadly, many children will not loudly declare their feelings, some will already have learned it is not safe to say such things. They may try once or twice, discover through verbal and/or physical violence that it was not a good idea, and promptly never try again. But some trans children will not truly, not for a long time, be able to maintain a crystal clear fix on what it is that is troubling them about the way they are presented to the world, about why they want to wrinkle their nose at being called 'little sister'. It will be like a mental gnawing sensation or an itch or a throb that is set off every time gender is specifically mentioned. That was how it was for me and probably a lot of trans adults who grew up in earlier decades. This is not to say my concepts of gender and of my gender identity were not formed at the typical developmental time but, rather, I believe children like me are sadly caught very early in the net of the enormously powerful notion that your assigned sex *must* be the same as your gender identity. It would come to override all of my early attempts at self-questioning to find an explanation for the discomfort I felt in myself. This was the fundamental pillar of belief that, in those early years, raised a blockade in my mind that made me think I could go no further than *wish* I was a boy, and for years stamped on the critical realisation, 'I *am* a boy.'

Although I believe there may have been a time in my very very early childhood where I did make it to this realisation. In one of my earliest, most fleeting memories, from around my third year, shortly after having ceased being forced to wear a night nappy, I recall lying in my 'big girl bed' and stuffing a small cuddly toy down the front of my pants. Alone, under the cover of darkness, I tried to correct myself to the physical form I knew was associated with my gender identity. I had seen what I was missing from the other boy, my brother, as we bathed together before bedtime. As he enjoyed his status as older sibling and thus purveyor of the spot closest to the hot tap, I was more interested with what I could see beneath the water as the bubbles dispersed. I have a feeling I tried my stuffed toy correction attempt more than once in what I have come to realise was my very first experience of gender dysphoria – the hideous distress caused by having a gender identity at odds with that assigned to you. Perhaps I hoped and believed, with all the conviction of a child's magical imagination, that come morning my toy would have transformed into my missing piece.

This would mark the first of many a comparison I would make between myself and James that would form the basis of a special secret personal rivalry experienced only by me. It was a type of rivalry that went far beyond the usual pains of the older sibling/little sibling dynamic, which from my perspective included the injustices of being made to sit at the colder end of the bath and of not being able to reach or climb or run as far and of forever being forced to play as Luigi on Super Mario. No, this was deeper, so deep I knew that if he found out about it and used it against me in an argument I would not have been able to deal with the feelings it would invoke. The simple fact is he had everything I wanted but couldn't have, not ever. This was not something I wold inherit from him in time or could wait until I'd grown big enough to manage; this was something we would never share. Because assigned sex was everything that mattered, he was the *real* boy and I was just *pretend*. In this world we could both like blue but only I was meant to like pink. We could both love dinosaurs but only I was bought dolls. We could both love super soaker fights, but only I would be told I couldn't do it without a top on. And as we neared puberty it was only I who would fail to take the right exit and go sailing off into that most particular world of pain and suffering. This secret rivalry, these secret injustices of being his little *sister*, that began as soon as I was old enough to recognise that we were supposed to be in different gender categories, would come to surround our relationship from my end in every respect as I shall detail as my story goes on.

◇━◦━◦━━━◦━◦━◇

It could not have been long after my night time experiments with cuddly toy anatomy replacement that I was captured into the notion that because of my genitals I simply *must* be a girl and became enclosed within that concept, as people we met in the street with me in my pushchair, my brother hanging off one side, exclaimed to Mum how lucky she was to have 'one of each'. Indeed, looking back, it is clear that, by the time I was a child of five with a freckled grin and strawberry blonde bob cut hair, I had formed a clear idea of who I was meant to be in the eyes of the world and had buried that identity conviction I had once had. As far as I or anyone else could tell, in my family, as in a classic story book, there was one mum, one dad, one boy and one girl and that is what I would draw under the crayon yellow sun.

Chapter 2

THE TWELVE DOLLS OF CHRISTMAS

ON THE NAUGHTY LIST

I didn't want to seem ungrateful. The 'Around the Tree' present-opening ceremony was in full swing in the living room in the afternoon of this mid-1990s Christmas day. Nan and Grandad sat, as they always did, in twin armchairs pushed together so that I might sit between them on the combined arms and rest my back against the warmth of the wall radiator. Perpendicular to this were everyone else squashed onto the brown sofa that made up the other component of this most 1980s of three piece suites. Our little Christmas tree, decorated in the haphazard way befitting the design talents of two small children, stood on the largest of a set of three wooden coffee tables against the sliding patio door. Presents occurred in two phases during my childhood Christmases, the first phase being the 'Great Sack' stuffed with presents that miraculously appeared at the end of my bed following my failed attempts to stay awake, and which I would use all my strength to haul into my parents' bedroom to be ripped opened. The second phase, 'Around the Tree' did not take place until after lunch *and* after all the washing up had been accomplished, which had me sitting on my twitching hands in agony for what was quite literally hours, staring hungrily at the shiny wrapping paper. I was to be unimpressed with what 'Santa' had brought for me however. Dolls. As I unwrapped each present, with my family looking on, I came across doll after doll, some big, some small, some with multiple functions, some with matching accessories. Among them were several Barbies, stick thin and expressionless, a creepy baby whose eyes would roll back in its head when I tipped it upside down and another baby which doubled as a hot water bottle. There were 12 in total and they comprised practically all of the presents I received. I remember doing my best impression of unwanted present excitement, but inside I was upset and confused. How could anyone in my family think I would want dolls? In fact, not just any dolls, but proper baby dolls which were, in my mind, the absolute epitome of dolls. I had not asked for them and I did not want them. But, then again, why not? It was surely a reasonable assumption to make that a little girl would enjoy such a present at the age of six or seven, especially one who had what was considered by Dad to be an excessive amount of cuddly toys.

These inappropriate and damaging gender assumptions made about children's interests and the toys based on them is one of the most pressing issues in the current fight against the ironclad grip society has on the gender binary and rigid gender norms. These assumptions and the biases they create in adults are damaging to all children but, additionally, to trans children they can wreak terrible havoc, sowing confusion, guilt and shame as they try to make themselves conform to the ridiculous expectations and restrictions of gendered toys. Indeed, this was an issue that came to permeate my early childhood and my struggles to grasp what so bothered me about my gender designation.

GIRLS' TOYS

Given the heaving bin liners that still sit in my parents' upstairs storage area, I may have to admit that Dad was right about the cuddly toys. But like a lot of people, whether they choose to admit to it or not, I find myself loath to completely part with many of the things that brought so much joy to my childhood. I was the proud owner of a veritable menagerie of stuffed animals from rabbits and rams to cats and cheetahs, each one with a name and a life of its own. The most important of these was a grey and white striped cat, which was actually a hand puppet complete with sound box that once upon a time would meow three times when pressed. He was given to me after my fifth birthday party by my brother Neil, and I vividly recall opening him under the gazebo in the garden and falling instantly in love. For some inexplicable reason I named him (for I decided he was a 'him') Charlie Snuggles and he sits on my bed to this day. My cuddly toys were everything, I was the type of child who had to find space in their bed to lie down at night (good training for cat ownership) and my parents were constantly trying to come up with space saving solutions such as a canvas shoe rack which they hung from the ceiling in my room and stuffed with the smaller toys, including my beanie babies, which later on I sadly gave away before they became a valuable collector's item!

Charlie Snuggles's status as Best Toy was further heightened by the clothes I was able to buy and dress him in. This had come about by chance when visiting Windsor, where I discovered a small shop that sold cricket jumpers, backpacks, sunglasses, waistcoats and bow ties for teddy bears. They were expensive but over several trips I accumulated all of these items for my cuddly friend and took great delight dressing him in them for special occasions. My enjoyment from this was such that the jealousy was well and truly real when walking through aisle upon aisle of outfits at the Build-a-Bear shops that appeared in every shopping centre just too late for me to truly appreciate them. Charlie would sit with me as I played with my other toys like 1980s and '90s classic Polly Pocket, back when Polly was a half inch choking hazard (she since grew larger but was discontinued in 2015 – RIP Polly – until she was resurrected in 2018). Charlie would also help me play with the small collection of My Little Pony dolls I accumulated including a green one with orange headphones and purple roller skates that Google tells me was called 'Hip-Hop'. My friend Victoria, however, had the entire stable and I was always bursting with jealousy when playing over at her house. The jealousy was even more severe, though, whenever I encountered a proper rocking horse. My parents' elderly friend, Joan, had a beautiful one in her sitting room, but it was more for ornamental purposes and I had to seriously restrain myself when left alone with it. This is the one toy I was desperate for and never received, although looking back I can understand why; they were very expensive and there wasn't really anywhere to put it, alas!

Throughout my childhood I also loved art and making things and became proficient in a number of old school crafts such as weaving, for which I had a toy weaving loom that I had asked for after a memorable school lesson. I also had a child's sewing machine after being fascinated with my mum's and having learned to hand sew at Brownies, gaining several badges in it. Although sadly I never got the hang of the machine, and broke it within weeks, in fact I would go on to be banned from using the sewing machines in my secondary school textiles class after leaving a trail of destruction! However, the craft I loved the most was knitting, which I learned from my mum and my godmother, Suzanne, when I was around 7, although I never progressed past making scarves in only one colour.

BOYS' TOYS

My obsession with Jason the original red Mighty Morphin Power Ranger was really something. Few people my age will not remember this massively popular show that featured a group of 'teenagers with attitude' who were imbued with special powers to save the world from the monsters that would rain down upon it from the moon base of Rita Repulsa and Lord Z. Such was its popularity that it spawned a movie in 1995, the first that I ever remember seeing in a cinema, and indeed, another 'grown up' version was released in 2017, no doubt to capitalise once again on its original, now young adult, market (it worked – I own the DVD). As Red Ranger, Jason was an incredible martial artist, friend and leader; I was drawn to him like a moth to a flame and my Red Ranger action figure became one of my favourite toys. This interest overlapped with that in another red character, Captain Scarlet, which was one of the 'supermarionation' shows of the 1960s, the most famous of which was of course, *Thunderbirds*. The BBC re-aired the show in 1993 and I loved watching the indestructible Captain Scarlet battle the mysterious Mysterons of Mars and I had the action figure and the dressing up costume.

Clearly, I loved action figures, including arguably the best ones of all, the transformer type toys. The greatest one of these I had was a robot that turned into a sleek silver motorbike, which was more than a little bit responsible for my love of motorbikes, the flames of which were further fanned by my brother Neil's real life bike collection. I vividly recall loving every minute of sitting on one of his bikes for a photo opportunity and having to stretch as much as I could to be able to reach the handlebars. This love of action figures was complimented by my love of remote controlled things and the advent of *Robot Wars* in 1998 was a huge deal for me and I watched it religiously. I was an ardent fan of Chaos 2, from Team Chaos, who had the first robot to be able to do a self-righting flip and which routinely threw other robots out of the arena on its way to becoming champion.

Many of these interests I shared in one way or another with James. His interest in Power Rangers leaned more towards Tommy the Green/White Ranger and we spent many a fun Saturday morning pretending to go on missions as Tommy and Jason. Missions were a large theme of our play together and we would often dismantle and rebuild our bedding and the sofa cushions into aeroplanes and submarines. James's primary love was aeroplanes and piloting them and I was his plucky co-pilot, who was occasionally not so subtly annoyed at never being allowed in the 'main' seat, but we always managed to work well enough together to succeed in our heroic endeavours. We also shared a love of LEGO® and co-owned two large boxes full of the stuff that were the jumbled up remains of many sets. Whilst James preferred following the instructions to try to recreate the actual sets, I was more of a random builder (or master builder as I like to think), except when it came to the big medieval castle set that was my LEGO® pride and joy and which I refused to put into the big boxes. James and I also co-owned the world's greatest games console, the Super Nintendo Entertainment System or SNES. This was another present from Neil, who passed it down to us one Christmas, although only with two games, one of football in the days where the ball was literally a square, and the other the legendary Super Mario All-Stars, which we played so much I can probably complete it in my sleep and I know for a fact that the theme music still haunts my mother.

GIRLS' OR BOYS' TOYS?

It's pretty clear to see that my toy interests were fairly eclectic, covering a range of things from construction and action to creativity and empathic animism. This, I'm sure, is true of all children and yet society has seen fit to drive a wedge between children by categorising some interests and types of toys 'for boys' and others 'for girls', as I have demonstrated in the previous passages. People who try to defend this extraordinary divide do so largely on the grounds that it is driven by some innate differences in ability and interests between boys and girls, that girls are innately wired for empathic, caring and animistic play, whilst boys are naturally drawn more to action and construction. This is an argument that I think everyone will have heard many times throughout their lives – so much so that it has become one of those things that people simply deem to be true. But the evidence does not support this notion and whole books could be written deconstructing this myth. In fact, they have, such as *Delusions of Gender* by Cordelia Fine (2010), which is a book I wish was required reading for all new parents. Decades of research makes it clear that girls are not naturally better at empathy, caring and communication and boys are not naturally better at logic and engineering.

The apparent differences are down to the opportunities and reinforcements provided from the very moment of birth, if not by the parents, by the adverts, book characters, toy packaging and everything else the child encounters.

But trying to get people to step back and think harder about this belief is a serious challenge. I've had several conversations with people who are adamant that it's clear how naturally the little boys go for cars and building toys and the girls for dolls, some with people who say they were on the fence prior to having or being around children as to whether this was nature or nurture. But is it any wonder that little boys would choose a car or building blocks out of a toy box if that's all they've ever been surrounded with their whole lives? How many of these little boys have a baby doll at home? How many have been exposed to the notion that it's totally normal and OK for a boy to play with dolls? Cordelia Fine speaks of the unconscious gender biases that live inside all of us and that manifest everywhere. It's depressing but not surprising to see people failing to realise the extent of the influence of these biases on the development of children's behaviour. The BBC conducted a fine example of this in a recent social experiment documentary called *No More Boys and Girls*. In this, adults were given a range of toys and asked to play for a while with a toddler assumed to be a girl or a boy. Each of the results shown had the adult attempting to engage the child with toys defined for the assumed gender of the child and the adults were shocked and a little horrified to be told the child was actually not a girl or boy and to be forced to come face to face with the extent of their own unconscious biases; that they chose toys for the child based on what they thought would be or indeed, should be, the interests of a girl or boy. It is not hard to see that it was this, the idea that as a girl and as one who had shown interest in some 'girl' toys, I must therefore like all other appropriate girls' toys that led my extended family to see fit to give me so many dolls that memorable Christmas day.

In the face of this, it seems I was lucky to have been able to play as I did with such a wide range of toys. But as a person assigned female at birth I wonder how much of my exposure to the 'boy's' toys was down to having a big brother whose toys were either passed down to me or which I was allowed to share play with. Whilst my parents were not overly zealous disciples of the gender rules for toys, as in they did nothing to prevent it when I was in full on Red Ranger mode, they were as furnished as everyone else with those rules and had spent their lives surrounded with reinforcing messages. I wonder how many hours of LEGO® construction I would have partaken in if the two big boxes had not been bought in the first instance for James and I wonder, if James were not around, whether Neil would have decided to give me the Super Nintendo. This is one of the things that made me glad to have had a big brother; he was my guarantee for access to toys designated for boys. Of course, in the same vein I also wonder if I hadn't been assigned female whether I would have received Charlie Snuggles or been able to accumulate a mountain range of cuddly toys, which were also deeply important to me and allowed me to develop empathy and caring skills. The fact that in different circumstances I could have missed out on many of the things I held so dear is worrying and disheartening, but I fear it is the reality for many children.

I read on Twitter recently a thread by a lady (@boguspress) who had worked as a children's face painter and who had been approached by a little boy who wanted a butterfly on his face. This little boy's mother however point blank refused, and made her give him something 'for boys', a skull and crossbones. This is not an isolated incident, as the book *The Gender Agenda* (Ball and Miller 2017) makes clear. This is based on the Twitter diary of a couple documenting how their small boy and girl were treated so shockingly differently on the basis of their gender. I read it from start to finish with my jaw on the floor. It was poignant too, to witness in the BBC documentary *No More Boys and Girls* how the children experienced newfound joy when given a toy that wasn't designated to their gender category. One girl who had received a construction toy mentioned how she liked it so much she had asked her mum for some more and a boy, who was seen in the programme to be the archetypal rough play boy, expressed sincere enjoyment of his teddy-making craft project. It truly shows how damaging it is to pigeonhole children into one of two categories that cuts them off from discovering and developing interests with important skills that they are perfectly capable of developing. As many people have pointed out, we spend years telling girls through colour, packaging and marketing that construction toys are 'for boys' and then decide there are so few women in engineering because of innate differences. It's crazy.

I think I was lucky to have been born no later than I was. It is clear that my chances of being exposed to and bought 'boys' toys' was much higher than if I were born just a few years later. On the face of it this seems a strange thing, after all we like to think of ourselves as more enlightened than previous generations, yet looking back at advertisements of the 1970s such as those highlighted by the brilliant 'Let Toys Be Toys' campaign (Let Toys Be Toys 2018), the difference is startling. Old LEGO® adverts and pages from bygone Argos catalogues are much more likely to show boys and girls playing with the same toys. To see these contrasted with the pages and pages of pink products played with only by girls in more recent editions is shocking and depressing. LEGO®, which was once marketed to all people of all ages, is now considerably split between boy sets and girl sets, which are made clear by their pink packaging and stereotypical themes.

I wondered when exactly this had happened. I know that LEGO® had slipped into being seen more of a boys' toy by my childhood in the 1990s so that I was conscious that my interest in it was seen to be boyish. I also recall being astonished, through having my associations challenged, that Mum had an elderly client, a slightly eccentric German lady called Dorrit, whose house was filled with LEGO® builds and who regularly had neighbourhood children knocking on her door asking to come in and play. The 'Let Toys Be Toys' action group, who campaign to break down the extreme gendering of toys, say this and the extraordinary 'pinkification' of girls can be traced to the explosion in merchandising of Disney princesses in the 1990s and that has ratcheted up ever since. Disney, which had been in bad shape for several decades, hit upon a winning formula in the year of my birth with *The Little Mermaid* (Falk 2014) and with the mountain of merchandising that followed. From then on Disney princesses came thick and fast and were plastered all over everything, marking certain lunch boxes, stationary sets, backpacks and much more as most definitely 'for girls'. It certainly seems that the big increase in the creation of specific girl and boy versions began during my childhood, that most major brands had realised the serious profit to be had if you could make it so that girls and boys had to have their own versions bought instead of shared. Indeed, I can remember the creeping in of these girl versions and of being very conscious that my choices were not the ones I was meant to be making. The shaming that took place for going outside the pink boundary was all around, it stared down at me from billboards, haunted me in shopping centres and confronted me in the playground. It became a sore spot in my secret rivalry, when being given or buying anything, that James could easily have what he wanted but that I was forced to navigate through a perceptible mood of societal disapproval.

The issue appears to have got increasingly worse over the last 20 years, to the point I feel a lot of people around my age, many of whom are now parents to young children, have been made oblivious to the fact that there was ever another way. Because it is all my generation have ever really known, they believe, sometimes very strongly, that there have always been pink-girl and blue-boy versions of everything, that it's one of those long-standing traditional things and that to challenge it is some kind of new political correctness or some kind of radical LGBT agenda. As someone who was damaged by this culture, I am thankful it is now being challenged, people have woken up and realised the direct connection between the messages given to children in the gender rules of play and the inequalities for everyone that develop in later life, despite all the equality laws we now have. The 'Let Toys Be Toys' campaign has had great success at getting retailers to remove explicit signage stating certain toys are 'for girls' or 'for boys'. But more still needs to be done. I have recently returned to toy shops, as James has begun his own family, and have been confronted with the walls of pink and blue that still exist, albeit minus the signage. Continuing consumer pressure is helping to take down these walls and have toys displayed instead by type with advertising showing they are available to all children. This is not to say that there is no place for pink or blue. They should simply be part of a wider choice and in a world where anyone is allowed to like them, without stigma. After all, a hundred years ago pink was considered to be for boys and blue for girls (Boulton 2014), which excellently highlights how these rules are totally arbitrary and completely ridiculous.

MAKE BELIEVE

In my early childhood, my ownership and enjoyment of all those girls' toys and interests was obvious and sincere. What followed from this sincerity would be another of the dangerous and sad consequences of stereotypes and the great gender toy divide: because I liked some toys designated exclusively for girls, it blocked any realisation that I could really have a male gender identity. Such thinking would come to form another pillar in the maintenance of the notion that I, my family and the world at large, couldn't possibly be mistaken in the truth of who I was. And it didn't matter how many boys' toys I liked, the extreme aversion society has towards boys having *anything* to do with girls' items, which is far more explicit than the reciprocal, had taught me that the liking of even just one 'girl' toy meant I could only be a tomboy and nothing more.

Tomboy. I would come to hear that word over and over again in the years that followed the first time I heard it at the age of six from my Grandma on one of her visits as she measured me in my room for a new cardigan she was to knit. I was confused by what it was supposed to mean...tomboy?... Was it like tomcat? But she explained that it was the name for a girl who 'acted like a boy' and 'liked to do boy things'. I mulled it over in my mind as I stood with my arms outstretched, a tape measure going from shoulder to hand. I wasn't entirely sure I liked the word or the concept. On the one hand it felt good that people recognised what I liked doing but, on the other hand, it didn't feel right and made me feel fake in some way that I couldn't really describe, a fake boy and thus a fake girl. I shook my head to scatter these confusing thoughts and feelings away for I did not know what to make of them in that moment and that made me feel afraid.

The one place where, ironically, I could feel well and truly real, was in my imagination. Imaginative play is the joy of youth. Adults look back with fondness and long for the time their imagination was so vivid, so wild and free and without the constraint of self-consciousness that dulls it through maturity. I engaged in imaginative play as much as possible in my early childhood, both in and out of school and both with and without company. My very earliest imaginative escapades centred on the adventures of *Budgie the Little Helicopter*, the TV series created by the Duchess of York about a rescue helicopter in a similar vein to Thomas the tank engine. There was also SuperTed, the teddy bear with special powers, the first 'super hero' I ever loved. Either alone or with friends who came around to play, I would dress up in my cape and try to fly like SuperTed by jumping off my dresser, which eventually broke under the strain of being a launch pad.

I have already mentioned my sofa cushion aeroplane missions in the living room with James, which also took place in the local park in a gnarly old tree, whose branch structure greatly resembled that of a cockpit with two seats. We would fly all over the world dropping bombs, shooting down enemy planes, as James was obsessed with the world wars from a very young age and, as pilot, he was generally in charge of what the mission was going to be. As co-pilot, not only did I learn to say 'Messerspit' very early and discover what the exact differences were between a Hurricane and a Spitfire, I was in charge of shooting backwards from the tail of the plane. Like all good make believe co-pilots, I modelled myself on many of the brave airmen I had seen on the hours and hours of black and white war footage James would also watch.

The Power Rangers, on the other hand, were decidedly more colourful and after every episode James and I would be jumping about doing our best martial arts moves, which I'm sure influenced our mum's decision to take us down to the local kid's karate club. James was always Tommy the Green/White Ranger and as such he owned the super awesome White Ranger Legacy Saba sword, which had the face of a white tiger on the hilt and which I would steal from his cupboard and play with when he wasn't around. But my spirit ranger was always the Red Ranger, Jason, and it was as him that I karate kicked the stuffing out of the sofa. So obsessed was I with Jason that, given a free choice of a make believe character in many of the imaginative games my friends and I would play at each other's houses and in the school playground, I would choose to be him in some way, at the very least by using his name. This same pattern was replicated in other characters I would become in imaginative games, such as Disney favourites Robin Hood, Aladdin and Simba. Indeed, the only Disney princess I ever felt a real connection with was Pocahontas, whose forest freedom I found appealing. I never felt the desire to dress up as a classic princess, to be Belle of the ball, and my only great interest in going to the Disney shop in the Harlequin shopping centre (now Intu Watford) was not to acquire the latest princess gown but to throw myself into the mountain of cuddly toys that used to be on the shop floor before Health and Safety.

I felt good when I was being Robin Hood or SuperTed, or a co-pilot war hero or Jason the Red Ranger, like the world made sense, like I made sense. I had a confidence and a pride in myself that felt real and true. It wasn't just acting; it felt different to that, as if I was simply showing the version of myself that otherwise stayed in the background, like clothes at the back of the wardrobe, which there never seemed to be an appropriate time to wear. My desire to play as, to be, a boy character wasn't lost on me, it felt wrong to play a girl, like I wouldn't be able to do a good job. This drive was such that I would not have played at all if the game required or I was forced by others to be a girl character, to be someone even further away from who I really was. If James had insisted I was a lady co-pilot or I had to be Kimberly the Pink Ranger, I would have told him to stuff it. Similarly, if a friend said I had to play as Jasmine, not Aladdin, I would rather have been the magic carpet. It never came to this though, my friend Victoria, whose living room floor was covered in a grand rug that looked just like the magic carpet, was obsessed with being Jasmine and once, as soon as I had come through the door, launched into a speech about how she should get to be Jasmine. She needn't have bothered, but I was glad I didn't have to explain my lack of desire for that role. Though at the time I did not truly make this connection, the imaginary world was my refuge, where the problematic restraints of my real life in my sex designation and my liking of girls' toys, could be bypassed. So long as I was someone else, I could be myself.

◇━◦━◇━◦━◇

In a better world my liking of girls' or of boys' toys would have said nothing either to myself or to others about my gender identity and I would not have raised that particular blockade into place that further obscured my vision of the truth of who I was in my early childhood. I would not have bristled with anger of unknown origin over being directed towards the pink versions of every item and I would not have been made to feel odd or wrong for defying the status quo. I hope the campaigning against the extreme and artificial divide that permeates the toy world continues so that the future will be a better world for children to live without being so ridiculously and brutally split into two categories that do an injustice to boys, girls and to the many children who do not feel like either.

Part II

WHEN I WAS A BOY

Chapter 3

WEDDING DAY BLUES

INVITATION

Summer is the best time of year, so they say. As a child I was inclined to agree given the exquisite timing of my birthday slap bang in the middle of July, to be forever sandwiched between BBQs and bike rides, water fights and weddings. And it is the latter that jolts me into another memory. I am holding an old photograph, one I have shown several times to psychologists in both private and NHS gender clinics, of my mother, my brother and me standing in the luscious grounds of Moor Park Mansion as the daughter of my father's second cousin tied the knot during the early summer of 1998. My mother, in an act typical of her carefree haphazard nature, is not looking at the camera in the crucial moment but away over my brother's shoulder, probably at another lady's outfit, judging upon whether it was better or worse than her own white ensemble. My brother himself is grinning straight at the camera in the way he does, using his whole face, that makes his eyes look almost completely shut and that only serves to make his excruciatingly 1990s blonde bowl cut stand out even more against his dark blue shirt. My eyes turn last to the image of myself, forever burned into the film of this pre-digital age camera. Even now I find it hard to look myself in the eye. Because who is it that I see? I could not believe it the first time I rediscovered this photo post self-acceptance in 2011. Just as in classic ghost films, when the protagonist spots someone in an old attic picture they do not expect to see, chills went up my spine as I stared at this photograph and caught sight of the boy Caspar looking dead straight into the camera. Defiance, stubbornness, tolerance, frustration, it is amazing how one look can convey so many different things. I had not realised until then just how obvious my real identity had become during this later childhood period, how close to the surface it had forced itself despite the cage I had built over it and the magnitude of the mental gymnastics I played to keep myself functioning.

I try to cast my mind back to that captured moment, what was going through my head? But that particular information is too decayed and I am wary of trying to force memories to return. But emotional recollection is strong and it is with clarity that I feel now, as then, the anger, the embarrassment, the sadness, for I stood there on that manicured lawn in a navy blue cotton tennis dress, my 'compromise costume'. When we had received the invitation my mum had laid down the law, 'You are wearing a dress to this wedding,' she said in her not-up-for-debate voice. I moaned, I ran up the stairs, I slammed my bedroom door, but I was nine years old and this was happening whether I liked it or not. My parents picked their battles, they were content to let me choose what I wanted to wear on a daily basis, but special occasions were a line in the sand. In my heart I know Mum wanted me to look 'nice' and that, to her, looking nice meant conforming to gender clothing norms. But there was a part of my mind that knew her desire also came from a place that would mean she would not have to explain to every person she casually mingled with at the reception that I was not her second son.

As I stewed in my bedroom, staring at the pastel coloured balloon wallpaper, a growing part of me wanted to give in. After all, the more I thought about it, the more I realised I had not seen many of the expected guests for some time, probably since the last time I had worn a non-school uniform dress. That had been an even more special occasion; Nan and Granddad's diamond wedding anniversary. It was a big deal to the family and reminds me to this day that true love can last a lifetime.

A huge celebratory party was held at a function room in Ruislip, which even my grandma in Yorkshire came down to attend. I feel the familiar knotting in my stomach as I recall being herded through British Home Stores in search of a suitable outfit for my starring role as a poetry reader for which I would be richly rewarded with a cuddly toy Andrex puppy Nan had collected tokens for. At some point, as we passed manikin after manikin, I decided I would surprise Mum and put up no resistance to the notion of wearing a dress. I had never liked dresses, not just because they were specific attire for girls, but because of the serious restrictions they create. But there is a part of every child that is desperate to please their parents and at seven I knew the joy this act would bring Mum and Nan too, whose day I wanted to make special. A part of me was also oddly curious, what would it be like to be viewed as a girl, to try to be a normal girl? It had been such a long time since I'd made an attempt, maybe it would be different this time. Perhaps, if I practised, I would come to understand and maybe come to develop the mind-set I was so clearly missing, that the other girls just seemed to have.

So when she stopped in front of a yellow sleeveless dress with flowers patterned over it I nodded and said, 'I'll wear this one.' Mum beamed, 'Great!' she said, 'You can wear your white sandals and we'll get some matching yellow socks. Look it even comes with a straw sun hat!' I had not anticipated the straw sun hat. Standing at the bottom of the stairs on the big night, I knew I'd made a terrible mistake. My severe dislike of being viewed as a girl and of having this difference from James so manifested, threatened to overwhelm me with what was most definitely dysphoria. Oh, how my heart ached with jealousy as James came down the stairs in his blue shirt and awesome multi-coloured 'Joseph'-style waistcoat and there was me looking like some Easter version of the French cartoon schoolgirl 'Madeline'.

HAIR CUT AWAKENING

I knew it was this image of the little girl with strawberry blonde hair in yellow dress with sun hat that my extended family would be bringing with them to the wedding. Well, there was nothing I could do about the hair. It was gone, cut off at the back and sides, replaced with as 'masculine' a cut as I could manage, which turned out to be some kind of feathering effect, to soften it, in the words of Karen our home-visiting hairdresser. Quite unexpectedly, I had burst into floods of tears when Karen had put my hair to the chop as I sat on a kitchen stool. I had made a huge scene, crying and wailing all over the place and demanded in my childish way that she stuck it back on. I felt terribly sorry for Karen, who must have been mortified at my reaction and confused over my behaviour. What had brought this on? Was I not desperate to have it cut off? Had I not begged, demanded, threatened to cut it all off myself if I didn't get my way?

I had become increasingly disgusted with my feminine appearance in the years prior for reasons I could not consciously comprehend or explain. Hair is a powerful symbol of identity and *something* in me was railing hard against my bob cut. I wanted to be rid of this social signifier of girl-ness, I wanted to spike it up at the front like every boy band member prancing about on *Top of the Pops*, like my favourite footballers, actors and gladiators. But I broke as I saw my new reflection in Karen's handheld mirror. A massive surge of vulnerability shot through me like a geyser from deep within, taking me entirely off guard and overwhelming me so completely I lost total control. For the first time I could see my reflection as a boy staring back at me. And I wasn't ready. I wasn't ready for this realisation of who, of what, I was; I wasn't ready to face the tumultuous waves of conflicting emotions crashing over my mind. Like a wound that had been exposed too quickly, I wanted to cover this boy, *myself*, up again.

It had been coming to this point all my short life and all the while I had managed to remain just consciously oblivious enough to these feelings that arose and grew stronger every day, of the desire to play as a boy character, to appear as a boy, to wish my anatomy was different, to not be thought of as a girl. All of this had operated covertly, circumventing my mental blockades, like water creeping through cracks in a dam wall. But it had been discovered; my decision to have my hair cut had put a mirror to my truth and, finally, I had stared myself in the face. But I could not handle the consequences of this truth, the blockades still stood, breached though they were, and it was simply too contrary to everything the world had said to me about who or what I was supposed to be. Years of social messages would not let me go and they mauled at my brain, screaming at me that I could not really have seen what I had just seen. But I knew it in my heart that I *had* seen it and this contradiction broke me so because it defied any explanation I could give, like the physics beyond the event horizon of a black hole.

I cried and cried and cried as I ran up the stairs to stand on my parents' bed to look at my whole reflection in the long mirror on the front of the wardrobe door. Tears flowed down my face as I looked at myself and understood that I was not *just* a tomboy, as everyone had repeatedly told me I was. But it was an impossible thing. I searched in my mind for an answer, for some semblance of comfort, but I found none. The bare-faced truth was clear: there was nothing at all to be done about this situation, and the panic and fear of this began to knot in my stomach and I held onto the bedstead as a wave of dry retching overtook me. The pain of this forced me to make a huge effort to calm down and slow my breathing, to stop the flow of tears as I simultaneously tried to accept this truth and push it as far out of my consciousness as possible. How could I even try to square it with everything I had been taught about sex and gender? There were no counter examples, no images I had seen or people I had heard of that showed me there could ever be another way. And it was pointless and dangerous to fester away on something I had no hope to solve, so I made the decision to cage it deep, to hide it in the back of my mind and not think of it more.

I returned downstairs and Karen hesitantly suggested feathering the sides, assuring me it would make it look softer, more feminine, how it was all the rage among strong female role models. I said I felt a bit better with the final result, partly in an attempt to make it up to Karen and to appease Mum who was mortified at my 'rude' behaviour. But I went to bed that night both extremely anxious and deeply alarmed. Anxious about the reaction I would get the next day in the school playground and alarmed at this new state of being I had now entered. I went to school in the morning with a baseball hat on, which I was forced to take off in class where my teacher, sensing my nerves, made a big show of reassuring me I looked great, for which I was grateful. My friends were shocked and curious but no one looked into my eyes and saw what I was trying to hide, as I had worried.

Gradually, I strengthened the protective mental cage around the knowledge of my gender identity. I accepted it but it would remain an unsolved and unsolvable problem. So I did not poke it, allowing myself only the certain expression of it that I had started with my hair cut and I instigated a total ban on probing thoughts that tried to get me to examine how this knowledge could fit into the world. Over time, the more I saw myself, the easier it became to deal with the sight of my reflection whilst fending off the urge to ask the *forbidden questions*. My new appearance was just enough of a vent that it brought a certain peace and comfortableness in myself I had only experienced before in imaginary play.

But the complications of my gender expression were only just beginning and it wasn't long before I realised my appearance 'confused' people. Despite the attempts to feminise my short hair, my general boyish manner and clothes was seeing me clocked as male regularly and I learned for the first time in my life the truth that people see what they expect to see even in the presence of conflicting evidence. It is something that has been both an advantage and disadvantage over the years. Shopkeepers and people in the street I asked for the time all began to call me 'son' or 'young man'. Every time this happened my heart would give a jolt of joy; being seen as a boy began to feel wonderful and I soon began to crave it.

But it brought with it a new looming sense of awkwardness. When I was alone and it happened I could not help being overjoyed, I revelled in it and I found myself doing everything I could to affirm their assumption. But when I was with my parents, a horrible tension arose. I knew the 'error' would be met with a correction and I began to feel the weight of the surprised 'oh', the raising of the eyebrows, the second, more lingering, look. I wanted to shrink away from their gaze, to unsee the cogs spinning away in their mind searching to answer why I did not conform to their expectations; it made me squirm physically and mentally. Because of this, as much as I knew Mum didn't want to have to correct people at the wedding reception, I also knew I didn't want her to have to. I couldn't face so many awkward instances of backtracking in one day. It embarrassed me, I embarrassed me.

And that was a home truth right there. The way I was, a girl by every standard that seemed to matter, but compelled by my gender identity, which I could cage but not completely silence, to refute that in my expression, made me feel different, abnormal and seriously problematic. Why was I like this? What about puberty? How was this to end? These are the questions I worked the hardest not to ask myself. This was 1998 and whatever awareness punctuated the trans information vacuum of the time, it did not trickle down so far as to be perceptible to me. Google may have been taking its first cyber breaths but down in my nine-year-old sphere there were still no answers to those questions and the thousand more I kept locked away.

◆━━◇━━━◇━━◆

So I was faced with the dilemma. Give in to a dress and relive the burning dysphoria I had experienced the year before with the yellow dress or resist and feel my skin crawl as my parents called me out time and time again. It was Mum who came up with something of a compromising solution. A burgeoning tennis fan, it was she who, much to mine and James's displeasure, hogged the TV at the end of June every year for hour upon hour of Wimbledon. 'How about a sports dress,' she offered. 'Like the ones Venus and Serena Williams wear. They're not covered in frills and it would look very smart.' I mulled it over and reluctantly agreed on the proviso it was a 'masculine colour' instead of white. And that is how I came to stand on the immaculate lawn of Moor Park Mansion in a navy blue tennis dress staring down a camera lens. But from now on things would not be the same.

Chapter 4

SUMMER SECRETS

SECRET DENS AND SECRET NAMES

The last two years before the turn of the millennium contain some of my very best memories. This was, for me, that golden period of childhood wherein one is old enough to go out by oneself and with friends without adult guardianship and so adventure in an unencumbered and not altogether wise manner. It was also the first time, and indeed, for 20 years, the only time in my life I truly felt good about the way I looked and presented. But this ability was marked by a serious battle: to appease my need for personal peace, happiness and self-esteem, whilst keeping the identity I had locked away out of conscious reach.

The end of the 1990s was, from my perspective, a great time to be alive and to be a child. I suppose everyone is to a certain extent nostalgic and whimsical about the time of their own childhood (if it was sufficiently happy), but I do truly believe it. This was the time when gadgets had made life easy and comfortable, but was just before electronic devices and the Internet became all encompassing, when it was possible to have a childhood spent more outside than in and where absolutely no one in the group had a mobile that could be used to order you home from the woodland. It was not seemly to give children mobiles then and my friends and I would often go out without even a watch and only knew it was time to go home because it was getting dark or by stumbling upon a passing dog walker.

My house was in a long, standard suburban street but with the added bonus of a fairly large oval of grass in the middle, which we called 'the green' and which was the perfect size for a game of football. Going left from my house and across the end of the road was the local park, technically named King George V Playing Fields, which was used for local league games and which had a fenced off children's play area in one corner, the one I used to play in with James in earlier days. At the far end of the playing fields was an entrance into a large farmer's cornfield that we would occasionally run through (Theresa May has nothing on me) towards a motorway that marked the border of our roam. Going right from my house to the other end of the street, and walking a few yards to the right from there, were two small fields on opposite sides of the road with trees and bushes around the edges. A small road into a block of flats down a hill cut one of the fields in half and the one across the road lay just before a school, St John's Catholic primary, and my own school, St Peter's Church of England (C of E), was opposite to this on the adjacent side of the field. It was in the thickets that surrounded these fields that we made our secret dens, numbering three in total. The primary one was named 'Kat's den' after my friend, who first discovered it and lay just before the road into the block of flats. The second was in the far corner of the field and called 'the treehouse den', which we visited less often and the last den was in the field opposite. Called 'the thorny den' it stretched the entire length of the back of the field and consisted of a mass of overgrown thorn bushes that mangled together along the fence that bordered off St John's School. We went there rarely, usually spending a couple of days of hard labour in spring and summer hacking a path through the thorny branches so that it was possible to run all the way through. When not at these dens we could be found skateboarding down the footpath on Coombe Hill or attempting to 'break' into each other's houses by climbing through open upstairs windows or building nuclear war bunkers in the back garden.

The 'we' of these crazy childhood exploits were principally myself and my best friends Katrina and David or Kat 'n' Dave, who I have known for most of my life. Dave lived in the same street as me with his mum, older sister Susan and Jack Russell terrier, Spot, at the end closest to King George V Playing Fields while Kat's house was in a street off the other end of mine and backed onto the field that contained the den of her name. She lived there with her mum and dad, Debbie and Steve, little sister Arianne and dogs Rufus, Hector and then, later, Buffy, a German Shepherd/Collie cross whose daily walks often consisted of joining us on our outside shenanigans.

Kat is most aptly described as a free-spirited person, who even from the earliest days has had a somewhat unnervingly lax attitude towards danger and disapproval that has allowed her to dare have a lot of interesting adventures. I have always been admiring of this and I know my worry of potential disaster means I wouldn't have had anywhere near as many crazy and hilarious life experiences if it wasn't for her. Among shared interests, I think we also gravitated together through some innate understanding of our differences to the rules of the heteronormative, cisgender world. She too was classified as tomboy and lived as I did, expressing gender in a manner confusing to others. Today she identifies outside the binary and lives in Brighton with her girlfriend and occasionally performs as a drag king.

Dave has always given off a teddy bearish vibe to me in both his kind-hearted nature and huggable physicality. He too had a penchant for creating crazy exploits but it's fair to say he was better at the planning than Kat ever was. On the face of things, he is the most normative of all of us, in that he now has twins with his wife, though, purely on the basis of his friendship with two 'girls', both mine and Kat's mums thought he would turn out to be gay. But he has never been a slave to masculine expectations and remains among the best men I know.

We were at those dens most days after school and through the summer holidays, either just us three or with many of our other friends, most of whom were our classmates at St Peter's. There we would spend hours playing the game of 'manhunt' around the fields or building huts in the den out of branches held together by nothing but luck and old bits of string and which had roofs thatched with old leaves and twigs to such high quality (if I do say so myself) they were practically watertight and which we would sit in when it rained. There was also a large tree just outside this den that, fancying ourselves as expert climbers, we would climb every time we were there and which I'm sure is still scarred with the carvings we made on it right at the very top.

There was also a much smaller, more horizontal and haggard old tree on the field where the thorny den was. It was here one afternoon that I first gave myself a different name out loud. Kat 'n' Dave and several of our friends were there, hanging out idly on the poor old branches, when the conversation turned to what we would have been called if we had been born 'the opposite sex'. I listened intently to the others whilst trying to think about what I would say. This was a topic I both loved and hated to think about. It pained me to dwell on 'the alternative' but I found myself almost morbidly drawn to musing upon who I could have been in some kind of parallel universe. I hesitated from joining in because I knew what, in all likelihood, I would have been called: Richard or Stuart, and I was not at all impressed with these choices. Mum and I strongly disagree on names and I wanted my name to be something cooler and less common and I had decided in my head that parallel universe me was called Jake. In an occasional weak moment I allowed myself to think about being Jake, which segued into acting as though I *was* Jake for a few minutes before I snapped out of it and berated myself, as I was doing in the exact moment I was brought into the conversation by my friend, Natalie. But despite some inkling of better judgement I couldn't help myself, as if saying it outside my head would make it more legitimate, more real, 'I would have been called Jake,' I responded. It was exceedingly unlikely that they would know I was lying but even so my heart pounded a little bit at the risk and at the thrill of sounding out loud a snippet of a secret thought. My friends didn't know then that, in that moment, the identity I kept under lock and key in the back of my mind was trying this name on for size. I realised I suddenly felt a bit sick, it was a violation of my rules and, as ever, the mental strain of keeping the issue away from my conscious thoughts made me feel nauseous. As I had learnt to do in these dicey moments, I endeavoured to change the subject.

A TOMBOY LIKE ME

In the very height of summer when the shining sun made it just about warm enough, Kat 'n' Dave and I would leave our dens and venture further down beyond our school to the back entrance of the Rickmansworth Aquadrome. There were several rivers here dotted all over with swans and herons and a couple of lakes, which were the water-filled remains of the holes created when gravel was taken to build the original Wembley stadium. In the first river, small and shallow, we would wade up to our knees in search of oysters and practised catching minnows with our bare hands. We would also make mud pies from the riverbed sludge and launch them on stick catapults at each other across the small bridge.

The second river was wider and deeper and was traversed by a tall metal bridge. This river was deep enough to submerge our whole bodies in and we would do so whilst still wearing our regular clothes and then lie on the bank drying in the heat. Sometimes we would bring my yellow inflatable dinghy and paddle a little way upstream, daring only once to go so far as to not feel the bottom with our long stick before freaking ourselves out and opting instead to tie the dingy to the bridge and float around eating the sweets we intended for our voyage, much to the amusement of passers-by.

Oftentimes, we would walk or cycle the mile or so home whilst still at least partly wet and then try to sneak past our parents before they noticed our river-sodden clothes. I would rinse mine out in the bath and hope Mum wouldn't ask questions. But of course she did, though, to my relief, she was rather relaxed about the whole idea. 'You're like "Swallows and Amazons" or the "Famous Five",' she laughed. I knew what she was really getting at with this. I always felt ambivalent towards the Famous Five books, which had long been terribly dated in certain areas, particularly in attitudes towards girls and boys, with George constantly striving to be seen to be a boy as if boys were superior. It irritated me to be compared to her partly because of that outlook and partly because I suspected I wasn't a tomboy like George was a tomboy. In weaker moments, like the ones that allowed me to act being Jake, I scoured those books for any hint that George's feelings went far deeper than that, but it was never made clear and I would wonder what became of George in her fictional adulthood and felt oddly let down after learning that Enid Blyton had based the character on herself in childhood, which to my mind put paid to any notion that George was really like me. As far as I ever looked into the possibilities of my own future, the presence of that cage in my mind meant I knew for sure that, unlike them, *I* would never shrug off the extreme gender non-conformity of my youth.

I began to think in this manner about Kat too. Of all the girls in our class and in other classes in the school and in the neighbourhood, she was the only one I knew who seemed to be different in a similar way to me. She too had short hair, which she had cut soon after I did, and we wore the same clothes (sometimes exactly the same) and shared the same style of behaviour. Sometimes I would find myself trying to examine if Kat was a tomboy like I was a tomboy. Did she too have within her a secret she tried hard to keep as much away from herself as from others? There was no way to ask without confronting my own secret and at any rate I didn't have the words. But knowing Kat as well as I did I was sure she too would not, as adults all arounds us would smile and suggest, reach the age of thirteen and suddenly *blossom*. I felt comforted by this knowledge and glad for the good fortune of having such a person in my life and, whatever her own truth, she made me feel less completely alone.

A FOOTBALL OUTING

Later in the evenings, after having arrived home for dinner, I would join James on the green along with some of the other boys who lived around its perimeter for a game of football. I always liked football and always deeply loathed the notion that girls were rubbish at it for some innate reason. It seemed pretty logical to me that the group failure of girls in this area was entirely down to practice. Being a decent player was important to me and I gave as good as I got on that green and developed into a pretty good left-footed player that earned me respect. However, it was a long time before I played for a proper team. James on the other hand begun playing for Chorleywood at seven or eight and, at least in the first few years, I went, sometimes begrudgingly, sometimes willingly, to watch him play. Part of me wanted to be on the team too, or I guessed, the one for younger kids, but there were absolutely no girls to be seen on any of the pitches and I assumed that I wouldn't be allowed.

I did however, participate in a football training camp one summer holiday when I was ten. James was there too, but in a higher age group, and so I joined my group without protection. James and I were not the best participants in summer club activities and such organised fun. We much preferred to be free range and on foreign holidays would flat out refuse to join hotel kids' clubs. But there were summer days when our mum needed some peace and so football camp it was. I was extremely nervous, both about whether I would be good enough and the awkwardness of my gender presentation in this group with no obvious girls. I hoped that I could just get away with the assumption I knew they were all making. We did a couple of warm-up activities to begin, during which I was pleased to assess myself as one of the best in the group and my anxiety eased. But then the trainers gathered us together and suggested we go around the group and say our names by way of introduction and because communication in a football game is important. My heart rate ratcheted up several levels. I loathed these situations with every fibre of my being but there was no way I could get out of it. I had to make a choice, Katie or Jake? I could go with the truth or I could go with the lie. But what was the truth and what was the lie? I could not say and the nausea enveloped me again. I fought to think logically for a moment and I realised I really had to go with the paperwork. I had seen that one of the trainers had at least glanced at the registration sheet he'd been handed and I couldn't be sure he wasn't expecting to hear what I was meant to say. And so I said it, in as strong and confident a voice as I could muster.

At once I saw the eyebrows go up and the jaws go down and I could feel a dozen pairs of eyes search me afresh, a dozen voices murmuring to each other. I tried to look straight ahead and act as though I was oblivious to the awkwardness while willing my heart to go back to my chest. The next kid finally said his name and the moment was over but I was left feeling completely upset. Now I was going to spend the day being viewed with different eyes, thinking if they were wondering why I looked the way I did, why I was so much more extreme than other 'sporty girls', wondering if they were secretly laughing at me for being this odd fake boy that had fooled them so and I could feel myself retreat into my anxious shell. It could have been different, I could have spent the whole day being thought of as a real boy and that buried part of me was angry about losing such a rich opportunity to escape the cage. But I was also consciously relieved I didn't have to find out if I could stand the stress of subverting my mental rules for such a long time or of worrying about being found out by paperwork. Above all, I just wished I didn't feel any of this, I just wished this wasn't how I had to live my life.

WHAT HAPPENS IN VEGAS STAYS IN VEGAS

Despite what this subheading might suggest, my family actually never went anywhere as crazy and happening as Vegas on our annual summer holiday. I am a proud child of caravan holidays, which is the best time in life to go caravanning given that you are too young to be responsible for emptying the chemical toilet.

We caravanned all over the Scottish Highlands and rural Wales throughout my childhood in our small Marauder touring caravan, which was old even then, a family heirloom having been passed down from my grandparents and aunt. But I loved it; the smallness made it extremely cosy and the lack of amenities present in more modern caravans meant our holidays had much more close-to-nature vibes than caravanning in recent years. On every holiday, James and I would take our bikes and roam the campsites before and after the days outing to local attractions. There was also often a play area on site and we would check this out and meet some of the other caravan kids. As the years went by and I approached my first decade, these holidays would come to be another opportunity for my secret self to escape into the outside world; after all, holidays are about escaping your real life and it would be so easy to let that secret part slip out to people who didn't know me and whom I would never see again. In the face of this, as time went on, I found myself weaker and weaker in the fight to resist the urge to allow it, which grew as strong as I grew weak, overwhelming the protestation of my rules and inevitably, I lost the battle.

The first time was one holiday in Wales, somewhere near Snowdonia, where we were staying on a beautiful site surrounded by forest covered hills. In one corner of the small field was a little children's play area containing a tall plastic treehouse with a green and yellow 'gingerbread'-style house roof and I spent hours lying on a plastic tree branch chilling in the tranquil open air. Most of the time I was up there alone but this time James had come too, lying on the branch on the other side of the roof. After a while I came around from a lazy daydream to see a small girl from a family who had just arrived coming up to the treehouse. It quickly transpired she was very precocious and extroverted and she wasted no time in introducing herself and bombarding us with questions about who we were, how long we had been on the site and what we thought of the area. I answered the latter two types of questions, hoping that my efforts to engage her in those topics might steer her away from the first but this was a vain hope, she was absolutely insistent that I tell her my name and I could think of no good reason to withhold such simple and normal information. I raced through my internal deliberations upon that subject but came to an abrupt halt when, through her continued chatter, she made it clear she had assumed I was a boy. In an instant my feeble attempt to think I should oppose this assertion crumbled into dust. But James was there and I didn't know what to do but sit there grasping the plastic branch with every last drop of my grip force. It felt like I was watching a train crash in slow motion. But he did not give me away. My heart seemed to give a great leap and I almost spoke the words I wanted to say. But I hesitated with them on my lips, with the sudden thought I did not want James to think I'd given this a lot, or indeed, any thought. And so, rather awkwardly, I told her I didn't want to tell her my name, instead she should guess it, like it was a game.

It was best to remain still upon the plastic tree branch. Adrenaline had just shot through my body and I was afraid I might lose my grip in a moment of panic. The girl, on the other hand, had accepted my proffered game, odd as it was, with enthusiasm and had already begun reeling off potential names. James seemed amused and my panic subsided as I realised he really was going to go along with this. I launched myself wholeheartedly into her attempts with an animation borne of relief and of a strange kind of unbridled joy at being *seen* by someone else, a person who existed in the real world. Though I knew this was just for now, just holiday escapism that I could have no hope of taking back to my usual life, I could not contain the sheer happiness I felt. Fortunately, before she ran out of names, I heard Mum shouting over the field that dinner was ready and we were to come now. I jumped down quickly from too great a height in my desire to be away from the situation before it could unravel and hurt my ankle slightly, but I adrenaline-ran ahead of James out of the gate and down the hill. 'We should give you a name,' James said, as we were halfway across the field. 'How about Josh?' he offered. 'Hmmm, Jake,' I said feigning as though this was my first time deliberating upon the subject, 'It's cooler.' *'Why was he so fine with this?'* I wondered. I could only think he really did just think it was funny, confusing and fooling the girl. And what was the harm in it; it just was a fun game between us and her, our little holiday in-joke. He didn't know the tumult of emotions the episode had caused me, so much so that I felt exhausted when we reached the caravan. It was a game for him. But it wasn't a game for me and I filed away another piece of secret jealousy.

Over the next few days I thought more about James's response, the fact that he had found it funny instead of weird and that he had not ruined it. Perhaps it was because he was well used to me appearing as I did, he was no stranger to my style, to my behaviour, to how unlike other girls I was. He had lived it as long as I had after all, sharing his toys, handing down his bikes and his clothes. I usually tried not to think about what James thought of me, it filled me with too much jealousy, but it was nice to realise he didn't think me so bizarre as to out me. However, it was much more shocking to experience Dad doing the same.

As fun as caravanning was, there were some perks of civilisation that were a wrench to be without. The lack of running water was a real irritation, as fun as it was to roll the barrel of water around the fields on the way back from the tap. It meant the washing up almost always had to be packed up and taken to the communal sinks on site and every other night I was dispatched to be the accompanying drying-up child. Though generally relaxed about what I wore and how I behaved, not in day-to-day life casting themselves as gender police within our home, my parents had never allowed the assumption of my gender by others to go unchallenged. It was astonishing then to experience this one evening at the washing up sinks. When Dad and I arrived, there was already a man there halfway through his box. He looked up at us and gave a friendly smile. 'The boys' turn tonight, is it?' he said. As always, the ice-cold sinking feeling washed over me, which was the sign I was automatically shutting out the outside world to weather the oncoming storm of awkwardness and embarrassment. And it came, but in a totally different form that I no preparation for. Instead, after a small pause, I heard my dad, in a quiet voice, say, 'Yes.'

I dared not look at him or at the man, putting all my effort and attention into unpacking our box and turning on the water to drown out the noise, both outside and inside my head. This was a different kind of feeling, I did not usually perceive my parents to be embarrassed when they corrected others over my gender, more irritated or apologetic, but now I felt like this situation had made Dad feel that way and that, for the first time, he didn't want to go into *it* with this stranger and I felt awkward because Dad had felt awkward because of my way of being. But I also felt again the unbridled joy of spending a few moments in the company of another who believed in the authenticity of my caged identity. There was joy too for the fact Dad had spared me the usual outcome and it had showed me he could deal with me being thought a boy, even just for a few moments, and this would be crucial knowledge that steadied my courage in years to come.

◇━◦━◦━◦━◇

These days of my childhood have stayed with me in great clarity, no doubt because I think of them so often. They were wild and happy days as any childhood days should be. But I cannot help to feel the sorrow of all those times my gender problem was thrown into the foreground of my life, complicating even the simplest of things. I have often wished I could go back and have those days again, not just for the usual reasons of carefree life and the exuberance of youth, but because, as glorious as they were, they were marred with a profound worry that other children did not have to bear. The desire to give life to Jake that grew from thought, to word to deed meant this time was the closest in 25 years that I came to being myself. But the mental and physical stress of this forbidden activity, framed as it was in my mind as a lie but not a lie, as a wrongness that made me feel so right, was always there, like a dark fog looming over my back. It placed a cloud over my carefree childhood that I could never hope to escape.

Chapter 5

GIRLS' TROUSERS TOMORROW PLEASE

ST PETER'S

Of course, my experiences outside of school are just one part of the story. A child spends a great deal of time inside the four walls of a classroom, learning far more than just the national curriculum. What I would learned about gender during my schoolroom years, from its uniform requirements to its use as an easy group divider, would cause its own waves of unnecessary confusion, anger and sorrow that blighted my otherwise excellent school days.

St Peter's C of E in Rickmansworth was a very good school. It was a classic primary, with only one class of 30 or so children per year group. It was old too, very old, the original main building having been built in the 1800s, along with the grand stone church that stood on the edge of the school playing field. This original building had been converted into the dining room and library long before I arrived there in 1994, but you could still make out the hooks and pulleys on the walls where curtains had once hung to separate the space into separate class areas. By my time, what hung in their place on one wall was a large ornate wooden board listing the names of all the old boys who had given their lives in both world wars, and I would eat my lunch thinking about them and the hundreds of children who had gone through this building over the years.

The newer part of the school centred on the main square hall which was covered in parquet flooring where we would sit in rows facing a small theatre-style stage. The classrooms were situated off the corners of the hall, either directly or down small corridors. The school also had its own nursery and two playgrounds, one for the infants and one for the older years, as well as a sizable rectangular playing field lined with old trees. The church was considered a part of the school as much as it was a parish church and was presided over by a tall, bespectacled man called Father Alan, with a ring of white hair, who used to swing incense in an alarming manner when we went up for services on specific religious occasions. For a time there were also a couple of actual monks who wore black robes tied with knotted rope and who would give us assemblies filled with moral stories. Otherwise, as is usual, the school staff consisted almost entirely of female teachers and support workers, save for one man, Mr Budd, who took me for years 4 and 5 (ages 8–9 and 9–10) and is for me that one teacher whose example stays with you for life.

I was always a reasonably well-behaved child who maintained a good balance of focus on work and messing around with friends. But I was never in any serious trouble and scored between average and above average in every subject. Kat 'n' Dave were in my class of course, but I seem to recall that in every classroom, and for most subjects, we were placed on separate tables, probably for our own good, but, ever resourceful, we developed our own catalogue of hand signals that allowed us to share jokes across the room! I liked school from the beginning, particularly the fact that we got to play for the whole afternoon in Reception (ages 4–5). But the tone changed sharply when I entered Year 1 (ages 5–6) with the foreboding Mrs Thomas. She was an old-style teacher who had clearly been one for decades, given her age, and who commanded a lot of respect, although some of this was gathered by preying on the fears of small children, such as telling us she had eyes in the back of her head to watch us constantly, which made me feel like I was under constant surveillance. She would also scare me near senseless with the declaration that the headmistress, Mrs King, would bite my legs off if I did not read well enough to her during the Year 1 reading assessment she conducted in her office. I cried the whole way down the corridor. I believed in this possibility partly because Mrs King herself maintained a frightening persona that made nobody want to be sent to her office or spend much time in her presence.

One of the most useful things about James being in the year above was that I could get an appraisal of the teacher and the work topics before the year began and would actively look forward to certain things, such as Mrs Bowden's Year 3 (ages 7–8) Romans obsession. My second favourite teacher, she was almost as old as Mrs Thomas but, in contrast, had the kindly air of a mother hen brooding her chicks and made sure to end each day with us gathered at her feet for a reading of a good book. My favourite teacher, however, was Mr Budd, who must have been in his 30s and was authoritative but kind and the best teacher I ever had.

UNIFORM

School uniforms are a big deal in the UK, a deal that I agree with given its ability to create a sense of smartness and of belonging. St Peter's school colour, as demonstrated by our uniform, was green, which meant green school jumpers emblazoned with the school insignia. Boys were to wear this along with a white button down or polo shirt and grey or black shorts or trousers. Girls could choose between the jumper and a cardigan option and pair this with a shirt and a grey pinafore, skirt or, in the summer months, a green gingham dress. The fragmented memories I have of my reception year make it clear I was a connoisseur of the classic grey pinafore with the square of four buttons on the front and a long sleeved shirt. I did not care for this pinafore, which I thought was a ridiculous item, so unlike anything else I wore or would consider wearing outside of school. I liked the shirt a little better but hated the fact Mum referred to it as a 'blouse' when I could see no discernible difference between it and James's shirts, certainly nothing to warrant another name. Fortunately it did not come with frilly sleeve edges, unlike the vests I was forced to wear in those early years. I hated them dearly and would lie about wearing them, as I would also only wear tights so far as the cloakroom before taking them off and hiding them under my coat on the peg.

My attitude towards clothes was complicated. As any child, I knew early on the gender rules of clothes and I would wear leggings, some with frankly outrageous 1990s patterning and complete with foot stirrups, without any fuss, as I would also love to wear the insanely shiny classic black buckle-up school shoes and was glad that these were allowed under my gender designation. But skirts and dresses were an absolute no from the beginning. One of my earliest clothing memories at age three or four is of delighting Mum with choosing to wear this pink corduroy skirt to a swimming lesson that I otherwise flatly refused to wear. I distinctly remember choosing to wear it entirely because it would make her happy. I disliked them principally, in those younger days, because they were a symbol of ultimate girl-ness that made me feel confused and uneasy and I hated the way they were presented to me as a possible option and never to James. In addition they were so restrictive of movement, you couldn't run very fast in them or climb or even do a cartwheel without risking showing your underwear and I hated feeling so exposed. But pinafores and skirts were school uniform, a binding requirement, and so they had to be worn, no matter how much I wished inside that I could wear shorts like James. Over time it became simply one of those things that I had to accept could not be changed. In this way I developed a strange sort of split set of standards towards clothes.

By the time I was considering having my hair cut I had banished all obviously 'girl' clothes from my wardrobe, the unease they brought forward within me from the way they made other people interact with me having proved too off-putting, so that Mum saw that it was a pointless waste of money to continue down the pink-lined aisles and, after the mental trauma of *that* haircut, there was no going back. Clothing was one area I had to allow my true gender identity to seep into the world. Post-cut, trying to wear 'girl' clothes in everyday life became so fraught with nausea-inducing self-consciousness that it was hard to concentrate on anything but the desire to rip them clean off. But it wasn't because I hated pink or butterflies or flowers, just that wearing them was so inexplicably linked to the girl gender designation, I couldn't bear it. Although this is one thing in which the extraordinary double standards for clothing is to girls' benefit. I could actually wear all the 'boy' clothes I liked in public, it transpired, without anyone being mean or angry about it or any brutal attempts to shame me for it, even if they knew I was meant to be a girl. Instead, there was a certain respect to it, part of the 'tomboy' label, a respect that is in no way given to boys who want to wear dresses, and I was very conscious of this double standard and glad to have been afforded by society this sliver of gender non-conformity allowance.

To dress how I wanted, I was more than happy to wear James's old clothes, preferring them to new ones if new ones meant girl clothes, but I vividly remember the first time I was allowed to buy a pair of khaki shorts from the boys' section. I had begun loitering in and around the boys' section on shopping trips and Mum, perhaps somewhat desperate to get me something new that I would actually wear, allowed me this time to pick out the shorts. I was so proud and wanted to wear them to the dens and to climb trees even when it was much too cold and I was so pleased to be able to wear them to a birthday party with my favourite one of James's old T-shirts, which was navy blue and had 'Brooker' stamped on the front in white letters. This became my favourite outfit and I wore it as often as I was allowed before Mum snatched it away for washing. I felt right and oddly powerful in my correct boy's social uniform in a way that filled me with an exuberance I rarely felt otherwise, because it increased my chances of being 'mistaken' for a boy.

Soon my wardrobe was filled with more 'boy shorts' and an array of Nike and Adidas tracksuit trousers.

At school, however, the girl's uniform remained. The pinafore gave way to a pleated grey skirt and white polo shirt in the winter months with the green dress as a constant part of summer. It stands as one of my most successful acts of mental pigeonholing, how this fact of life did not drive me to distraction and sap my capacity to concentrate. It was fine because it was school, it wasn't reflective of the 'real world' or of my own free choice, and so long as I framed it that way it was somehow alright.

CHARACTER BUILDING

However, there were moments where a degree of free choice was afforded and I took every advantage of them, despite the unease and later outright struggle to allow a release of my gender identity from its cage without asking the forbidden questions that hovered all around it. Mrs Bowden's love of our Year 3 Roman history topic extended into our art lessons and into drama and every year one day was designated as 'Roman Day'. In his year James had gone dressed as a magnificent solider with golden armour and helmet complete with red plume made from paper and cardboard that Mum had copied most accurately from a history book. James also made himself a large Roman shield, which he let me help colour in before proceeding to hit me with its embossed front. When my time came, a part of me wanted to have the same costume, but James would not have liked me to copy him. The only alternatives were to be a 'well-born lady' or a slave. There was no contest; I was categorically not going to voluntarily be a lady, well-born or otherwise. I gladly put on my rags and set about envisioning a whole life for my slave self – a young foreign prince who had been captured in battle and forced to work for a rich Roman family. We slaves were required to wait on the rich patricians who reclined on our cushion-covered class tables and I enjoyed losing myself in my fantasy despite Mrs Bowden's constant referrals to me as 'she'.

Because of the Victorian origins of our school, several times in my years there I also took part in a Victorian Day in which classes were conducted in the strict Victorian manner with everyone suitably dressed. Mr Budd was astonishingly effective in his role as an imposing Year 4 Master and I recall a slightly scary morning of counting in shillings and sixpences as he walked up and down with a cane. As with the Roman Day, I could not bring myself to wear the requisite girl attire, long dark dress with some kind of petticoat and bonnet hat. No, I was a street urchin boy in ripped trousers, James's old waistcoat and Grandad's old flat cap. In the afternoon we lined up outside to have our class picture taken but I was dismayed to find it was to be split between a girls' photo and a boys' photo. I had to remind myself firmly this was a custom of the time, but it still made me angry. I did not want to be lumped with girls even despite my clearly being a street urchin boy, because it wasn't just a costume, not to me, and again I had to fight the unease and the forbidden questions away. The only consolation was that Kat, dressed as a chimney sweep and also in a flat cap and shirt, would be in the picture too. But I wasn't going to let the embarrassment of being different get to me this time, I was going to own it, I was going to make them see how ridiculous it was to put me here. So I knelt for the photo, right in the centre of the front row, head up and proud to be the street urchin boy in a group of little maids. Years later I would show this photo to a psychologist at a gender clinic and she would laugh out loud at the obviousness of my conviction.

This wasn't the last time I would stick to my guns on such an issue. Mr Budd's interest in dressing up for historical reasons didn't end with Victorian Day. In fact, our curriculum in Year 5 seemed to be largely centred around history, with everything from English to art to drama to music incorporating the Tudors in some way. In music we learnt to make Tudor music with old-style instruments, in art we made a huge model of a Tudor house and in English we created a class newspaper called *The Tudor Times* for which we each had to write an article. Mine was an advertisement selling a luxury house like the one we'd envisioned for our class model and I took the opportunity to engage in some more of the make believe that acted as an outlet for my real self. I signed my article as well-respected fictional Tudor real estate agent, Edward Wallop.

Later on in Year 5 we had the opportunity to attend a living history experience day for which we were all to go dressed as a character. I had already been a Tudor monk on a freezing class trip to Hampton Court, for which I wore the brown bed sheet that had previously served as my shepherd's outfit for a Nativity and is a day that is seared into my memory as the coldest I have ever been. Never ever go to Hampton Court on a freezing day dressed only in a bed sheet. But this time we were to choose a name for our character from a list and one afternoon Mr Budd went around the room asking us to pick. I was immediately uncomfortable; this wasn't like with Edward Wallop or the monk, this was to be shared with others outside the school and I suddenly felt very nervous of that idea and embarrassed about having to ask for a boy name, instead of simply naming myself in private. I felt very self-conscious, like it would be a clear signal that my tomboyishness was different to the actual meaning of that label and again I worried it might make the other kids or even Mr Budd ask me difficult and probing questions. 'Why do you want a boy name?' was simply not a question I wanted to engage with in class. As expected, all the girls were asking for girl names and I had the panicked thought that I might not be allowed a boy name anyway, if there were only so many. So when it came to me I blurted out a girl name, but even as I said it I knew I couldn't go through with it, my stomach had tied itself into knots and without a second more of thought I said, 'No, can I be called Henry?' I actually hated the name Henry and I don't know why I chose it, I guess it was just the first name that popped into my head. It reminded me of gross old Henry VIII who killed his own wives and was so disappointed in getting daughters instead of a son. But in the moment Mr Budd said it was fine, I felt it to be the best name in the world. In the end the trip was cancelled but

I had learned once again that my overwhelming drive to grab opportunities for a snippet of my hidden self to be exposed was ever present and would never go away.

GIRLS' TROUSERS

An extraordinary thing happened as I entered Year 6 (ages 10–11); we were informed the school management had made the decision to allow girls to wear trousers. I do not know whether this was purely an internal decision or whether there had been any parental or student pressure to prompt it. Certainly Kat and I had moaned amongst ourselves for several years, but there had been no obvious protest that I had been aware of. I was totally ecstatic and couldn't wait to tell Mum, who, with some dubiousness, allowed me to commandeer a black pair of James's castoffs. I hung them carefully in my wardrobe and looked forward to the morning as if it was Christmas day.

There was much curiosity when I arrived in the playground, from boys who seemed a mixture of amused by the novelty and slightly put out and girls who seemed equally interested and accusatory. Several kids put on an indignant expression and exclaimed, 'You can't wear them!' But I replied robustly that actually I could, they'd just said girls could wear trousers so here I am. In truth, I had been feeling self-conscious all morning, from the anticipation of their responses and from the cage I felt rattling in the back of my mind the minute I looked in the mirror. But as the day went on people lost interest and my sense of joy and of belonging increased rapidly, to look down at them, to catch my reflection, to see myself wearing what boys wore to school, it just felt so right.

Mrs King entered our classroom sometime in the late afternoon and went to speak with the teacher. Kat 'n' Dave and I were busy tidying up after an activity and were messing about slightly in the process. We failed to notice Mrs King coming our way until we heard her reminding us to stay on task. Still a bit scared of her, even after all those years, I quickly got back to tucking under chairs and watched her move towards the door. But just as she was about to leave, she turned to me and said, 'Oh, and Katie, a skirt or girls' trousers tomorrow please.' I was crushed. In an instant all my confidence and self-pride evaporated into nothing. It felt like I'd just been subjected to a public shaming, I had strayed too far from the acceptable bending of gender rules and I had been slapped down. Yes girls could now wear trousers but only on the proviso they were suitably 'girl-ified' versions, suitably different from those worn by boys. I felt so stupid. How could I have thought anything else? How could I have allowed my expectation of the clothing world outside school to have crossed into this domain? I pulled out my chair and sat down, now deeply self-conscious of my bottom half and feeling utterly miserable.

I didn't have any girl school trousers and had never even really seen any, nevertheless, I had a vague idea of what the signifiers would be, the same things that usually signified girl trousers; pointless, fake or too-shallow-to-be-useful pockets, a random selection of buttons on the front just for effect, jewelling on the waistband or else hearts or feminine category animals sewn onto the belt loops and shaping. It was the shaping that I hated above all else. Girls' trousers should be figure accentuating, contoured to your lines because it's all about maximising your looks, even in your school uniform. I hated the way they made me look, the way they outlined my hips and flared slightly at the ankle. Furthermore, they were thinner and felt less robust, like one rough game of football later and I'd have a hole in them. I even wondered if they made me feel better or worse than the skirt, every day they showed me the edge of the boundary I was not allowed to cross.

One thing they did have over the skirt was less risk of exposure. I vividly recall the rumbles of sniggering that went through the assembly every time a class was sat up on the stage steps for a class presentation. Always there was at least one girl who sat on a step with her feet on the step below and with her knees open so that the whole school in front of her could see up her skirt and at her knickers. I would sit there feeling so sorry for her and willing her to realise, but she never did.

When my class were up on the steps it was always in the front of my mind, keep your knees together! I hated the worry too, whenever I ran as fast as I could, whether my skirt or dress was flying up at the back in the wind; it created an unnecessary and irritating complication.

This is something that several equality campaigns have taken up in recent years and not just because of the issues for trans and non-binary children, this needs to be made right for all children. Why should girls have suffer these kinds of disadvantages? Given that my school had adopted trousers for girls, albeit with the girl-version only restriction, way back in 1999, I could not believe there are schools where a trouser or shorts option for girls is still categorically banned. Fortunately, campaigns like 'Let Clothes Be Clothes' (Let Clothes Be Clothes 2018) have sprung up to fight this and are doing a fantastic job in creating change, highlighting not only how this requirement is contrary to workplace dress codes in the modern day, but also seriously undermines a girl's ability to be active in the playground. They have also taken on the depressing sexism that exists in girl and boy school shoes, with parents now waking up to the fact that many girl choices are flimsier than those for boys and stamped with patronising names, as was demonstrated by the Clark's shoes outlets' 'Dolly Babe' versus 'Leader' range fiasco (Chapman 2017). I really did like my ultra-shiny shoes, but I would have liked them even more if I could have kicked a football in them without risking a toe fracture.

These campaigns are also highlighting the extraordinary sexism that exists in the rest of children's clothing choices, not only the colour-coding obsession, but also the types of slogans, messages and interests. As with the great toy divide, it is warming to see more and more people challenging retailers to please explain why dinosaur-adorned clothing is 'for boys' and butterfly-covered clothes only 'for girls'. What is perhaps most shocking, however, is the slogans you see printed on t-shirts and tops. In a society in an age where the government, the law and all morally conscious people are striving to close the gender pay gap and end the stereotyping of professions and roles, how it is that we allow such an obviously sexist disparity between the things written on children's clothes.

Whilst the rigid gendering of clothes did allow me blissful moments of being gendered as a boy when I wore clothes in the boy category, I lost something too, as does everyone under this system. Personally, I would have loved to have also been able to wear pink and purple and not have been automatically gendered as a girl. A world where clothes are for anyone who likes them would be a better place. Soon I hope to see that every child is given the option of a trouser or skirt uniform without gender prejudice.

STEREOTYPES

It was while watching the BBC documentary *No More Boys and Girls* that I experienced, for the first time in my life, the overwhelming urge to throw something at the TV. The girls in this class of seven-year-olds were almost all of the opinion that boys were better and really the only thing in which girls could claim to be top was in 'being pretty'. I could not blame them, though, given the world in which they have lived, bombarded with messages about how they should behave. Watching them say those things made my stomach twist. This was the product of the extreme gendering of toys and clothes that has taken place, sitting nicely on a chair, facing a television camera, expounding with total sincerity how 'men are better at being in charge'.

I do not believe it was this bad when I was young, at least it did not seem to be in my experience; we were rarely divided up for activities by sex and there were no girl/boy coat pegs or tables. Even so I had such anger hearing some of the boys in my class assume they were better in a myriad of ways and how many of the girls just capitulated to this like it was a universal law of physics. I hated the attitude of some of the girls, I wanted to scream at them that it was not true and whoever had told them that was a damn liar. I wanted the girls to know they were strong, to know they were clever, capable and not to accept this notion of being less good or second best. Whenever I encountered it I felt personally offended at the easy attitude to this, it was so obviously untrue.

I have never forgotten the looks on the faces of everyone in the class as Mr Budd came to the very end of *The Turbulent Term of Tyke Tiler* (Kemp 1977) one afternoon in Year 5. This story about a child's struggle to fight for their best friend not to be sent to another school, and fending off bullies in the process, is told entirely without explicitly alluding to their gender. It is only at the very end that the reader learns 'Tyke' is short for 'Theodora' and the protagonist is apparently not the boy everyone thought they were. I was sitting opposite my friend Josh and I can still see his eyes widening as far as they could go as I heard several exclamations of 'WHAT!' around the room. The idea that it was a female person who had done all the things Tyke had done, physically fought with bullies, climbed to the top of a school building, surely not! The challenge to these stereotypes was glorious to behold, but I was also ashamed of myself for having fallen into the trap, for my own face contorted too and my heart gave several massive thumps. It showed even with my deep irritation at and fight against stereotypes, they were so hard to escape entirely. I was shocked too by the revelation for another reason. Was Tyke a tomboy like I was a tomboy or just a girl who liked 'boy' things? I was suddenly flushed with a great thrill at the prospect of the former. This was the closest I had ever seen to a portrayal of myself and I have never forgotten the power that being able to relate can give and how I longed for it, for an answer, to be the same as someone else. But, as with George of the Famous Five, there was no way to tell and I remained tantalisingly bereft.

But even as I tried to resist stereotypes about girls, I fell into others. I saw how boys were not allowed to cry or show strong emotion that wasn't anger without being physically, verbally and socially battered for it. Such notions made me worried and confused for my caged identity, because I knew there was a softness in me, a softness that boys apparently didn't have and then where did that leave me? And even as I knew it was rubbish, because I had seen such softness in James, in Dave, in Dad, it was difficult to shake, I felt infected by this stereotype and deeply pressured, even by my own self, to harden.

✦──✦──✦

A few years ago, a friend posted an image of our Year 6, class of 2000, photo on her Facebook page and someone commented, 'Why is there a boy in a dress?' Oh, how I laughed the bittersweet laugh of someone who had come to gain the gift and curse of hindsight. Because that is exactly what I was, a boy in a dress in a time when being in a dress could only mean you were a girl. Primary school was a good time for me, when the work was fun and the exams weren't serious. But I do wish we hadn't been so gendered by uniform, that I didn't have to suffer the disadvantages of a skirt and then the disapproval of my choice of trousers that kept me from breaching the gender clothing divide. Just as outside school, in those later years before the turn of the millennium, my true gender identity became harder to control and my desire for and enjoyment of clothes that had me gendered correctly, be they at home or as a historical re-enactment in school, grew with me.

Chapter 6

TOILETS OF TERROR

WE MAY HAVE WON THE BATTLE

I was at my desk in our lab's overflow office space plugging away at my PhD thesis when the term 'bathroom bill' first entered my consciousness. It was mid-2015 and LGBT rights in Western countries had just received a huge boost. The USA had passed nationwide marriage equality after a monumental years-long effort, the last leg of which I avidly followed during breaks from my graphical analysis. However, I had been astonished as I followed the progress of marriage equality in the USA to discover it has no federal equality law that covers sexual orientation and gender identity. It is difficult to square this fact with a country characterised as the leader of the free world and that self-proclaims as the greatest place on Earth. I think that's a dangerous thing for any nation to claim about itself and whilst I believe the ideals the USA was founded on are the best ideals, the reality so far falls depressingly short of them (even before Trump). It was hard to swallow how, though marriage equality was now the law of the land, the fact remained that in many of the states if a newlywed gay couple's employers and landlord found out about it they could be fired and evicted if it was to their displeasure. This realisation reduced the sweetness of seeing the White House lit up in all the colours of the rainbow. However, this sweetness would be utterly soured a few days later when my lunchtime Twitter scroll brought me to a litany of articles collectively proclaiming 'ANTI-TRANS BATHROOM BILLS ARE THE NEW CONSERVATIVE BATTLEGROUND!'

It appeared that now that marriage had slipped beyond reach, like the great eye of Sauron, the unrelenting gaze of anti-LGBT extremists was to descend on where transgender people go to the toilet. Though this had caught me unawares, such bills were not new in the USA, particularly in some of the most conservative states, but now they were to enjoy national and international attention and serve as a rallying point for the extraordinary fury of those who felt rebuked by Justice Kennedy's majority opinion. I sat back in my chair and furrowed my eyebrows in a moment of worry. Then I googled the Equality Act (2010) just to be sure and gained a measure of relief. The law was clear, in the UK trans people have the legal right to use the toilet they feel comfortable with. *'Well then, I shall be alright,'* I thought and immediately thereafter felt a wave of shame. None of us shall be truly free until we are all free, I reminded myself sternly. That is a fundamental lesson from history, repeated time and time again, and it is simply not good enough to sit pretty basking in the freedoms of your own green and pleasant land while others suffer. Particularly since a number of the worst anti-LGBT laws still in force around the world are the fault of the British Empire (Godfrey 2016).

What's more, there is still truth in the idea that US culture heavily influences us here in Britain. Discourse around these US bathroom bills has caused and continues to cause an explosion of articles and debates, many of them ill informed, that are stirring anti-trans toilet sentiment in this country. This is exacerbated by a general trans rights ignorance. Your average British person is likely to understand that the Equality Act prevents a bakery from refusing a wedding cake to a gay couple but ask them where the law stands on transgender people and public facilities and you're more likely to come across some hesitation. It is also true that an awful lot of transphobia can spew from a person's face before you've managed to shield yourself with the Equality Act. For all the above reasons, this new rallying cry that's been made by anti-LGBT activists needs to be met with the most robust response possible.

So what exactly are these bathroom bills? The general premise centres around making it a legal requirement for people to use the public facilities corresponding to the gender on their birth certificate. Unfortunately, it is often not a simple case of transgender people changing their birth certificate as many of these bills go on to specify *original* birth certificate and make further reference to 'sex assigned at birth', some even go so far as to contain an explicit mention of chromosomes. They often come with little to no mechanism of enforcement, with those that do requiring some kind of bathroom attendant or security guard stationed at the door to interrogate anyone trying to enter. Penalties for breaking such laws range wildly from nothing to large fines to prison time (National Conference of State Legislatures 2017).

The most notorious of these bills is North Carolina's Public Facilities Privacy and Security Act or House Bill 2 (HB2), which was rammed through in a one-day specially called session on 23 March 2016. It was set out as a response to what was seen as overreach by the city of Charlotte, which had passed a pro-LGBT non-discrimination ordinance (Kopan and Scott 2016). I followed the quick proceedings with a heavy heart and a confused mind. Could they really be this stupid, this blind? Surely they wouldn't actually pass it, not after the huge backlash to the anti-LGBT 'license to discriminate' law passed in Indiana the year before (Heath 2015). House Bill 2 was signed by Governor Pat McCrory the very same day and a cloud descended over North Carolina. Proving that they really hadn't learned from Indiana (that brazenly discriminating against a minority will not be tolerated given the successful protests that occurred in Indiana after they passed SB101), it was clear that the sponsors of the bill had not reckoned on the level and scope of the protest. One thing everyone can understand is money and businesses small and large, music acts and sporting bodies all made it clear they would blacklist the state until this law was repealed (Graham 2016). This was extremely heartening to see and shows the majority of US people are nothing short of disgusted by these laws. So unpopular was HB2 that it very probably caused the end of previously popular Governor Pat McCrory at the election, with his successor, Roy Cooper, promising repeal (Christensen 2016). However Cooper went on to accept what was considered to be a weak compromise by activists (Jarvis and Campbell 2017). Attempts to completely recover from the damage of HB2 are ongoing.

Like HB2, many of these bathroom bills are pushed through hurriedly and as secretly as possible, in tacit admission that they know what they are doing is not just extremely controversial but built on a foundation of animus. Any rounds of open public consideration are always subject to the same twisted assertion, which is that allowing transgender people to use the sex-segregated facilities they identify with will put women and girls in danger of sexual violence within them. There are two arguments through which this assertion manifests. The first argument is thus: transgender women are an explicit threat to cisgender women in female facilities because they are actually still just men. This is the 'no such things as trans / trans women are merely sexually deviant men' narrative. It represents the crux of the matter for a lot of people; the lack of acceptance that transgender women *are women.* It is employed with shocking levels of wild abandon in state legislatures with not a single hint of subtlety. The second argument however is framed more softly within the concern trolling narrative: allowing trans women to use female facilities would lead to cis men exploiting the law by claiming to be trans, dressing as women to gain access to female spaces for the purpose of committing criminal acts against women. This is the 'bathroom predator' argument employed by your brighter bigot, the ones who understand that obvious animus towards an established minority group tends to lead to crippling rounds of legal challenges.

Both arguments however are fatally flawed. In Britain there are very clear established laws that state *anyone* who goes into *any* facility specifically to conduct an act of violence, of sexual misconduct, of voyeurism against another shall have committed a criminal offence. After all, no female spaces have ever had some kind of invisible force-field across the entrance that prevents anyone with an M on their birth certificate from entering. In the same way, I've lost count of the times that I've seen women slip into the men's toilet when the queue was just too long at festivals, theme parks and theatres, particularly at the Fortune theatre in Covent Garden. I've noted it on every one of the many trips I've taken there with whoever I could cajole into coming with me to see the world's greatest play, *The Woman in Black.* The fact of the matter is that if a man or a woman or a non-binary person or anyone of any kind wanted to go into a women's or any other toilet for a nefarious reason they can actually just do that. That is why there are criminal laws covering specific acts within them. Pushing the idea that allowing transgender people the right to go where they feel most comfortable would undermine these long-established criminal laws or make offences more likely is inexcusable. What actually happens when such bathroom bills are enacted is no change to the level of assaults against women in female facilities but a skyrocketing in acts of violence against transgender people by actual or self-appointed Toilet Police. As a case in point, at the time of writing the Texas legislature is debating Senate Bill 3, a bathroom bill, which many commentators say is the reason for the calling of the whole special summer session. However, there is a heart-warming level of protest, not least from the police department, who have taken to the steps of the House, alongside campaigners and survivors of assault, to denounce the bill as 'a solution looking for a problem'. The police representative spoke with passion when he said he'd searched back to 2014 and found not one case of assault in a women's restroom by men claiming to be women and that he'd rather police resources were not pulled into pointless policing of bathrooms when there's violent crimes they need to solve. It is worth noting that violent transphobia does not currently constitute a legal hate crime in the state of Texas (McGaughy 2017).

It is also interesting to note, from a UK perspective, that the right to use the facilities with which you identify is a part of the Equality Act and thus a protected right. In the years since then, how many people can name a 'predator' case of a man using this as a way to gain access to women for criminal behaviour? Anti-trans campaigners try to scrape together what scant cases there are from across the globe as proof of some kind of major issue but, if you look for it, you can find practically any type of criminal behaviour in women's segregated facilities by any type of person, including by cis women themselves, see, for example, De Vaal (2018). In each case the perpetrators were subject to the force of criminal law and that is why the laws exist. So where are the hordes of perverted men who claim to be trans to gain access to these facilities? The answer to that is simply: in the imaginations of anti-trans bigots.

You may have noticed the above discussion makes almost exclusive mention of the effect of such bathroom bills with regard to trans women and spaces designed for women and girls. This is deliberate. You don't have to be a trained scientist to be able to take even a casual glance at this issue and observe it is almost entirely conducted without any reference to trans men and trans masculine people. I find that there is still a lingering view that the trans population consists purely of those assigned male at birth who transition to female. It seems the very concept of trans masculine people escapes realisation in what is probably a consequence of the misogyny of patriarchal society, much in the same way as throughout history that there has been considerable disparity between the penalties for lesbians versus gay men.

To be a gay man was to be 'more like a woman' and that, for a man, was an utterly shameful thing, so the rhetoric generally went. So for a 'man' to say she is actually female and to take steps to align her body with that truth is beyond the pale for many. Why would a man want to become inferior? Why would a man wish to give up all the privileges of his gender? This kind of fascination is what I believe largely drives the social and media obsession with transgender women and from it the toxic conclusion that the only reason a 'man' would to do this to 'himself' is because 'he's' a psychopathic sexual deviant. As an extension of this, there are still a huge amount of people who maintain the idea that a transgender person is exceedingly obvious to spot, that it's just a matter of looking for the 'man in the dress'. They lack any understanding that medical science has made any progress. Whilst it is not and nor should it have to be the aim of every trans person to 'pass', the fact is that, in the twenty-first century, those who wish to pass have the best opportunity to succeed. Nowadays it is routine to meet a trans person and only know they are trans because they have told you so. This is true for trans women and trans men, as many famous examples attest, although it is the case that trans men in general have always found passing easier.

The fact that trans men exist and the fact we are likely to be indistinguishable from cis men only adds to the ridiculousness of the bathroom debate. Proponents of the laws make a huge deal out of not wanting their wives and daughters to have to share facilities with men whilst completely failing to realise that by passing such measures that is exactly what they are going to get. They don't understand it is more frightening to occupants of women-only facilities to see a man, perhaps bearded, wearing male-assigned clothing, trying calmly to say in their deep voice, 'Don't worry madam, I have to be here, there's an F on my birth certificate and I've probably got two X chromosomes.' There have been a number of protests based on this fact across the USA (Molloy 2015) but they've fallen on deaf ears and blind eyes. They fail to understand that forcing trans men to go into women's facilities would provide a far easier mechanism for rapists to enter these spaces – they could just claim to be trans men. But possibly the easiest excuse of all, if they were so inclined to even bother to look for one, would surely be to just take advantage of the signs that hang in practically every service station women's toilet I've ever been in, which read along the lines of 'male cleaning attendants may be operating in this facility.'

GET OUT!

Perhaps the most distressing aspect of this whole issue is the effect it has on trans and gender non-conforming youth. As mentioned above, many bathroom bills are targeted at use of school facilities and make it clear that trans children should be banned from using the facilities with which they identify and present. When reading about this as I sat at my desk I noticed my pulse had quickened, for stored away in the recesses of my memory are many distressing experiences of run-ins with gendered facilities.

It was shortly after my hair was cut that I was thrown out of women's toilets for the first time. It was at a campsite somewhere in the wilds of the Scottish highlands where my family had rocked up on one of our caravan holidays. I am a proud product of childhood caravan holidays and all the trimmings that come with them but the trips to the site toilet and washing facilities were about to become fraught with a worry no nine-year-old should have to bear. Yes, I was dressed head to toe in my brother's hand-me-downs and yes, my short hair was spiked up at the front but I was apparently a girl and these were the girls' toilets. I walked in without a second thought and, just as I was entering a cubicle, caught the attention of the lady cleaning the basins. She barked at me in a gruff voice that made me think she was probably a 40-a-day smoker, 'What do yer think yer doing? These are the women's, get out with yer.' I tried to mount some kind of response but she waved her cloth at me and repeated, 'Go on, go on!' I ran out the door back into a patch of Scottish sunshine and looked around, hoping no one had seen my panicked escape. But there was no one about and so I slid round behind the toilet block and tried to gather myself.

What the hell had just happened? *'You look like a boy,'* I reminded myself. *'But I need the toilet!'* And for the first time in my life it crossed my mind that I might use the boys'. *'You can't do that!'* I thought. That seemed true enough. *'It must be against the law and what if James or Dad comes in!'* I searched around for an alternative but the only one I could think of was to bite the bullet and go and confront the cleaning lady. *'But I can't,'* I thought hopelessly, annoyed at my own childish shyness. *'And you don't really want to...'*, that small voice in the back of my head said. I tried to grind that train of thought to an immediate halt. I knew where it was going but that, of course, was a forbidden mental destination. It was true, though, mixed in with the fright and panic and confusion of the cleaning lady's rebuke of me was a ping of joy. She had thought I was a boy and, as always, I wanted to keep it that way. It was easy to run away from that thought this time, though, as my bladder's protesting pushed itself to the forefront of my attention. I moved back around to the toilet entrance, there was no sound coming from within so I went in slowly and darted into a cubicle. Mum has commented many times on the speed with which I can use toilets, this is where it began. I was terrified the cleaning lady would be back and ran out without stopping to wash my hands.

From this point on I lived in a new era of my public life. It was now dangerous, as I saw it, to use public toilets. If I used the boys' I could get in trouble, but the same was also true of the girls'. On subsequent toilet trips on that campsite I began hanging about the entrance, waiting until I knew there were no other occupants. For the reaction of the cleaning lady had jarred me into the reality that all or at least many women were likely to respond the same way and I really didn't want the scenes it would cause. What if they really shouted? I couldn't take being shouted at in any situation and had the usual response of bursting into tears, which I was desperate to avoid. Going to use the showers was alright, as Mum came too, but I started to feel like I was stepping over a breach every single time.

I had the same feeling, only significantly amplified, the first time I ventured into the boys' toilets on another campsite somewhere in the wilds of the Welsh countryside. I was in my usual position waiting around the entrance but the group of women that were in there were not being quick about coming out. I could see them at the mirrors, brushing their teeth, doing their lips and eyes. I needed to go and I was getting angry. Angry at them and angry at the situation that I bet no one else in the whole world had to deal with. I was pretty sure there was no one in the boys'; I had been standing there for at least five minutes. Dad and James were back at the caravan and hadn't indicated they'd be coming over. I was older and bolder than I had been before and so I looked around and glanced down the lane to make sure no one was coming and then crossed the threshold. The first thing that alarmed me was the urinals. I don't think I'd really seen one in real life before then. They were ugly looking things and the idea of weeing openly like that was a horrific one to me. The next thing that alarmed me was the fact there was only one cubicle. There were four in the girls'. Was this typical? I darted into it and all the while worried about what I would do if it was occupied and there were men at the urinal? What if next time I was wrong in thinking no one was in there? And if men wee at the urinal then they only go into the cubicle to do the other thing but if I'm in and out quickly are they going to wonder why I didn't use the urinal? This was rapidly becoming exhausting. I was freaked out enough to not dare go in there again. But I had felt excited by it too, partly from the general thrill of doing something risky but also from the thrill of going where all the boys go.

Of course there were many situations where it was impossible to wait until I was sure the toilets were empty or risk it and use the male option, either because the place was swarming with people or my family were close at hand. Family trips out to theme parks, museums, the cinema, shopping centres, restaurants, every single one of them now a situation where toilet terror was never far from my mind, where my otherness of gender could cause a ripple of disturbance at the mere opening of a door, where, like Agent Smith of *The Matrix*, agents of the Toilet Police could be anywhere and anyone. I'd had my first direct brush with one at the campsite in Scotland and, naturally, my second warning would be an escalated threat.

I was hugely excited to go to the newish attraction of LEGOLAND® Windsor in the summer of 2000 with my mum, brother, sister-in-law Cathy, and three young nephews.

In particular I was absolutely desperate to get my hands on one of the giant foam LEGO®-style swords, largely to fight James with it. But I was less keen on having to use the park toilets. I tried three times to go down the short corridor into the female toilets, each time beaten back by overwhelming paranoia and self-consciousness. Need eventually drove me in but my worst fear was realised on the way out when I was snared by a teenage girl who put her hand on my shoulder and let me know in no uncertain terms that she'd caught me, that I shouldn't have been in there and that she could tell on me if she wanted. As a teenager myself I would have given her a piece of my mind, but at ten that piece had yet to form and I once again found myself unable to speak. I ran from her without risking a backward glance and busied myself with teaching my nephews how to walk along the edge of a raised kerb, hoping the girl had disappeared into the swarm of people. I left the toilet area burdened with the sense I'd done something wrong and I'd been caught, tried and convicted, like a criminal.

ARE YOU SURE?

And so it went on. Between the ages of nine and thirteen I was pretty defenceless against the Toilet Police, as many a child would be in the face of the open hostility of strange teenagers and adults. Maybe if I was more assertive or self-confident I could have put up more of a fight, maintained composure, explained myself. But there's the rub. How many people have to consider the possibility of having to explain their right to be in a facility, at eight, at ten, at twelve years old or, indeed, at any age? I wonder what would come of it if cis people took a step back and thought about what it must feel like to have that conversation with yourself, to have to go thus armed into a gendered space. To have experienced the horror of the infamous female toilet queue full of irritated women looking idly about them. To understand what it feels like to have those bored eyes scan across you, dart back and transfix. A look that makes you know you are being assessed, every inch of you, the 'this' and 'that' of your appearance each weighed and slotted into either the male or female column. To pray that you are given enough points in the female column to avoid an accusatory confrontation, to avoid the making of a scene and a memory that will stay with you forever.

I was not so lucky one Saturday in 2002 when out in Watford High Street with Kat. We had stopped to have lunch in the 'big' McDonalds (the 'small' option being around 400 yards up the street – quite why one high street had two of the same shop in such close proximity always amused me). It was busy on the ground floor and so we collected our food and claimed a table upstairs. I immediately regretted this decision. The only other occupants of this floor were a group of quite rowdy teenagers. I hated being anywhere near this sort of teenager; they intimidated me just from their very presence. We did our best to ignore them and for the most part they ignored us too, save for the moment I had been dreading; part of coming to McDonalds was the convenience of using the toilets there. I was 12, puberty had started and though I still had short hair and was wearing 'boys' clothes, sprouting breasts had made me lose much of the confidence I once had that I could get away with going into the boys' toilets. And it was out of the question in this moment, the stakes were too high. The thing was, yes, the chances of passing had reduced but that wasn't to say it had gone completely and it was impossible oftentimes to tell in advance what gender casual observers had assigned to me. In light of this I had made the decision it was safer to go for the female option, that way, if there was to be a scene, I would have the all-important anatomy card to play to my advantage that meant I'd be safe from any accusations.

Kat's appearance matched my own and this was a conundrum we shared and it was together that we made our way past the teenagers as quickly as possible and through the female door. I think I heard one of the teenagers shouting at us as the door swung closed. *'This is going to be one of those days,'* I thought. There was someone else in the toilet. I cannot remember whether she was already in there or whether she entered after us but just as we were at the door to go out, she stopped us. Her uniform and badge marked her as a member of the McDonalds staff and my stomach dropped. It hit the floor at the exact moment the door thumped shut. Kat had bolted. Fight or flight. Though I have faux moaned about how she ditched me, I don't blame her for going, I'd have liked to have joined her, run away so fast I'd have left my skin behind like they do in cartoons. But I was too far back and hesitated too long and now I was face to face with an angry employee demanding an explanation. 'I'm a girl,' I managed to get out. She did not look convinced. 'Are you sure?' she responded. I have thought about this moment many times in the years since. What the hell kind of a question was that! She said it with such an accusatory tone that I was seriously put aback. I had been asked my gender many times before but this kind of response was new to me. This was a person not satisfied with my own assertion. She wanted proof about my own gender and I was required to give it to her. 'Yes I'm sure,' I said and raced through options in my mind. I didn't have any ID on me, I was twelve. I didn't walk around with my passport or birth certificate; I didn't have a driving licence or a student card. So I did the only thing I could think of, I pulled my oversized hoodie around my back, tightening it to expose the presence of the tell-tale lumps I hated so much. She let me go. But there were still the group of teenagers to face. I stared straight ahead at the stairs and walked as fast as I could. Shouts of laughter and 'Wrong toilet, mate!' followed me as I went.

I came down the stairs to see Kat waiting for me, leaned up against the big sculpture of a hornet on the street just outside the door. We didn't really speak about what had just happened, we were just too used to it being a fact of our existence: part of the game of Russian roulette that was travelling through life as a square peg wedged inside a round hole and today, quite simply, we had lost. I stayed quiet on the way home trying to shake the bubble of dysphoria that burst up from the depths of my mind where I kept it. I felt like I'd been violated, physically and mentally, in the kind of way that results from having to defend the core of your character. I'd had to pay a price to this lady for appearing the way I did, for not conforming to the prescribed gender rules. That price had been a forced demonstration of my body. I was shaken in another way too; once again the mental cage I'd placed over my gender issue had been rattled violently. The fact is, as I stood there facing her expectant eyes, I wasn't at all sure. I wasn't sure of who I was, I wasn't sure I could live my life this way. I just wasn't sure.

JUST WASH YOUR HANDS

This last memory is the one I most often return to when engaged in the trans toilet 'debate'. It really hit home recently when I came across an article about a girl who said she had been thrown out of a McDonalds for using the women's toilets and had the police called after being mistaken for a boy (Hartley-Parkinson 2016). Fifteen years later and it's still happening. It was another reminder that it isn't just trans or non-binary people who suffer under Toilet Police surveillance, but anyone who does not conform to a rigid set of ideas about what a woman looks like or what a man looks like. Got a thick coat on, trousers and short hair? Well, you just better make sure you can prove you're a woman. Several such reports have surfaced, particularly in the USA (Richardson 2016) and are notable as being an eye opening experience for those who suffer them. After all, there's nothing like being physically dragged out of a female toilet by a large security guard to make a cis woman appreciate the gauntlet trans women face. Something may not be a problem until it happens to you. No one wins when toilets are policed, because it occurs as a direct way to police gender expression in general. It's interesting to note that proponents of these discriminatory measures are usually those who are also proponents of maintaining rigid stereotypical gender roles and say things like 'It wouldn't be a problem for them if all women looked like women and wore dresses just like the little symbol on the door say they do.'

I cannot count the number of times in my life I wished there were gender neutral facilities. As a latent trans boy, I often think on how many of my horrible toilet memories could have been avoided in a world where I wouldn't have had to worry about the Toilet Police or plan out a defensive speech or carry ID or make Mum come with me or alter my clothing choices. It was always a joy to know the train/aeroplane toilet was not gendered and I could just use it without any mental baggage. I wished this situation could be everywhere. I have wished it in more recent years too, as I went through the awkward stages of transition. Fortunately the rise in trans awareness has brought this issue and the concept of non-binary people to the public sphere for the first time and people are waking up to fact that, for some people, choosing one or the other requires an identity compromise and that there are a lot of other people for whom a neutral facility would be really helpful.

However, the idea of gender neutral toilets has caused its own stir. I sat in my kitchen on 1 December 2016 and watched the first ever trans debate in the House of Commons. Although I was depressed at the sight of the many bare benches, it felt good to see this representation of progress and the passion with which the speeches from those present were given and I couldn't help juxtaposing it with the disgusting debates in US state legislatures happening at the same time. Nothing in politics is ever smooth sailing though and so it came to pass that Labour MP Caroline Flint brought a little taster from across the pond. She appeared to have succumbed to the bathroom predator argument and wished to sound the alarm on gender neutral facilities. To do so she raised the case of a student at the University of East Anglia who had gone into one such toilet and there placed devices to secretly record women and therefore such places were not safe. But she failed to relay that this student had also gone into women-only facilities and carried out the exact same illegal acts in an example of how a man can just walk into female places without needing to bother claiming to be trans. If there had been no gender neutral toilets at the university he would have simply been restricted to conducting his voyeurism in the women-only places (Duffy 2016). I am not someone who advocates for the total end of such segregated facilities, some people prefer them and that's fine, but I see no reason why an additional gender neutral option should be a problem. On this issue, in my opinion, the bottom line is that there is no good reason why gender neutral facilities should be denied to those who want, need and deserve them.

There is another feeling among some people that trans and non-binary people should have to use single stall facilities if they want to go somewhere gender neutral or not have to use the segregated place they were assigned at birth. Fortunately the Equality Act speaks against this. Acceptance of gender identity cannot be partial. Why should trans women be denied the ability to go into the women-only toilets with their group of friends on a night out? Why should they be denied access to the summit conferences some groups like to conduct in these club and bar toilets as they block other people's access to the sinks and mirrors? My personal grumblings about that phenomenon aside, it is simply not acceptable to force trans people to have to go elsewhere on their own. It is not OK to single us out for different treatment, especially when such treatment may have the effect of outing us as trans against our will and in places where that could have serious consequence in this unequal world.

The place where this particular issue is felt most keenly is in schools. According to most US bathroom bills that target use of school facilities, trans students are banned from using those with which they identify if they are multi-user, which they nearly always are (National Conference of State Legislatures 2017). Instead such trans students, if they are not to be forced to use the toilets they were assigned at birth, are required to use alternative accommodations. In practice this often means staff/nurses' facilities or single user facilities only. This not only treats them differently and potentially outs them but in many cases severely limits their access. Oftentimes they have no choice but to either hold it in or use the wrong facilities and face bullying and ridicule. It's one of the reasons trans kids drop out of school.

As a latent trans boy I never faced a battle with the school administrators over which toilets I should use. Perhaps this was just as well since it was before the Equality Act (a reminder of how recent this Act actually is). However, in the early years of secondary school at the beginning of this millennium, I did face routine harassment and intimidation whenever I used the girls' toilets. I can easily recall the banging on the cubicle door from the groups of girls who accumulated in there during breaks, the shouts that I was in the wrong place. The force was such sometimes that I didn't dare even try to actually use the toilet, so afraid was I that the old door wouldn't hold. I'd just stand there on the other side listening to the sound of their violence until they got bored and left and the only sound was that of my heart pounding as if in my throat.

Eventually I admitted this to Mum who called my form tutor. He called me out of class one afternoon and sat with me on the stairwell to discuss what could be done. He was a young teacher and a good one too, though, unsurprisingly, he didn't seem to have any experience on this issue and could offer me only general assurance that I shouldn't have to worry about using the toilet and to tell him if the bullying persisted. I was thankful for that but I felt so awkward even having the conversation and went away with the sense that I was the problem and that really the only way it was going to end would be if I stopped confusing people about my gender and conformed to other people's expectations. If only people weren't so ignorant about gender, if only there had been a gender neutral option. If only.

◇━◦━━◦━◦◇

In all likelihood I could fill an entire book with toilet terror stories, those presented here being only the ones bearing most significance. I'm sure this is equally true of any trans and gender non-conforming person; my friend Kat, for example, carries a number of her own. The fact that I remember them so clearly, even after twenty years in some cases, underscores the stress, worry and fear this issue has held for me over most of my life. The stress, worry and fear of being forced into confrontations with a society at odds with gender differences and of being made to bear their consequences, forced too into confrontations with my own mind upon the very nature of who I was, but unable at that time from fear of others to embrace the consequences of that knowledge. It shouldn't have had to be this way and I'm so glad awareness around the gender spectrum and segregated facility use is becoming part of common life. But with that the inevitable hysteria has to be dealt with of people so scared of hypotheticals that they lose any ability to see the reality. We must deal with the uneducated and the miseducated who worry upon this issue and we must stand strong against those who wish to subvert such worry to push bigotry and hatred.

I am hopeful for the future here, for the truth cannot be destroyed and the accumulation of experience through time and education is seeing more and more people opening their eyes. Bathroom bills don't protect women; they are an attempt to legislate trans people out of existing in public life. Embracing trans rights does not alter established criminal laws and thus does not compromise the existing rights of others. I am confident that this brand of trans panic will be made to fizzle out and will be consigned to the history books of minority panics and I hope that sharing my perspective and experiences here will help make that happen. During the writing of this chapter I saw a photo of a little trans boy crying on the floor outside the office of the Governor of Texas as their latest bathroom bill passed the Senate. We don't have any time to lose.

Part III

ISN'T IT TIME YOU GREW UP?

Chapter 7

BREAST IS BEST

TICK TOCK GOES THE CLOCK

I remember wondering, one summer day when I was in Year 4 as I made my way with Kat 'n' Dave out to the field, how many more years I had left before my breasts would begin to grow. For how much longer would I look in the mirror and like what I saw? When would the tell-tale lumps start to protrude from my chest, smashing my ability to be gendered how I wanted? I thought, based on what I knew of puberty, which was a reasonable amount, that I had maybe three years left, if I was lucky. I had realised even before then that my body was a ticking time bomb and every day in the back of my mind was a quiet refrain – tick tock, tick tock, tick tock. I could no longer get far away from the incessant knowledge that this was to be in my future. It was becoming an ever closer threat, the sands of time were now more in the bottom than the top and I was absolutely powerless to stop it. I knew, one day, my time was going to run out.

I did not want them. I had never wanted them. If I knew only one absolute about myself then it was this. Ever since the day I discovered that it was what happened to girls' bodies, I had repelled the idea away in revulsion. For a short time it was a successful strategy to ignore this information, it seemed so extremely far in the future, in almost the same cosmically distant time period as the idea of dying. But whenever it was plucked from that expanse and thrust into my young face, a swell of serious anger would erupt from the very heart of me. Mum tried to convince me of their coming, to break it to me gently, as did Aunty Sue, though she did so in a perhaps more matter-of-fact way.

In one memorable episode, we were upstairs in Aunty Sue's house in Yorkshire, with me lying face down on a bed as I called on her nursing skills to remove the large rose thorn that had imbedded itself into my bum cheek from the bush I had backed into whilst trying to catch the rugby ball my cousin Josephine had thrown to me. It was a deeply embarrassing situation, but Aunty Sue had told me not to be so silly, we were 'all girls together' and remarked off-hand how it can't be as painful as being stabbed in the boob with a rose thorn. I must have been demonstrably irritated by this comment as Aunty Sue then said 'You will develop them, it is going to happen.' I felt a burning, passionate anger that made me ball my fists and clench my teeth. This knowledge was by far the biggest and most painful thorn I could ever feel, it pierced me right through the heart. I moaned and muttered tersely into the duvet, 'I don't want them.' But they heard me and launched into a lecture that made me want to sink into the bed and through the floor and not hear how 'It happens to all girls,' 'Girls are excited to get them' and 'You're just going to have to accept it.'

Accept it. That was all there was to do. As sure as day turns to night and night turns to day, this was going to happen to me. But I still hoped so much it wouldn't. Sometimes I would stand for long periods of time in front of the bathroom mirror with my top off and examine myself. I would run my fingers across to make sure everything was still flat and turn sideways to see if I could detect a difference in my side profile. As I turned ten I began to obsess over this and started trying to surreptitiously compare myself to my friends whenever we were in the changing rooms for our school swimming lessons, just to see how likely it was that things were altering. I felt mentally under siege from this extreme worry and paranoia, like I was on the verge of a war that I knew was definitely going to happen and that would utterly upend my entire life.

How do you live day to day with that threat, just waiting and waiting, with the only uncertainty being precisely how bad the situation will get?

I began trying to prepare myself by estimating how large they were likely to grow. My interest in biology had ignited a couple of years earlier when Mum was studying anatomy for her beauty and massage exams, when I would let her borrow my spine after she'd read me a bedtime story. She'd tickle all the way up my back counting and naming the vertebrae as she went and I ended up being able to name all 206 bones by the time I was eight years old. I tried to apply some biological principles and looked to as many female members of my family as I could to make an informed guess. Things did not look promising. Not one of these family members had what I considered to be small breasts and some, like those of both my Nan and Grandma, were quite large. This was not what I wanted to know and I pushed this distressing information away, refused to admit it could be what awaited me. I clung to the hope that observations like this could only take you so far and there wasn't really any method available to me to know for sure. For better or worse, I was stuck with that gnawing uncertainty.

THE FORK IN THE ROAD

In the summer of 1999 my family went on our first proper foreign holiday to the island of Majorca. It was the first time I was to go on an aeroplane and I was unbelievably excited about the whole prospect, sun, swimming and outdoor resort theatre shows awaited me. But what also awaited me was the start of the biggest and ugliest challenge to my relationship with James, which would lead to an utter overflowing of bitter jealousy, that in the years to come I would battle constantly to prevent from pouring out of me. He was almost two years older than me and by the summer of 1999 had gone sailing off into the pubertal sunset.

James is very good-looking; he always has been. To Mum's delight, his bright blond hair looked to be staying blonde and he was gaining height and muscle and a preoccupation with fashion. He made sure his luggage went on that plane packed with cool flip-flops, swim shorts, designer sunglasses and metal dog-tags that made him remind me strongly of Val Kilmer in *Top Gun*. On our second day at the resort, we walked the short distance from our apartment to the beach. To save time, and because it's a perfectly reasonable thing to do when you're on holiday in such sunny and exotic surroundings, we went dressed only in our swim wear. I had on my black swimming costume with green stripes up the sides, sandals and a baseball hat so that my scalp didn't burn under my strawberry blonde hair. James on the other hand was decked out in his cool flip-flops, shorts, sunglasses and had forgone the dog-tags for a newly acquired shark tooth necklace. I walked the whole way trying to avoid the trail of ants that stretched all along the sidewalk railings and the sight of James's bare chest and nascent six-pack.

I had always loved the musculature of the male torso and was attracted to it in every possible way, in contrast to my view of the female torso. Part of my distress at the thought of what was to come was the knowledge it was not going to involve the development of this form of beauty. I was not going to become angular; I was going to become curved. And, what's more, I was to be closely taunted with what I could not have, it was to be dangled daily in my face. I would have to live every day knowing James had taken the other fork in the road from which I would be barred and which put him on a parallel path that I could see but never touch. *'It's not his fault, it's not his fault,'* became my mantra in times like this. I hated feeling the way I did then, seething with poisonous jealousy that twisted my heart. I loved my brother and I didn't want to boil over with bitterness and sadness every time I looked at him.

I also hated having to wear this swimming costume. The skin-tight nature of it meant that, like skirts, it felt far too exposing, which was odd given the messaging that girls had to be more covered up than boys. I could never understand why I could not be topless in public, either in regular clothes or in swimwear. What was there to see? My nipples are the same as his nipples! For children, I could not see why this was the way things were. But I had never been brave enough to challenge it; the weight of social disapproval was more than enough to make me scared of breaking the status quo. That changed on this holiday, spurred on by the sense of urgency from impending change, I knew that it had come to now or never. So one morning, I snuck out early from our apartment and jumped into the swimming pool a few metres away, dressed only in a pair of shorts. I surfaced and quickly looked about me to see if any of the few people already on sun loungers were giving me a funny look, but they were more interested in absorbing the sun's rays than the goings on around them and I tried to shake off the vestiges of paranoia. The first thing I noticed was how unexpectedly different the water felt now that so much more of my skin was in direct contact with it. It felt silky over my back and chest in a very pleasing feeling but which stabbed me with anger that I had been denied it before. I swam around, pushing off from the side, feeling marvellous and free, pretending I was a merman. I was glad I did it; at least I would have that memory to take with me on the miserable journey down the other fork in the road.

We returned home as the summer drew to a close but almost immediately I went on holiday again on the Year 6 (ages 10–11) week-long class trip to Little Canada adventure centre on the Isle of Wight. Here we stayed in log cabins and learnt abseiling, tunnelling and climbing. And it was here that I first heard girls talking excitedly about the pubertal changes they were experiencing, one morning in my cabin as everyone was having showers and getting ready. I couldn't understand the excitement and felt completely at a loss with the conversation in a way that made my stomach tense. So absorbed was I with warding off thoughts of my own changes, the idea that others would be approaching them with totally the opposite outlook and feelings was something of a shocking realisation. I chided myself; of course they would be excited! That was the *normal* response and I was decidedly *abnormal*, a strange type of non-girl who had a secret veiled away from the world and which I still could not bring myself to consciously confront. No one would understand me. I was alone with this pain and that is how it would remain. I stood there getting ready as quickly as possible, trying to bury the feelings of guilt at my feelings of dread that mixed with this hideous sensation of difference, excited chatter about periods ringing in my ears.

I realised then that I had sounded the alarm to begin closing down emotionally, it was now time to batten down the hatches for real, changes had come to some of my friends and they were coming for me too. It was time to start saying goodbye to myself. I had my sleek, black camera with me on this holiday, which I had been given for my birthday and Kat 'n' Dave and I had been having fun photographing random things and posing with silly faces in our free time. Kat and I had also purchased these little toy animals from the gift shop which had googly eyes, hers a starfish, mine a regular fish, and for some reason I decided to get her to take a photo of me kissing it in the way I'd seen fishermen do to prize catches. As I posed, I made the very deliberate actions of holding the fish up to my face with both hands raised so that my arms were drawn across my chest. In this way I blocked my upper chest from view so that there could be no possibility of the tiniest of bumps, that I otherwise fought ferociously not to acknowledge, being visible in the shot. I also tilted my chin up to a degree rather greater than was really necessary in the hope of displaying my strong angular jawline, the likes of which were sported on James and all the older boys and men I admired and which I loved about my own face. I wanted it on film, to capture it before it was lost to the softness, before it became a casualty of war. I was most pleased with the picture when I eventually saw it on the way home from the Kodak shop. It would be a fitting memorial for whom I had once been, how I had once looked, and I inscribed as much on the back in gold pen: *Best picture of myself, October 1999, aged 10.* Yes, it would be another cherished keepsake on the sad trudge down the other fork in the road.

CRUSHING PRESSURE

On the last night before the end of our time on the Isle of Wight, a disco was held in the main hall to which the other school in attendance at the centre that week were also invited. I was a little annoyed at this, I didn't like fraternising with other schools and it felt like they were gate-crashing our celebration. But it also made me extremely tense. They would, of course, assume I was a boy and, as always, the joy I felt at being gendered correctly, that glorious feeling of gender euphoria, was slowly eaten away with worry at being 'found out' – of being 'outed' for what I 'really was'. As I grew older, the fear of this had started to become more extreme, the way people responded to me in those moments, and the possible consequences of it, were getting increasingly serious. A very young child displaying gender non-conformity is excused some of the direct disapproval or disdain, this being reserved for and addressed to their parents by confused or downright disgusted observers who presume, since the parent or guardian is meant to be in control of all aspects of the child's life, that, at worst, they are the ones instigating this behaviour, or, at best, allowing it to happen. As the child grows older, the attacks – for that is what they are – start to become aimed straight at the child, as the child is expected to be past a certain point of maturity, of 'knowing better' than to still be behaving like this.

There was no way I was not going to outed as a girl to the other school. Members of my class and teachers present would, at some point, be overheard calling me by my name or else addressing me as 'she' or 'her'. Failing that, it was likely at some point in the course of the evening I would need to use the sex-segregated toilet facilities. I always made a point when entering a new place to familiarise myself with the location of these facilities and would spent time deciphering when might be the least busy times to use them to limit the amount of toilet terror I was to face that day. Sometimes there would be more than one and I would note which of them was the most hidden away and least likely to be overlooked at the entrance so that I might slip in to whichever toilet I had the nerve to use, unobserved. But there was no such luck on this night. The toilet doors were inside the main hall area, not even in a vestibule, and so it was going to be with the largest audience possible that I would have to go through the door emblazoned with the faceless figure wearing a dress. The stage was set for the night's outing.

I was still determined to have a good time. Stay away from the other school and have fun at the disco with Kat 'n' Dave, that was the plan. We loved our school discos, from running around the pulsing patterns of light, to making up crazy dance moves, to running out of the hall in mock disgust at yet another Spice Girls song. I did my best to connect to this sense of excitement and enjoyment on this occasion but it was a struggle. The hall wasn't very large and it proved pretty difficult to stay very far away from members of the other school even though we had separated as seamlessly as oil and water. Something else was happening, however, that began to push against this separation. It became apparent that some members of my class and of the other where egging each other on to go up and mingle with members of the opposite class, who they had told their friends they found attractive. Little groups of giggling girls and sheepish boys were forming around the room. I did not want to get involved with this development, either there in the hall or anywhere else. Attraction or having crushes was very decidedly an aspect of growing up, a function of puberty, and I did not want to engage with it at all. To do so would be an unacceptable concession to the knowledge that puberty had come for me. My biggest concern in that moment was trying to ignore it, trying to shut out the fact that my classmates, my friends, were engaging in this pubertal game. The idea that I would be drawn into it, even as a passive participant, escaped my consideration entirely.

It was whilst I was standing in a corner with Kat 'n' Dave, behind the gaggle which was pushing my friend, Rebecca, towards a boy from the other school, when I noticed one of the smaller groups of girls flitting looks at Kat and I and giggling and whispering to themselves. My hackles went up immediately. I presumed they had discovered my 'true identity' from overhearing a use of my name and Kat's too, her being my companion in gender non-conformity, and were now carrying out the usual post-outing conversation filled with shock, confusion, amusement, disgust, disdain and mockery. But it slowly dawned on me that they were in fact shooting us the same *interested* looks that other groups had been exchanging. I didn't know what to do, but, curiously, riding behind that wave of shock was a sudden feeling of intense happiness; they believed I was a boy and, what's more, they found me to be an attractive boy. That realisation burst through my barrier against the concept of crushes and flew straight into that cage in the back of my mind, which swelled with something close to pride. I did not return their interest, but that didn't matter. As I tried once again to rapidly repair the barriers between the front of my mind and the back, I became aware of other feelings that had flowed over me. This was a previously unexperienced and unexpected situation for which I had no plan, but I could already sense the danger it put us in. These girls were going to find out we had 'tricked' them and they were going to feel angry and embarrassed, the very emotions that made people lash out the most.

It was in that moment that Kat asked me to go to the toilet with her. We often did this together because our nerve sometimes failed us when the act of opening a certain door had to be done in full view of so many potential members of the Toilet Police. A problem shared is a problem halved. But I really didn't want to this time. I was awash with panic and fear of this act of outing in a way more complicated and serious than I ever had before. The consequences on this occasion would be the group mocking of a wall of hostile faces and very likely some embarrassed and/or angry girls and that was bad enough, but it occurred to me that at other times, in the future, this could lead to real violence, physical and mental. When people start feeling that you're messing with their feelings, all manner of next level nastiness can be unleashed. And what of my own attractions, how was that even going to work with me seemingly being one gender but yet another? I went with Kat in the end because I'm not a bad friend and we faced our wall of mockery, but I went to my bunk bed that night with my head swimming in the complications of this other aspect of growing up and which I tried to push aside, for now.

INTO BATTLE

My eleventh birthday was taking place at the Baptist Church down the road from my school. It was an absolute scorcher of a day in mid-July of 2000 and, unlike many of my birthday parties, which were paradoxically conducted at the ice rink in Hemel Hempstead, this one was to capitalise on the hot weather with all out super-soaker war waged on the field in the grounds of the church. James and I were highly skilled super-soaker fighters, which was a serious pastime in the 1990s, and we each had in our possession what is obviously the greatest super-soaker to have ever been produced – the XXP-275. It was a double-barrel shooter with each barrel fitted with a nozzle that could rotate through four different shapes from slits to sprays to beams. These were operated not by a little trigger, but by a big yellow pull-down lever which sprayed out the water under the pressure you had pumped into it with the front hand pump according to the reading on the top pressure gauge. The water capacity of 2.7 litres was so great in the huge green tank on the back that its total weight meant I really needed the large black strap that held it around my neck like a guitar.

The war was set between the mighty forces of all my friends versus the feeble threat of James's motley crew (history is always written by the victors). Kat 'n' Dave and I had been preparing tactically for this for weeks and were organising the troops into an efficient water balloon production line when I spied James setting up his position on the other side of the field in his swim shorts, XXP-275 in hand. Something in me snapped. I left the water balloon assembly in Kat 'n' Dave's capable hands and went into one of the small side rooms of the church and took off my swimming costume and went out only in my shorts.

I don't know why I thought I could get away with it, perhaps because it was my birthday and, by virtue of being fussed over, felt pretty high and powerful, as if on this day like no other, I could do what I wanted. The lumps had grown in the months since the Isle of Wight the previous October but only a little bit, and in my opinion were within the bounds of *acceptability*. I thus strode out with my XXP-275 and with confidence borne of defiance headed the first charge towards enemy forces.

It lasted for maybe five minutes before Mum appeared out of the safety of the church and came up to my side, putting her arm around my shoulder. She guided me back into the small room, all the while whispering into my ear, 'You need to wear your swimming costume. The thing is you are a girl and you are developing now and you have to wear appropriate clothes, I'm sorry but that's the way it is.' I tried to argue it was my birthday but she was adamant I was not going back out there until I complied. I returned to the battlefield feeling as though my wings had just been held to a fire and burnt off, my heart bubbling with bitterness and anger. I picked up my super-soaker and rejoined the fray at the start of the next wave of attack. James and I met in the centre of the field and I pulled my lever down releasing the twin jets of pressurised water straight at him with as much force as I could. I wanted to hurt him. I wanted to make him pay for having everything I couldn't have. For his perfect body and his perfect future that seemingly stretched out like a golden trail before him. The pain of the reciprocal jets of water actually felt good; they took my emotions away as well as my breath.

That night, I stood in front of the mirror in the bathroom wiping away tears and wishing with all my being there was something that could be done to stop this, some pill or injection I could have or even some kind of magic that could be performed to take them away in a flash of light. Like practically every child alive at the turn of the millennium, I was fully ensconced in the world of Harry Potter. I am a proud member of the first generation of Potter fans; the fans that began reading as the books were being published and suffered the agony of the three-year wait between books four and five. Kat 'n' Dave and I were equally obsessed and longed to get that Hogwarts letter, to be whisked off to that magical world and we would act out scenes in the playground with me, given my hair, obviously taking the role of Ron. But I wished for a Hogwarts letter for another, very different, reason to other children. Daydream after daydream I would spend imagining having the power to make these bumps vanish from my chest with some spell, or I would dream of going to the hospital wing where Madam Pomfrey would give me some terrible tasting potion to drink, but which I would take gladly and marvel as the bumps slowly melted away before my very eyes.

But in the cold light of day there was nothing. I lifted my arms above my head to see if my nipples still appeared to flatten back as the skin was stretched tight. *Just*. There was now barely any sand left in the top of the puberty timer. I was taking the other fork in the road as if some invisible force had me by the legs and was dragging me kicking and screaming onto that path. But for me, as one who did not belong on it, I could see only darkness ahead and could only hear the gut-wrenching sound of oncoming war.

SECONDARY CONSIDERATIONS

In the changing rooms of Marks and Spencer, Watford, James was visibly distressed. 'You cannot wear *them*, you WILL be bullied!' he exclaimed. My heart sank. That was real concern in his voice, the kind that told me he wasn't just trying to ward me off from buying the boys' trousers I had on as an act of sibling cruelty, but out of genuine fear for what it would mean for me in my first days at secondary school. I had high hopes of trying again at this new school after the failed attempt at St Peter's and had utilised all my assertiveness to get Mum to agree to letting me even try them on during our Back to School shopping trip in late August, but James's almost panicked protestations dissolved my willpower completely. It would be wise for me to take his word for it; he had already completed

Year 7 (ages 11–12) at Westfield Community School and was thus well-placed to know what the reception would likely be to a girl in boys' trousers.

I had always fully intended to take up my sibling priority slot at this school despite the sadness of it meaning I would be separated from Kat 'n' Dave. It was the only secondary school in the area that had trousers as a part of the uniform for girls and that constituted almost all of the requirement criteria I had for my new school; league table results or quality of facilities be damned. The other important factor was James's presence, which meant I might have the option of using his popularity as trading capital to repel potential bullies, which I considered a distinct possibility. At that time Westfield did not have a reputation as a particularly good school; it did not have any kind of selection criteria, unlike the grammar schools or St Clement Danes, which Mum and Dad had tried to get James into. Mum had wanted me to sit the entrance exam for Watford Grammar School for Girls, but I made it clear I'd have rather sawn my hands off and she did not push it, although she would occasionally comment wistfully that I could have got in. Maybe so, but I shudder to think what it would have cost me to try and survive at an all girls school with pleated skirts and pale shirts that would have made it blatantly obvious if I wasn't wearing a bra.

I took off the boys' trousers as my mind began slowly filling with vivid scenarios of bullying and constant run-ins with the Toilet Police at the new school. After all, there were going to be so many more people in my year and in the school as a whole; gone were the days of safety in small numbers where everyone knew you. I thought hard for a few moments, maybe it would be a good idea to go entirely the other way with my uniform choices, to pre-empt this situation. In this school environment there would be no joy to be had from letting or encouraging people to presume I was a boy, which they would do given the blue polo shirt and thick blue jumper I would be wearing. If I wore a skirt then it would settle the matter in people's minds so that I would not have to navigate through constant awkward situations and dozens and dozens of people coming up to me demanding an answer to 'Are you a girl or a boy?' I settled for a very plain looking black skirt, which I made myself promise to wear for the first few days, after which I could swop to the best I could find out of the available options of the obviously tight-fitting/shaped girls' trousers.

Everyone's first day at secondary school is a very momentous occasion that is certain to find a place within the long-term memory. Mine tells me that I was scared for all the usual reasons, but also terribly anxious about my appearance. This day was going to be scary enough, new people, new buildings, new subjects; I didn't need to have yet another and very costly drain on my reserves of confidence. Placing my difference on full display in this act of self-preservation was probably going to take it all. But I had promised myself and went again through how it would be a good thing in the long run. I had to remind myself of that over and over again as the funny looks came at me from all directions, some people even double-taking and pointing. I felt so self-conscious and angry, which built higher throughout the day and just hoped it would be worth it. But there were a lot of people in the school and a lot of things to take in and, even after managing through two more days, it appeared that my efforts were not to be entirely rewarded: BANG BANG BANG, went the toilet cubicle door.

◆━◎━━━◎━◆

It is a most exquisitely hideous thing to understand that you are going to change in ways you know right down in the very core of your being are categorically not what should be happening. And further, to know you have absolutely no control and no recourse to stop it. By the end of the first year of this vibrant, young and hopeful new millennium, I already felt exhausted, old and hopeless. I had been beaten into submission by the fact of puberty. I felt like I was slowly dying during this time, counting my time left in days and weeks, checking over and over for more signs of the coming of the time when I would no longer recognise who I saw. There was to be no bright and sunny future at the end of the path I was forced to take. I couldn't even envisage what might be at the other end.

But I couldn't tell anyone how I felt, quite simply because I had no reason to believe there would have been any point to it. I still had no knowledge of any other person as me and thus what 'as me' even really meant. I had seen no television programmes, I could read no books. In the feeble attempts I had made to voice these deepest pains to those closest to me, they had not been able to give me anything more than yet another rendition of 'You're just a tomboy.' So I was to be dragged along this wrong path, and all the way the emotional cavern inside me would fill with the poisons of bitterness, anger, deceit and jealousy until I could hold no more.

Me in a frilly pink number (1990)

*Wearing my navy tennis dress with Mum and
James at a family wedding (1998)*

Fun in the Sun with Mum and James (1999)

*Kat 'n' Dave and I running away from another
Spice Girls song at a school disco (2000)*

*As the inscription on the back still states, this is the 'best
picture of myself' taken on the Isle of Wight (1999)*

Inappropriately dressed on the London Eye during a hot summer's day (2005)

Tuxedo selfie (April 2015)

Chapter 8

NOBODY MUST KNOW

NOWHERE LEFT TO RUN

There was nothing I could do. It was the summer of 2001 and I was trapped in the car as Mum took the turning into the King's car park next to the Harlequin Shopping Centre. She had just spoken those few dreaded words that had me feeling as if I'd been rammed through with a spear, 'We're going to Marks and Spencer to get you properly fitted for a bra.' It was always going to come to this, but I had pushed it violently out of my conscious thoughts, clinging to the desperate hope that they wouldn't grow large enough to make it necessary.

Why was it even necessary? For health? For function? It certainly wasn't for the tribeswomen I'd seen in the *National Geographic* in many a doctor and dentist's waiting room. Clearly it hadn't been for the thousands of years human and other female hominids had existed back in the archives of time. No, this was about the obsession with aesthetics. In this world you've got to look a certain way or you will be judged. If your breasts move freely on their own, even a little bit, you will be judged. If they are allowed to be a natural teardrop shape and not perfectly spherical mounds shoved right up next to your armpits, then you will be judged. Some people may say it's a free choice, but that could not be further from the truth. Ask yourself, how many people assigned female at birth are given it as a free choice? No, they will be told they must wear them, for fear in this patriarchal world, of inciting sexual advances and to prevent sagging. They will not be told there is no good justification for that assertion whatsoever and will become among the huge majority of people who still believe that bras prevent this natural consequence of aging.

'No! I don't want to!' I begged, I pleaded as Mum locked the car and began marching me towards the shops. 'You don't want them to sag!' she said. 'And it's not nice for *other people* if you don't wear one! This is not a negotiation!' I stood in the little fitting room cubicle engulfed in anger and humiliation. I'd just been measured by a brisk but professional lady with half-moon spectacles and a tape measure around her shoulders who'd duly gone off to fetch some try-outs. Rooted to the spot, I folded my arms firmly across my chest, defensive until the last. At least I had won the argument about underwire. There was no way in a thousand hells that was going to happen and Mum was shrewdly aware of how far she should push her front line. Perhaps sensing what she was up against, the lady returned with a selection of fairly utilitarian looking bras. They were not 'training bras' as I had seen some frilly triangles labelled in the rows we passed on the way in. Training bras; what an odd phrase, training for what? To cope with the mild to extreme discomfort you are going to have to put up with for the rest of your life? But I'd successfully staved off this moment for so long I was deemed to be past those sizes already. I put on a white contraption as the lady told me it should be clasped on the second rungs, not the first.

The mental and physical reaction was quick and violent. The cage in the back of my mind felt like it was on fire, like it was being burnt at the stake and the pain sent out a shockwave down my body that tensed every muscle. This was visceral anger and I could not make myself relax. My shoulders screamed under the burden of being so painfully tensed underneath the straps that lay on top of them, every bit aware of the weight they were suddenly holding up. My torso felt as though it had just been caught in a vice and I could feel the line digging into my skin all the way around from front to back. 'Are you sure this is right?' I asked as I became overwhelmed with a BURNING,

PASSIONATE RAGE to rip it from my body like I was Bruce Banner turning into The Hulk. 'Yes', the lady said. I could feel myself collapsing internally, my happiness, my self-esteem, all of it crumbling into nothing. Tears formed at the sides of my eyes. So *this* was to be my fate, this unbelievable level of discomfort, every day, for the rest of my life. 'It's important to wear ones fitted correctly, it's about comfort,' Mum said. *'It bloody is not,'* I thought venomously.

Yes, I am aware my aversion to bras is largely a product of gender dysphoria for their obvious association with breasts and mine isn't the typical response of a person who finds themselves growing breasts, but I genuinely think there are more than a few people who have simply learned to put up with the irritation, the discomfort, put it down to 'one of those things women have to deal with'. I think it is an unspoken truth which you sometimes see snippets of in memes, articles and stand-up comedy routines: *'Ladies, the best time of the day is when you can get home and unclasp that bra, am I right?'* *cackle* *chortle* *laugh*. I wasn't laughing.

How was I going to cope with this parental and social requirement? How was I going to concentrate at school or even function from moment to moment in daily life whilst combating The Rage caused by this discomfort? I could barely stand it. This was a level of dysphoria I did not think was possible, although of course, I had no word to attach to the feelings I believed no one else in the whole world had ever experienced. The bare truth of my changing body was now glaring at me from three differently angled mirrors and it was so completely *wrong*. How could this be happening to *my* body? And now this wrongness was to be further highlighted; not only was the bra so disgustingly uncomfortable, it made them more visible, put them up front and centre for everybody's viewing pleasure, the absolute opposite of what I wanted. But I was persuaded to try several others, Mum hovering about interjecting how, 'Sometimes you just need to find the right one,' but every one the same response; the same shockwaves of primal agony at the discomfort of bra and breasts upon my body. *'I can't do this, I can't do this, I can't do this,'* ran unceasingly through my panicked mind. But I wasn't getting out of there without at least one, that I knew. So I picked two at random, one white, one light purple, and left the shop feeling like my life might as well be over.

That night I locked myself in the bathroom and pulled out a bandage from the medical supplies in the cupboard under the sink. I wrapped it around my chest and pulled the ends tight. The flattening effect was somewhat effective but the discomfort from the bandage could not be ignored and I knew this was never going to work. It also made it harder to breathe in and out completely and I felt The Rage mounting again at the reason why I was trying to do this. I knew I could not get away forever with not conforming to the requirement of bra wearing, the social pressure was far too strong. But I couldn't wear one, I just couldn't, the dysphoria brought on from the discomfort and the way it made me confront the presence of these breasts upon me, made it utterly impossible to function. With every fibre of my being I wanted these illegitimate breasts gone, removed right that very second and in that moment I didn't care if it meant hacking them off with a kitchen knife.

The seriousness with which I had that thought unnerved me deeply. It felt like my mind was spiralling down into a well of darkness and I was conscious that if I fell in, I might never get out. I hurriedly took the bandage off and stuffed it back into the cupboard and then ran into my room where I stood and gave into the urge to beat myself repeatedly in the chest until I cried out in pain. The emotional release felt good, as did the thought that maybe if I damaged the tissue then they wouldn't be able to grow any bigger. The worst day of my life up to that point ended with me crying myself to sleep curled up in a ball of despair.

BRA BATTLES

The next few months were hell on Earth. Every day I'd wake up to a mind already swimming with worry of getting through the day ahead without having to wear that contraption of torture, constantly thinking through what deceits I would have to commit this day and just how many layers of clothing I would have to keep on to prevent these lumps from being seen. Mum would try to make sure I was wearing it before I left the house for school, by looking or even running her hand down my back. But I quickly got into a routine of passing inspection and dashing to take it off in the bathroom before running out the door to the bus stop. I was glad of my school uniform, the comfortable royal blue polo shirt and thick jumper made it a lot easier to get away with this social taboo, so long as I kept the jumper on. However, after school, at weekends and events I would find myself cornered and it quickly became a constant battleground characterised by shouted demands and screamed refusals, anger and crying. I'd be sent to my room and not let out without it on. All the while James sat downstairs watching TV or playing a video game, making me seethe with jealousy and overflow with embarrassment. I hated him knowing I had breasts; I hated him knowing I hated them and the bras that went with them. I would lock myself in my room, crying out the pain and anger until I was nothing but an empty shell. These were some of my darkest days, in which I was consumed by the fog of despair. I have often wondered how or if I would have been able to go on like that for much longer than I did if I hadn't made a desperate and very important stand, or if my parents had been harder, more ruthless on this matter. In this regard I was lucky.

Things came to a head on our second big foreign holiday to Canada. After the death of Nan and Grandad, Dad had been the sole inheritor and, as well as splashing out on a sports car, had decided to take us all on a 'caravanners-at-large' holiday in a campervan around Canada. The first stop was Vancouver and the hospitality of some of Dad's old Christian friends from years gone by, a sweet old couple called Tom and Cynthia. Whilst we were there Tom was extremely excited about taking us to visit his church. Mum cornered me in my makeshift room as everyone was getting ready, 'You are wearing a bra to this service,' she said. Mum is a small and bubbly person, but there is steel in her too and I knew it as she pointed her finger and narrowed her eyes at me that I would have to at least have it on my person in some way. I had learned during earlier fights that I could lessen the dysphoria if I had it unclasped as much as possible or ,when it was done up, pulled at the back or the front of it with my hand under my shirt. But that was hard to do surreptitiously and the service was long. I was emotionally spent by the end from trying to keep a lid on The Rage that began as soon as that clasp was closed around my back and which manifested as severe irritability that soon made me snap and project an attitude easily interpreted as rudeness. I took it off in the toilets as the service segued into coffee and cake but it was barely a minute before Mum took me aside and told me to put it back on. I flat out refused. I had reached the absolute end of my emotional overdraft. This was a battle I simply had to win for the sake of my mental health, which was now straining under the burden of the constant worry of forced bra wearing events. Mum relented. At the end of the day, she wasn't a sadist. This was our big holiday and she wasn't up to spending it locked in combat with me. As wilful and steely as she was, on this issue, upon which my happiness well and truly depended, I could not and would not back down.

It was a serious relief to know I could have respite from that particular struggle, but these breasts were on me every minute of every day. There was no respite from that relentless mental ache and anguish, the constant stress of having to deal with the searing dysphoria and trying to exist successfully in a world hostile to my predicament. It was hot in Canada, very hot, too hot to wear a jumper, and I began to devote a lot of mental energy to developing strategies to get through what were, for other people, basic life situations. For everyone else they were simply daily deliberations on what to wear, what outfit suits the day or looks the best, but, for me, every choice now solely centred on how I'd be able to hide these breasts, how best I'd be able to simply get through the day without people knowing I (a) had breasts at all and (b) wasn't wearing a bra. For example, to combat not being able to wear a jumper in the heat, I took to pulling at the bottom of my t-shirt, walking around holding it stretched taut slightly outwards from my body to give the illusion there was nothing there. This was reasonably successful but would take away one of my hands from other uses and made my arm ache after a while, building up frustration and sadness within my inner emotional cavern. As did the sight of James, ambling along, arms freely by his side, experiencing not one single iota of this misery. Bitterness and jealousy flowed in too.

This calculating shame behaviour continued as we returned home and time and physical development went marching on. Under the blessing of the coldish English climate, for which I gave thanks every morning, I encased myself within layers of material. So great was my need to hide, I would push myself to the absolute limits of endurance, refusing to take off my jumper even as the mercury soared. I would walk around central London in high summer done up to my eyeballs and would take family trips on the glasshouse pods of the London Eye in a zip-up fleece with fur-lined hood. If I did remove an outer layer to narrowly avoid fainting from heat exhaustion, instead of tying it around my waist or draping it around my shoulders, I would fold it up and hold it against the front of my chest to act as a visual barrier. I grew used to having the use of only one arm as well as the horrible feeling of the sweat caused by the jumper obstruction, which would collect under the breasts and run down my stomach as I walked.

I began to seriously hate summer and dreaded its arrival. It meant an enormous increase in my mental load and the possibility of not being able to properly enjoy situations and events I otherwise loved; in some cases it meant having to pull out of participating altogether. I would be invited to go on days out, such as to Thorpe Park on a glorious summer's day, and would have to turn them down, knowing full well it would be an event in which I would not be able to apply my coping strategies effectively. But, worse, in order to get out of going I'd have to either fake a family commitment or fake an illness, which made me feel awful, a deceitful, cheating liar.

Even hanging out just generally with Kat 'n' Dave became difficult. I would consciously try to steer our decisions on what to do to be an activity that involved staying indoors and not moving very much, such as watching a movie, which was one of my favourite activities given that it allowed me to sit hugging a cushion to my chest. A sad departure from the outdoors adventure-loving child I had once been.

I felt so ashamed, but I couldn't tell anyone. This issue was so personal it was well beyond anything I could share even with my closest friends. My hopes about Kat being like me had increased as she too had seemed to struggle with her physical development and the wearing of bras. But I couldn't even begin to broach the subject and, at any rate, it wasn't too long before she managed to figure out what I seemingly could not and took to wearing bras and being, if not proud, at least comfortable with this aspect of her body. I remember how crestfallen I was the moment I realised this. It meant I really was alone with feeling this certain knowledge that my body should not be doing this and thus, even among other gender variant people I knew, I was different, an outcast from literally all of society. I was at least glad that Kat's breasts were becoming as sizable as mine, which meant I was spared suffering the concern that hers would be small and I would be consumed with that particular painful jealousy. Interestingly, my jealousy towards Dave remained quite mild; I never developed the same level of burning inner vitriol towards him as I did towards James or boys in my class. I'm not quite sure why, perhaps it was because I was aware he wasn't having the best adolescence himself at his own school, which meant my jealousy at his body developments was overridden by concern and anger on his behalf.

My body's developing continued unabated. It was now moving beyond the point where it was possible to hide their existence, even in a jumper, and I worked hard to build supporting walls in my mind to deal with this threat to my stability. Something was going to have to be done, as time began to run out on even my most cunning strategies and I took to devoting all of my free mental time to the solving of this escalating problem. I had already established that bandaging was a no go (a fact I'm very glad of given what I now know of the dangers of binding with bandages), but one day I hit upon the idea of wearing my swimming costume under my t-shirt to stop them from moving around – a sensation I hated deeply for it reminded me they were there, and to create something of the socially acceptable chest shape.

This had a chance, I thought, because I could still bear to wear my swimming costume, although only when under the water; any time out of the water required an immediate covering towel or top or else the use of my forearms drawn right across my chest so that my fists rested under my chin. I would stand for ages like that as we waited on the winding stairs for a go on the flumes in the fake tropical paradise that was Aqua Splash in Hemel Hempstead. I went out wearing my swimming costume as an undergarment a few times with Kat 'n' Dave, skateboarding down a very steep red brick lane we called 'Jordan's Hill' around the back of the local leisure centre up by the playing fields, revelling in the recovery of a small part of the joy and freedom I once had at the comfort in and use of my own body. I hoped they wouldn't notice I was wearing a swimming costume, but of course they did, in hindsight it was ridiculous to think they wouldn't, and the wind blowing up the bottom of my t-shirt as I rode my skateboard down the hill certainly made it very clear. It was a reasonably successful strategy in terms of managing the mental anguish, but overheating from the skin-tight nylon soon reared itself as a problem and after Kat 'n' Dave had teased me as 'swimming costume girl', I abandoned the practice in panic.

THE CROP TOPS OF SHAME

The single greatest thing Mum has ever given me in the whole of my life was a navy blue Nike sports half-length crop top. She had bought it for herself, but had given it to me as a possible solution. It extended half way down my torso and had no tight elastic band on the bottom, nor any specific 'cup' areas, it was merely a tight tank-type top. I was severely dubious, but the situation was getting extremely desperate. It was early May 2002 and I could feel the brain-melting burden of summer drawing ever closer once again. It was now at the point where there was absolutely no chance of taking off my jumper at all. If it came to it I was simply going to have to faint. But when I put that Nike top on in the bathroom, The Rage rumbled, but did not erupt. I put on my t-shirt and found that not only did it stop the movement, it also created a passable 'socially acceptable' shape. The relief that flowed throughout my body was extraordinary and burst out of me in waves of tears and laughter befitting the fact a massive mental cloud had just been removed and I could see the blue sky again. It wasn't the ultimate solution, I knew, but it was enough to allow me to function in the world for the foreseeable future at least. I asked Mum to get me another so that I could have one to wear when the other was in the wash. I could now go out in a t-shirt again and give the appearance of a normal bra-wearing adolescent who wasn't consumed with hatred towards their secondary sex characteristics.

The first time I tried it out was at the cadet weekend of the St John Ambulance division, of which I would rise to become Sergeant Leader. During this weekend, we would sleep over at the hall and work towards a 'proficiency' in a first aid-related subject. We were called in for the exam one by one on the sweltering Sunday afternoon, while everyone else engaged in a game of volleyball in the yard. I stood for a long time in front of the long mirror in the toilets, staring at my front and side profile; would it pass the test? There was only one way to find out. To my utter relief, no one looked at me funny or made any comment as I stepped out in my red England away kit shirt. The relief and joy of simply being able to take part in a game like that was unreal. It gave me a piece of vital hope that there was indeed a way forward. Even so, I felt a severe need to keep them a secret; I was ashamed of them as I was of having these breasts and, if people had to know about the latter, I was desperate to make sure the former remained for my knowledge only.

Despite this breakthrough, trying to play sport was a different situation and required a different solution. It was now a completely horrific experience, which was a serious issue given that I was a member of Watford Girls Football Club and had been press-ganged by my school Physical Education (PE) teachers to try out for the Hertfordshire county team, for whom, quite to my shock, I was selected to play as left back. I still loved football and had been persuaded a year before to join Watford by Dad. My friend Sarah, who had also gone from St Peter's to Westfield, was already there and so I felt somewhat comfortable trying to fit in with the team. But now it had come to the point where I could not go on without exposing myself to serious ridicule. To my pain, the navy crop top proved to be no good for serious sport and anyhow I was terrified of breaking it lest it be impossible to find another replacement. However, my deep aversion to engaging with this problem meant I was left in a massive panic the night before my first county game, desperately trying to find a solution. I found it the form of Mum's bright orange sports bra, which I took out of her gym bag in the back of her wardrobe. I tried it on briefly to make sure it fit and then threw into my own kit bag in relief and disgust. The whole way to the match I was moody and stressed, trying and failing to contain the pain and anger I felt at being in this situation, at having the enjoyment of this game sucked out of me.

Wearing the sports bra in the match was every bit as mentally straining as I had expected, especially since it wasn't wholly successful at stopping the movement and my anger at their presence upon me overwhelmed my ability to concentrate, which led to a number of anger-relieving fouls, one of which earned me a yellow card. As a coping strategy to the hideous irritation, I also began to purposefully stop running around as much as possible, doing the absolute bare minimum of work. I gave a poor performance, which unsurprisingly marked the only game I would play for the county team. Playing football had now become a thoroughly miserable experience and would continue to be so for the rest of my playing days as I moved with Sarah to Garston Ladies Football Club. It would have been easier to stop playing, but I didn't feel like I could do that, I didn't think I could just say I didn't want to play anymore and I had got it in my head it would be letting the team down, as a naturally left-footed defensive player, I knew I was fairly valued.

So the horror continued as I grew out of Mum's sports bra and was forced to take myself shopping for a replacement in the form of a white Nike sports crop top that I made sure was too big so that the band was as loose as possible. This was so that I could bear to wear it on the journey to the pitch, which was often just in a field, and thus the chances of finding somewhere to put it on were I not already wearing it were slim and I didn't dare risk being caught out. I couldn't play with it so loose however and so I stuck a large safety pin in the band, which I used to hold it at the back where I had pulled it together. Just before the game started, I would have to scramble about at my back under my shirt and brace my mental defences to fight against the rage of dysphoria. I could have played better, I could have been so much better than I was. Breast dysphoria well and truly took football and indeed most sports from me in the end and I was glad when I eventually managed to use the excuse of mounting A-level workload to extricate myself from it. I wished so much it didn't have to be that way.

VICIOUS CYCLES

So distressed was I at the development of breasts, I had forgotten almost entirely about the concept of menstruation and was caught off guard when it arrived shortly after I turned 12. It was easy to forget; it's not something that is seen or even talked about in 'polite society' no doubt because a lot of men can't deal with it or don't want to hear about it. Mum had kept her sanitary items well out of sight in the bathroom and the discussions and anatomical diagrams used to broach the subject in my late primary/early secondary sex education lessons were easy to keep at a mental remove. The dysphoria during these times was unsurprisingly high; it made me confront, for the first time, the nature of the *inside* of my body, reminding me with every cramp-ache that I was filled with such structures. And further, I was forced to confront the fact they were now active and that I was capable of *being pregnant* and *giving birth*. The idea of those things was terrifying to me because they represented states about as far away as was physically possible from that which I wanted my body to become. The idea that I was capable of reaching those states was met with violent opposition from the back of my mind and I snatched those thoughts from my consciousness and banished them away into the darkness. Such things did not and would never apply to me! And that was final. I couldn't be grouped with those girls in my class who were excited and proud to have achieved this ability. I felt happy for them in their joy, but it was a joy completely alien to me and I could not attach it to myself.

It was harder to get away from the realities of menstruation and the days preceding it where the peaks and troughs of hormones caused chaos to my emotional stability, as if I was a marionette being made to dance by an unseen force. I had already studied and duly memorised the classic diagram showing the changes in the levels of the four hormones throughout the menstrual cycle in relation to the state of the womb lining and it made me angry to think of it going on inside my body for the fact it meant my bloodstream was overflowing with that most hated of all hormones, oestrogen, knowledge which only further ratcheted my anger at the exact time my emotional threshold had been lowered. I knew my reaction was different, others just got on with it. And though no girls I knew enjoyed these symptoms of premenstrual syndrome (PMS) or the way it was made fun of by boys and men, I knew none who appeared to attach the same type of hatred to the underlying causes as me. They were angry at the inconvenience of it all; I was beyond angry at the fact it meant I had a womb.

That's not to say I wasn't also angry at the inconvenience it caused as it intruded into my life. Following on from our 2001 carvanners-at-large holiday in Canada, the next summer

I found myself tenting on a holiday park in France. The heat on the continent was unreal, the type of dry and unrelenting heat that makes you want to submerse yourself in a large body of cool water for the entire day. But, alas, the cycle had decided now was the moment to puncture my carefully constructed equilibrium. I sat on the edge of a sun lounger watching James belly flop into the pristine turquoise water, which glistened enticingly in the glaring sun, anger burning a hole in my heart. He kept asking me why I didn't want to come in. I couldn't bear him knowing why I *couldn't* go in, I couldn't bear him knowing this was occurring to me. He splashed around, lying in a blissful starfish on the surface as I sat with the heat bearing down on my neck, sweat accumulating under the carefully hidden breasts.

I boiled over. As fast as I could I bolted from the pool and back to our tent where Dad, after some quiet time, was sat reading in the shade. As soon as he asked me what was wrong I collapsed into a fit of uncontrollable tears. He picked me up and held me in his arms on the chair as I tried to say through racks of sobs how I hated not being able to go in. He seemed to know why; I suspected Mum had told him. I cried and cried and cried tears that signified a deep, long held pain, the type of tears that come because there is no more space inside for them to stay, the type of tears that mean you have finally come face to face with a searing grief. I needed to cry those tears. I needed to grieve for my lost body, for my once dysphoria unburdened mind.

I suspected he thought it was my first one as he rubbed my back soothingly and told me gently how it was all part of growing up and how that wasn't always easy. Indeed it was not. He had always been able to fix everything; it had always been safe in his arms, but he couldn't save me from *this* pain. Not this time, not anymore. I was alone with this heartache and I always would be. At least the emotional release had spared me a mental breakdown and I clung to his shoulder exhausted, trying to shut the floodgates once more.

ROUND PEG, SQUARE HOLE

I was 14 when I last openly wore a t-shirt in public. To my continual horror, the breasts had now grown beyond a D cup and were still growing and every day I burned with jealousy towards those girls who moaned in the changing room that theirs weren't as big as they wanted. The navy crop tops of shame, as I called them, had stretched to adapt and to my complete relief, still operated well enough to keep the movement to a minimum, but to my deep sadness, the passable 'socially acceptable' shape I'd had was lost and in a t-shirt it was completely obvious I was flouting this cultural norm. The crop tops were now only a half solution and I was back to being unable to walk around freely in a t-shirt. Once again I enveloped myself in layers of material, like my denim jacket, which I wore almost every day for three years, its heaviness proving to have a pleasing flattening effect on the front of my chest. Back again came the tests of endurance as I pushed my body as far towards heat exhaustion as I could go without collapsing. Back again came the holding of coats and bags in front of my chest and the frustration of having the freedom of my arms so curtailed. Back again came the resort to the devious deceits of fake illnesses, fake commitments and how I'd 'forget' to put on sun cream, which, as a very fair individual, meant I couldn't possibly risk taking off my jumper.

As I grew older, the pain of having this secret, that I was not conforming to this social standard like everyone else and the underlying reason why – that I hated what was happening to my body, that I had locked a critical aspect of my entire being away in the back of my mind, which now felt as though it was rotting into a foul and dangerous mess inside its prison walls, began to grate on me harder and harder every day. As teenagers, people are always a paradox; desperate to stand out as individuals, but also desperate to fit in with the crowd. I was no different, I wanted so badly to fit in, life would be inordinately simpler if I could just be like everybody else. I wanted to be free as I had been before and not be weighed down by this burden of dysphoria *all the time*. It's like having to wade through sludge while trying to keep up with everyone else as they skip along merrily on a clear path. You burn with pain from the effort and cry and cry with the never-ending exhaustion of it all.

I also wanted to fit in because of the rising social preoccupation of everyone around me with dating and the exploration of romance, which form a huge part of most people's lives. I wanted it to be a part of mine too, I wanted to experience the highs and the lows and learn the lessons your teenage years are meant to teach you about relationships and love. But whenever I thought about it, my secrets and underlying dysphoria would grab hold of those thoughts and squeeze the life out of them. Though I had been able to think about it enough to know with certainty that I was attracted to boys, which of course I had expected, given that it was the early 2000s and we were still under the spectre of Section 28 and years away from the Equality Act. I was taught absolutely nothing about gay people in school or out and my knowledge of it was limited to a 'rare deviation' that you could and should laugh at. It was still acceptable to have a serious debate on whether being gay was a lifestyle, newspapers still outed people on the front page and I couldn't name a single singer or actor or sportsperson who was willingly open about this part of who they were. It's quite shocking to think back, just a few years really, to that time when there was such a lack of visibility in mainstream culture and at how normal we thought it was to consider homosexuality as a joke, as an insult. I include myself in that. The messaging was all around us all the time; it permeates into you as an unconscious bias and the phrase 'that's so gay' became a part of my vocabulary as it did with everyone else I knew. Thus one was not primed to entertain the notion that the heterosexual expectation would not be fulfilled.

So I was a girl and therefore I would like boys and, right on schedule, I found this to be so. But I discovered within the fleeting moments of imagining a relationship with these boys that I could not stomach the idea of being thought of as a 'girlfriend' in any of the ways that that manifested. This was hardly surprising, but, as always, I did not allow myself to probe into it any further. I should have, but I had not anticipated the fight I would have on my hands to engage in the arena of attraction without slamming repeatedly into the bars of the cage in that forbidden mental place. I could not deal with it, the anger and mental danger it caused was too much and so I withdrew myself very forcefully from the arena. But the pain of this action would not go away, nor did it dull with time. I didn't want to spend my life alone, the thought terrified me deeply; to become an adult that was, at best, naive and unpractised in these matters, or, at worst, genuinely unable to love in this way – to create or maintain a functional relationship. You are meant to go through trials and tribulations in your teen and early adult years for a reason and, if everybody else did and I did not, would that leave me on an unequal footing, dangerously unprepared in my later adult years when the stakes are arguably higher? The fear of this, perhaps more than any other, made me desperate to try harder than I ever had before to fit in as the world told me I should.

SECOND TIME LUCKY?

I had had enough. One day in May of 2004, as I struggled through yet another sex-segregated PE class filled with 'who's dating who' gossip, whilst refusing to take off my red PE jumper, despite the river of sweat, I snapped. *'I can't do this anymore,'* I thought with anguish. *'I can't do any of it.'* Puberty and its irreversible, powerful hormones, which were seeping into my bloodstream every day had my body at their mercy. I had clung desperately to the few things still in my control: my hair and my clothes. But, to my body, the damage was done; the fork in the road had long disappeared out of sight behind me and it was time to stop hanging on to the past, I needed to face the future, prepare for it so that I stood any sort of chance of a fulfilled life. And so in the changing rooms, as I hurriedly engulfed my torso in my purposely too large blue school shirt and jumper and contorted my arms painfully to remove the red jumper and white t-shirt I was still wearing underneath, I knew it had come to this. I had to try and conform to expectation, and the small vent of gender expression that relieved the pressure from the cage in my mind, would have to be closed. I must completely cut off the route into that cage, there must be no more life, however feeble, breathed into the notion of this other way I ought to be. I told myself forcefully that I was a girl, I didn't have to be a 'girly' one, but I did have to completely accept that. Maybe then I'd be able to successfully overcome this terrible dysphoria. To do this, I decided it was time to go back to the bra shop and it was time to regrow my hair.

Mum was demonstrably happy that I had agreed at last to her desire to take me back to the Marks and Spencer store to try again. She had hit upon the idea of sports bras, having realised I was stealing her orange sports top, but I had fiercely resisted for months. We made the trip after a school day which saw me learn absolutely nothing from dread and worry. I had built a fortress out of bricks made of loneliness and fear around the back of my mind and I spent the whole time hoping that it would hold and I could do this. Standing in the cubicle, The Rage was rumbling, but the walls held as my conviction to conform burned harder than the The Rage. The sports bra was never going to be completely comfortable, but I could see a way of functioning in day-to-day life with it on and that's all that mattered. It made me feel relieved and uncharacteristically relaxed to think my life was about to become incredibly simplified to a degree I could barely remember.

I also had another very pressing reason for being deeply relieved it could work this time; I was to go on holiday to Tenerife with a friend from school. She was an only child and her parents had said she could bring someone on the family holiday to share the experience with her. I was flattered to be asked and excited to go on a holiday without my parents, one that was intriguingly hotel based instead of caravanning, but I was also terrified of the hot conditions and of being in the company of adults I didn't know very well, who would not be expecting me to display odd coping behaviours. I maintained my conformity conviction strongly throughout the holiday, ignoring with every fibre of my being the moments of pain as The Rage beat down upon the walls of my mental fortress, instead focusing all my energy onto those moments of unbridled joy at experiencing, for the first time in years, the simple act of walking around in heat in only a t-shirt with arms free, to walk around not caring what others thought about how I looked, to have some semblance of comfortableness in my own skin.

It wasn't to last. Almost as soon as we were home, I saw the cracks in the fortress walls as I exhausted all my strength to hold back the feelings beating upon them. It was never going to hold up, built on a foundation of lies as it was, and, like all things thus created, it came tumbling down. My feelings of bodily hatred were now stronger than ever for having been so constrained and more than ever I couldn't bear to look at myself in the mirror, at what my body had become. For all my strength and determination, I had failed in my quest to make myself be a regular girl, to make myself believe that it was so. I was once again plunged into the festering pit of coping mechanisms as summer swept in. Back I went to hiding from the sun like I was a vampire, shutting myself away in my room to ferment in my own moodiness. There, I tried to come to terms with the likely nature of my future.

I was going to be stuck with this half-life, this pained existence, these burdening coping mechanisms for rest of my life. And further, it was overwhelmingly likely, it seemed to me, that relationships and love were not going to be an option for me and it would be best if I did not dwell on the idea any longer. I could not be a girl who was loved by a boy, I could see no type of straight boy who would be interested in what I was: someone who flew into an internal and sometimes external rage every time they heard 'she' and 'her' and exhibited every refusal to be placed in that category for reasons they could not articulate. Nor could I be a girl who was loved by a girl, for the same reasoning and of course because I simply wasn't attracted to them, despite the assumptions of everyone around me based on the common conflation of sexuality and gender expression. But nor was I a boy who could be loved by a boy, as my understanding of homosexuality began to be thankfully reshaped by the growing education of society. What did I have to offer a boy thus attracted? The situation as I understood it then was hopeless. Sadly, I did not have the luxury of awareness of the concept of wider sexual diversity and of the surprising nature of love. From the options I knew were available to me then, I could see no hope and so I made a diversionary route for those feelings that led straight into the emotional cavern in the back of my mind into which they would enter and never return.

A* IN SELF-LOATHING

My self-esteem was now incredibly low. I hated almost everything about myself and had no sense of hope for a happy and fulfilled future. The only thing in which I had genuine pride was my academic ability and achievement. Whilst everyone else was out having fun in the sun, going on dates and getting 'fake drunk' on bottles of cheap cider in the local park, I sat in my room and read widely on many subjects, devouring textbooks and revision guides alike. This became my principle defence mechanism against the maddening body and life-hating thought cycles: drown them out in attempts to understand quantum teleportation and in the memorisation of the entire periodic table.

Up until this point I had been reasonably academically successful, always in the top quarter of the class for every subject but never really at the top. However, in time for the lead up to my GCSE exams I became an academic obsessive, caring little for the notion of work–life balance, which I decided didn't apply to me as it was reserved for people for whom it was actually an option. Clearly, the easiest way to become a perfectionist is to achieve perfection and, once I had done so, assimilating knowledge and skills and acing every test became my life and the more it happened, the more I needed it. I hung my entire self-worth upon it and anything less than perfection in this area wounded me deeply. In this way I grew a reputation for being super smart, which went some way to plugging the gaping hole inside me left by my failures in the areas of love and physical confidence. Crucially, it was an area in which I could have something that I didn't wish to swop with James, who, even in the year above, paled to my knowledge in many areas. I was going to decimate him and others with my exam results and I would live off the self-worth-saving feelings of academic superiority for many months.

Despite my failure to make myself believe in the idea I was a regular girl, I kept to the plan to grow my hair out and in fact did so longer than it had ever been, right down to my shoulders, in some kind of attempt at overcompensation. I did not enjoy the way it made me look or the way it laid to rest the very last of the possibility I had to be presumed a boy. Though I had to admit the new found safety I had gained from the clutches of the Toilet Police was a relief. I was no longer a prime target for bullying and made it out of secondary school without any further incidence, but it had taken hiding myself in conformity to do so. Looking back at the photos of my sweet sixteen birthday party, the last I would enjoy at the ice rink in Hemel Hempstead, I was about as far away from the young adult I wished to become as it was possible to be.

<hr />

The teenage years are the hardest time for most people, but mine were filled with a type of exquisite pain that cannot really be known by anyone who has not experienced it – though I have done my best to give a flavour of the daily struggles that, unlike other teen problems, had no end in sight, no future adult time when things would be different, be better. To be clear, I do not and have never thought that there is anything inherently wrong or nasty about female secondary sex characteristics and I can and do appreciate the beauty of the feminine form. It is just that they were not meant to be happening to me. Everything about seeing them on my body was wrong, the breasts, the hips, all of it just didn't belong.

The slow torture of being a helpless bystander to my wrongly changing body and juggling the mental and emotional burden of the shame it invoked took a terrible toll on the quality of my life. I was no longer free to run and jump and play. The dysphoria from the breasts and the coping behaviours I had to implement left me feeling as though I had become disabled in some way. The mental burden was extraordinary, just to get through the most mundane of average days. Further, I am left with a profound sense of sadness for what dysphoria did to the development of my personality. I became shy, introverted, shrouded in melancholy and deeply concerned with my inner state, which was as fragile as a candle in the wind and forced constantly to lie and deceive. I am a fantastic liar, but I was not born with that skill, it developed in the years I spent faking illnesses, making up family engagements, encasing myself in jackets and jumpers, pretending I had forgotten to put on sun cream. These are the twisted, deceitful and conniving things I had to engage in to survive gender dysphoria. It felt awful having to lie to my friends and family but I had no choice, I could not bear the alternative.

I feel incredibly fortunate to have made it through this time, a time when many have fallen, but as I settled into my melancholic shadow existence, observing but never fully participating in the ordinary rites of youthful life, I could not see clearly how my life would unfold from here in any way that made it something to look forward to.

Part IV

BECOMING MY OWN MAN

Chapter 9

THIS IS NOT A DRILL

ONE OF THOSE PEOPLE

It was one evening when I was 13, after the plates had been cleared off the table, when Dad sat back down opposite James and I and told us we had a sister. I was at once shocked and thoroughly confused, so much so that I furrowed my eyebrows until they hurt. Mum was now well over 50 and I knew for a fact she had entered the menopause, so that was out of the question. Perhaps they had done something extraordinary in the spirit of their religion and adopted a child from a developing nation? But surely they would have discussed it with us in advance? Dad waited a few moments longer as I ran through ever more unlikely scenarios, before calmly telling us that his eldest child from his first marriage was 'a transsexual and was now transitioning to a woman'.

It took some seconds for that information to be processed in my mind. This had not been among even my wildest speculations of moments prior, but I was struck at the same time with a faint thought of something having just made more sense. Unlike Neil, Dad's other grown-up child from his first marriage, who was firmly established as a part of my sphere of extended family, I had only met my oldest sibling a few times in the whole of my life, doing so for the first time at our Nan's funeral when this thin, dark-haired figure had come up to James and me and introduced themselves to us. Despite my shyness, I was immediately curious at the fact this person seemed so very different to Neil, both in build and demeanour, speaking softly and quietly and hardly at all, in a way that did nothing to dispel the air of mystery I had built up around the concept of my missing sibling.

There had been a divorce, I was told, sometime when I was six or seven and, somewhere through the messiness that surrounded that, Dad's relationship with his oldest had fractured. The pair had rarely spoken in the time since then and I didn't get the sense it was a good idea to pull at that thread. It was evidently full of adult burdens and long past grievances years before my time, which I probably wouldn't understand. But by the time I was ten, some effort was being made to reconnect, which culminated in a meet up on one of our caravan holidays. There, the mystery began to unravel as I learned more about their life in the missing years, but still I was struck by this person, who seemed to me to be very different to anyone I'd ever met before in a way I couldn't quite discern. So, when Dad made that announcement across the dining room table, the sharp initial shock at the unexpectedness of it gave way to something else, a small sense of explanation, of understanding.

But this did nothing to abate the next emotion I would feel: worry. My understanding of 'those people' was extremely sparse and confined to a mangled acknowledgement of such things as 'Hayley' from the television series *Coronation Street*, drag queens like Lily Savage, pantomime dames and the appearance of Eddie Izzard in several of the comedy videos Kat 'n' Dave and I would watch when it was miserable outside. True 'transsexuals' (I did not hear the word 'transgender' until at least a decade later) were weird people, far weirder than anyone else in the LGBT categorisation, as if the T was some kind of much rarer and darker subcategory that was on the very *very* fringes of society and was a concept most definitely not for children. They were outlandish caricatures of people whom it was most definitely fine to ridicule. I thought back to the only time I believed I had ever seen a trans person, in the car park of a motorway service station when I was maybe eight or nine. I had looked out of my window and seen what I had considered to be a man dressed in a white frilly-edged top and a denim skirt talking on the phone outside their car. To my eternal regret, I had gasped and then squealed to James to look at the '*tranny*' out the window and we had pointed and giggled our little heads off. I am just thankful they had turned to face the other way and this went unnoticed.

By the time I was 13 my understanding of trans people had not developed much beyond this point, although I would no longer have so actively pointed and laughed. But still, this was an issue to be weirded out by and mistrustful of and not openly speak about, partly because it was going to involve 'sex-change surgery', which had always been presented to me (such as it had been), as a radical and disturbing form of self-mutilation. Sitting opposite her across the table, I could tell Mum was not the biggest fan of this news for all the things stated above and for 'what it would do to Dad'. She has always been very forthright with her thoughts and opinions whereas Dad has always remained measured and reserved, but from both of them I got the impression then, and in the first couple of subsequent years, that this was seen, to a certain extent, to be a selfish act; that this member of our family had decided to go down this *strange* and *disturbing* path with no consideration of the emotional consequences for everybody else; 'Think what this is doing to poor Dad!' He did struggle with it at first, for sure, although his internal emotional nature made it hard to discern that first-hand. I was kept informed by Mum, who would tell me such things as that the first time we saw her on another caravan meet up Dad had had to, 'Go behind the caravan and hold on to it.' Silently and subconsciously, I filed those comments away.

What I did not do is make any comparison between my sister and myself. Looking back, it is difficult to understand how, despite my close adolescent exposure to the concept of being transgender, I did not make the realisation it might explain the knowledge and feelings of discomfort I had had about myself all my life. Perhaps there are several reasons for this. First, I have seen it is not altogether uncommon among trans men my age and older to have never made the logical leap as children, to have never realised that the existence of trans women would suggest the existence of trans men. The way it was presented in society as I grew up (such as it was presented), 'transsexualism' only involved those assigned male at birth, as did 'transvestitism' as was apparently displayed by Eddie Izzard, even though, as I watched Eddie walk on stage in fishnets and high heels, I myself was clothed head to toe in things from the boys' section. Instead, people like me were tomboys and then later, if their cross-gender predilections continued, were expected to become butch lesbians (to the point where I gave up trying to convince people I was not a lesbian). In that way, gender non-conforming girls and women were entirely accounted for. But even as I knew deep down that such an explanation did not account for me, I still did not make the leap.

The fact of the matter is I simply did not want to be 'one of those people', to become a joke, a deviant, a member of such a stigmatised minority group. To become something which both society and my close family had suggested to me was beyond comprehension, disappointing and hurtful to others. And what's more, if I were to be one of those people my sexuality would also be reclassified. I would become a member of not just one stigmatised minority but two. If I stayed as I was I could at least try to have a *normal* life filled with almost every privilege going. Subconsciously, perhaps I understood this and had that back part of my mind silenced by the powerful fear of experiencing such possible hardships. I knew I was relatively soft in the face of the young adult world; my dysphoria-stunted development and my abundance of privileges had made me so. Could I cope with being labelled with two massive targets? The answer then was no.

This held true even after I had seen a trans man for the first time, on a documentary sometime around 2003 or 2004, which I think must have been to do with the proposal of the Gender Recognition Act (2004). In the brief time before Dad changed the channel, the narration made clear that the middle-aged, heavily bearded man whom the documentary appeared to be about, had not always been considered a man. He spoke sadly about how painful it was to be interacted with correctly in certain situations up until the point they saw some of his ID. The narration also made it clear the man was about to go for surgery to gain a penis. The last thing I saw was the image of him being wheeled down a corridor in a hospital bed.

I did not hear exactly what kind of surgery it was and assumed, based on my burgeoning interest in medicine, that it was a penis transplant. I was intrigued but also slightly horrified by that idea, not least because from what I knew of transplantation, it was much easier to take something away than to add it and it would mean a reliance on immunosuppressant drugs. Mixed in with the messaging I was already influenced with of this surgery as self-mutilation, the idea of it troubled and scared me. I wanted to look it up, was it ever successful? And what of breast removal, was that possible? But at that time I did not have my own computer and there were no smart phones. The only Internet connected device in the house was the family computer, which sat in plain view against the wall in the dividing space between our open-plan living/dining rooms. Besides, I'd heard enough in the playground about Internet search history to ward me off typing in words of this nature into any computer. Instead, I filed this experience away into the Compartment of Dangerous Knowledge. At any rate, this was all academic, I told myself firmly. I was absolutely adamant I wasn't one of those people. It wasn't 1950 after all. I could wear anything I wanted to wear and do anything I wanted to do and for the sake of a safe life that would have to be enough.

DRIFTING

I had settled into my melancholic existence, moving through life while never truly living it to anything near the full extent. I sat in my room with my textbooks as James came in and out of the house with the standard stream of girlfriends. I did my best to be involved in the drinking and music club experimentation nights out in Camden with Kat 'n' Dave and others, despite how awkward and out of place they always made me feel. Dysphoria, my unwanted companion, was ever present and I kept to hiding myself away and distracting my mind with the latest research on stem cell therapy and in the memorisation of Shakespeare's sonnets and the constellations of the night sky.

I left school after Year 11 (ages 15–16) and moved to the local Sixth Form College to do the A-levels I wanted, which were not offered at my school, although I had spent all of one day as a member of the Sixth Form at the Boys' Grammar School. In an attempt to stay at Westfield but also do the courses I wanted, a proposal had been made, as had been arranged in the past for other students, to split my time between there and the Grammar School where I could study chemistry and biology. I was not alone in this situation, my friend, Katy, was also going to be undertaking this arrangement, which I was glad of for the moral support. I don't think I would have made it through the front door without her being beside me whispering words of reassurance. It wasn't so daunting for her; she already knew some of the boys there and was dressed perfectly in the appropriate formal attire expected of the Sixth Form. I myself was rather less well dressed in a mix 'n' match outfit of semi-formal white trousers, shirt and white knitted jumper, which I had stolen from Dad's wardrobe and for which it was of course, far too hot. In short, I looked ridiculous, but it was the best I could do under the burden of dysphoria. Nevertheless, my appearance and my knowledge of its inappropriateness made me very stressed.

Furthermore, I was anxious of the reception that awaited us. I was acutely aware we weren't going to be members of the 'Boys' Club' that can occur in groups of males who spend periods of time together in whatever setting (school/workplace/sports clubs, etc.) with no or very little female influence and I fully expected to be viewed in terms of that (which can range all the way up to complete misogyny). I hated meeting any groups of new people, but groups of teenage boys in particular because of this reason and because they usually wouldn't know what to make of my appearance. These things almost always led to mocking, either outright or whispered. Being juxtaposed with Katy didn't help in this context; next to her demonstration of femininity, I was very clearly different. Such situations as this always agitated my dysphoria to such a degree I was barely in control of my emotions. Being around so many examples of the physicality I wasn't able to have was completely horrific. And despite the fact the boys actually turned out to be lovely and mild on the toxic 'Boy's Club scale', the searing discomfort of my struggles with the formal attire requirement and the acute hatred of my body in that environment made me desperate to abandon the entire arrangement. It would be easier to take my chances at the local college.

I had a good experience there in spite of some of its shortcomings, the worst of which was the necessary resort to teaching myself large amounts of the Human Biology course material after various teacher failures. Kat was also there, although we shared no classes, and I found myself in a nice group of misfits, who amongst other things, would go and play laser tag in our free periods. I was glad to be comfortable within a social group and not subjected to any acute bullying, but I remained shut out of all rites of passages and increasingly looked for excuses to extricate myself from difficult situations that challenged my clothing secrets and filled me with dysphoria-induced anxiety. I tried to avoid such situations at all costs given that my emotional cavern, where I buried the pain of every such experience, was filling up at quite an alarming rate.

I was still telling lies, like the big one that got me out of going for dinner with my family on the cruise holiday around the Mediterranean when I just couldn't take another moment of demonstrating the existence of the breasts. It's true what they say; all the best lies are those which contain a modicum of truth and it was true; I really had suffered from sea sickness five years previously in Canada when we went whale watching on a small boat in a tumultuous sea. However, this was a massive cruise ship and the sway was pretty minimal. Nevertheless, the truth of that whale boat experience lent enough credibility to my complaint to see it fully accepted and I curled into a depression ball in the darkness of my cabin as everyone else dined the night away.

Kat would say to me one day after college, as we sat at the magistrate's court waiting for her mum to finish work as a court usher so we could grab a lift home, 'You know, I haven't seen you in just a t-shirt for years.' I laughed nervously and gave a vague, evasive answer. I wanted to tell her, with her own growing sense of queerness and her frequent trips to Brighton to explore herself, but I could not. Even with everything I imagined she'd seen in Brighton, I had no assurance that she would understand my situation, to which I still attached no label and could still not point to any previous examples. Drawing my arms over the front of my chest, I sighed quietly and changed the subject.

A UNIVERSITY CHALLENGE

I began at the University of Leicester in October of 2007 studying medical genetics. As do most new students, I opted for the experience of living in halls accommodation. Mine was a new build, John Foster Hall, which, with its wooden blocks of flats dotted amongst trees and greenery, made me feel as though I lived at a Centre Parcs. The blocks were divided into sex-segregated flats of five rooms and a kitchen/common room. I was extremely nervous of entering this new period of life, not only for all the usual reasons of being away from home, fending for myself and studying at a higher level, but also of what it would do to me to try (and very likely fail) to fit in with the girls in my flat. I tried precisely once, on the first night in fact, to maintain the pretence that I was a regular girl just the same as the rest of them and went out to the freshers' night club events taking place at the student's union. But of course I was dressed in a zip top, which I could not take off, and thus pretty quickly the atmosphere became challenging physically as well as mentally. I would have got drunk to soothe my pain if I hadn't sworn off drink completely before I was ever allowed to buy it for fear of spiralling into a mental pain-relieving addiction and for its tendency to loosen the tongue. I had secrets and it needed to stay that way. I could not afford to lose control of my mental faculties, but being around so many others who were, by stark contrast, letting go of themselves with wild abandon, only served to twist the knife into me even further. I left early and returned alone to my room. That simply wasn't going to be something I could do regularly for three years. They were lovely girls, but in the end it was far less stress to spend most evenings shut away in my room with only my new textbooks for company.

The course itself was a joy and I threw myself into academic life with as much rigour as I had for the last few dysphoria-fuelled years. It was vital to my self-worth that I achieved a first class degree and scored highly on every assessment and I made damn sure that happened. My lack of social life, even as I moved into a house with five friends from my course, made it easy to devote practically my whole self to this goal. It was always for others to go out on nights out in town or to be a member of a society or go on dates or host their partner at our house for the weekend. I did feel terribly guilty; Mum had had such high hopes for my university days, having never had the opportunity to go herself. She had squealed with delight on every open day we attended at the thought of all the groups and clubs I could be a part of, all the experiences I would be able to have that she never could. But the truth is I never could either, even as they were dangled in my face. My appearance, my dysphoria, made it impossible to engage with the world. I was 18 years old and had emerged from my adolescent chrysalis completely wrongly formed and, from this truth, unprepared and unable to strike out and forge my own path forward in the adult world. I would say to people, in that jokey way which hides the fact what you're saying isn't a joke at all, that my development had arrested at the age of 12. It was true, that was the point at which I had gone down the wrong path upon which I didn't belong. I could not thrive and I was not thriving there. All my fears of being disadvantaged in so many ways from being unable to engage in the world because of this were now coming true as I watched those around me cultivate serious relationships and thrive in their personal independence and maturation. In the end I earned my first class degree, but in many ways I squandered my university days in all the other ways that make them so rich and gain them the title, in many people's eyes, of the best days of your life.

I did come out of it with some excellent friends, though, for which I remain thankful and who have gone on to play a part in many of the critical days of my story. My friend Katy, from Westfield and the Boy's Grammar, is one of them. Having lost touch after that day, it was a moment of bizarre serendipity when we discovered, after spotting each other at the Rickmansworth 'Ricky Week' parade in which I was representing my St John division, that we were going to be on the same course at the same university. During our time there we grew closer and shared in friendship with Gemma, Anne, Kelly and Jess in a group that has come to be known as the 'MedGen Girls' after our course. I never dreamed I would ever feel comfortable in a group of pretty feminine girls, trying to fight against and mask my feelings of illegitimacy in that sphere and being unable to engage or relate to many of the experiences and perspectives they share with each other. There have been times when these things have reared their ugly heads in my mind, but I have found in their presence a completely welcoming sense of calm and of escapism from the chaos of dysphoria-depression. And, in the geographical unavailability of Kat 'n' Dave, I have taken some of my most frightening transition-related steps in public while in the safety of this group.

Being around Gemma was a particular blessing. She is the bubbliest person I have ever met in my entire life. Just being in the presence of her exuberance was relaxing, as was sharing in the joy of her relationship with her now husband, Tom. Through her and the other girls in turn, I pieced together a sense of what it might be like to function within such a relationship. It was Gemma who also came with me in my third attempt to buy and wear a party dress to the university end of year ball.

Everyone else was going and I was desperate to join in, to experience something of a good university night out. I don't know why I thought I could do it, given my last two attempts had ended so badly. The first attempt, for the first-year halls of residence Christmas ball, had ended in the first and only hangover I have ever experienced after I broke my own 'no alcohol' rule, caving into the desire to deaden the burning dysphoria. On that occasion I was downing 'snakebites' to drown out the fact I had decided to go hard and was wearing a £100 red floor-length ball gown and makeup – applied by my flatmate to complete my look. I woke up the next day with a face full of pillow, a head full of pounding and a mind full of even worse dysphoria than I had before the alcohol. The second attempt saw me spend another £50 on a silver cocktail dress for an Easter ball but, after a week of nausea-inducing dread, I couldn't bear to go through with it and faked a bad case of cold to get out of going.

Gemma volunteered to go with me to shop for the third dress and matching shoes. This one was pink, white and black, as if it had been attacked by an abstract painter, and had a big black belt around the middle. Gemma was so excited as I was trying it on and I found myself desperate to find one that pleased her, gave me a sense of kinship with her and furnished me with a sense of accomplishment at having done something like 'one of the girls'. But I was once again gripped with dread at actually going through with the wearing of it and it was a total relief when the group decision was made not to attend the event for logistical reasons. In the end, I would eventually wear the silver dress to a Biomedical Society masked ball just before the end of fourth year. The fact that I was wearing two masks that night wasn't lost on me.

Gemma's patience would also go a long way to bringing me out of the extreme train journey anxiety I suffered after our first year. I had spent the day in London showing the sights to two non-London friends on one of the hottest days of the summer. Central London and the Underground in a heat wave are hell on Earth, but of course I was zipped up to my eyeballs in several layers of breast-hiding clothes and was unable to peel them off no matter how hot it got, gripped tightly by dysphoria as I was. I came within inches of fainting from heat exhaustion on the tube, on the Metropolitan line between Baker Street and Finchley Road stations, to be precise. The terrifying tingling sensation of the oncoming loss of consciousness had reached all the way up to my neck before my panicked pleas for help from the other passengers saw someone shove a cold bottle water into my lap, which I then proceeded to pour down my back and into my mouth. It was only at *this* point that I could bring myself to take off my hoodie.

I suffered a complete emotional collapse in the car when Mum came to fetch me from Rickmansworth station, having in that moment forever lost the 'immortality of youth'. This newfound sense of the fragility of my own life would destabilise my mental health for the rest of the summer and see me become fixated on the idea that I could just die at any moment. I refused to leave the house and shut myself away from even Kat 'n' Dave, but I also begged never to be left alone and if I ever was I would phone Dad at his work just so someone would know if I suddenly passed out. Travel, even to the corner shops, was out of the question. I was put on benzodiazepine for this anxiety, but took them only once after discovering the juxtaposition between my falsely relaxed muscles and still frantic mind to be even more disturbing than the alternative. Instead I sat in the house for weeks festering in the anger of having got myself into this state through an act of total stupidity. It must have been over 30 degrees on that tube and I had ignored every ringing alarm in my brain telling me to get myself cooler – and why? – because I was a prisoner of the desire, the *need* for these breasts not to be seen or acknowledged by myself or by anyone else. I wondered whether I'd even be able to go back to university, but thankfully I was forced onto a family caravan holiday in

Wales, which finally gave me something else to focus on and I slowly began to stabilise myself. I did make it back to Leicester, but I could not see how I would ever make it back onto a train. Unfortunately, I had begun the process of applying for a year's placement in medical industry and train travel to interviews was a must. Fortunately, Gemma was applying too and I have never forgotten her careful patience with me on that first train journey, though it would be several years and a number of therapy sessions before I could travel by train alone and in any form of comfort.

I did manage to win a place on a year in industry placement, which I completed at the Sanger Institute between the second and third years of my degree. For this, I had to move down to the Cambridge area entirely on my own. I chose the small and quiet chocolate box village of Saffron Walden and a small flat in what used to be the village inn. It was an extremely daunting experience to live so far away from my parents, who had now swapped the hustle and bustle of the South for a retirement in the calm sleepiness of rural Northumberland. When they left, having brought down and assembled my newly acquired IKEA furniture, I shut the front door and cried my eyes out. My stunted personal development had left me feeling totally unprepared for what was serious adult living. I felt like a child who had been left home alone and was to remain so for many months. I was 20 years old. I should not have been feeling like that, I should have been embracing my new found freedoms and revelling in the joys of young professional life. But, sapped of self-confidence and shrunken inwards by dysphoria-induced self-consciousness, I could exist but not truly live. My enjoyment of the placement is what kept me going through this year as did the lovely team of people within whom I felt well integrated, perhaps owing to the fact that, as one of the youngest and the most junior member of the team, I was meant to occupy the role of the inexperienced student learner. But, outside work, I spent the weekends stumbling around the village square on my own feeling like a child who ought to have been looking for their mother in the crowd.

ROCK BOTTOM RELEASE

I began my PhD (doctorate) at the University of Sheffield in September of 2011. Aside from my love of biomedical science, my decision to pursue a PhD was also driven by the fact my entire sense of self-worth was still derived from academic achievement. In the beginning I found the experience difficult. Not only adjusting to a new city and new work expectations, but in the realisation that I was an adult now and this sad melancholic existence, this sad half-life state I was in, was not a drill, this really was going to be *it* for the rest of my time on Earth. Late 2011 marked the loneliest I have ever felt in my life, I was listless and lost. I didn't even feel real. I spent every day hiding my body and myself away as much as possible from everyone, my housemates, the other members of the lab and the other PhD students in my year group, with whom I was trying to become friends. Inevitably, my listless, melancholic state bled into my capacity to work properly and one day my supervisor took me into his office to chat about his concerns over my progress and my attitude. My dislike of my voice had meant for years I had spoken as quietly as possible, to the point where I didn't even realise it was often below many people's comfortable hearing capacity, and he commented on this too, warning me that it is a difficult thing to be a 'wallflower' in science.

I headed home with my head swimming with the growing consequences of my inadequacies at being a functioning human being. My ability to hang my self-worth on academic achievement was now in jeopardy and had already been attacked by the fact I had become just a small fish in a big pond. I was sliding into a serious depressive state that seemed to be leaching all of my energy, mental and physical, and once again the gnawing from deep in that far buried place pierced into my consciousness. I was filling with the instinctive awareness that the answer to my life, how it was that I had come to be like this, lay in the breaking down of all of these long-standing barriers, the opening of that cage and the direct confrontation with what I kept within it. But the fear of doing this was so extreme it induced an almost reflexive panic and I ran away into entirely the other direction, fighting furiously to push away that instinctive knowledge. I would make one more attempt to be whom I thought I should be, whom being would, I thought, solve my problems whilst keeping life simple and safe and without trauma for myself or others, trauma I feared would cascade out of that cage like an ever-flowing river.

The panic was so great that I resolved to start this new attempt by doing something I'd never done before – a relationship. Paul was a friend of a friend from undergraduate days whom I had got to know throughout the course of my last year at Leicester. He was quirky and kind, with a zest for exciting and often random new experiences, such as participating in social media flash town centre pillow fights. That February he'd sent me an anonymous Valentine's Day card, the first I'd ever received, which I had deduced was from him, being that he was the only person I knew who lived in the town where the card was postmarked from. As we were both fans of snail mail we'd been writing each other letters since the summer, each one hinting ever more at possible romantic intent. I had serious misgivings, but I couldn't help being intrigued. Here was a boy who was interested in me and, as much as I found that hard to get my head around, I wanted it to be true and I encouraged it. But the more rational part of me was worried about this development because I knew his interest, at least in the physical sense, was largely based on a false portrayal of who I was, with my long hair and vague attempt at feminine clothing and demeanour. Though, in my panic and in my longing to be wanted and rescued from the lonely life I could see stretching out before me, I shoved all that aside and allowed myself to be swept along into the arena of romance. But my misgivings were soon hammering on my mind and the guilt I felt for worrying I might be leading him on like that into believing in this version of myself meant I oscillated wildly between interest and disinterest. He came for two weekend visits from London before phoning and saying he didn't think it was going to work, ostensibly because of the distance. I was not sorry for the experiences I shared with Paul, only for the way it truly hit home the fact that I could not be a woman in any relationship.

Still, the panic remained and I took to another thing I had never done – physically marking myself as feminine by way of having my ears pierced. On a visit home, Mum took me to a shop in the local high street where I held my hands together tightly as the gold studs were shot into my earlobes. It was maybe a week before I realised they were infected. It was nobody's fault but my own; I had made a hash out of caring from them as I had been told to do in the first days. I had not stopped myself from fiddling endlessly with them as if as compensation to withhold the urge to pull them out completely for the way they made me look so feminine combined with my long hair. I went to bed on a cold January night resigned to a trip to the GP (doctor), but I woke up with a bigger problem: the left stud was gone and I could not pull off the back clasp. I scrambled all through my bed looking for it, but eventually sank into the realisation I could not find it because it had gone *inside* my earlobe as I slept. *'This is bloody poetic,'* I thought as I sat on a chair in the minor injuries department while a lovely nurse doused my ear in anaesthetic spray and proceeded to jerk and jolt it about. *'It's like my body is trying to tell me something'*, I thought, grimly.

That night, I sat in the otherwise deserted living room of my shared house and looked at the retrieved stud and its less well-travelled partner. And, in that moment, everything fell apart. I cried my heart out alone there in that dreary student house living room, having finally and truly wised up to the fact that I could drape myself in the extremes of femininity all I liked or I could throw on my previous uniform of 'The Tomboy', but all these things would never be more than a costume based on a lie. And I knew, until I allowed myself to look into the truth of what, of who I really was, I was never going to be happy, never going to be able to drag myself out of this pit of hopeless circumstances my life had become. I had finally hit rock bottom and, as I sobbed into my depression, that instinctive feeling I had had of what I needed to do to rescue myself grew louder in my head, as if my mind knew by some unconscious mechanism, some kind of survival instinct perhaps, that if I did not figure this out soon, the consequences might be catastrophic.

I opened my laptop, brought up Google and typed in *'girl who feels like a boy'*. One of the first things I saw was a link to a short video from a documentary about an American child who was *transgender*, who had been assigned female at birth, but as a young child had been able to communicate to his mother that he was actually a boy and wanted to live openly as just that. His mother had listened, had taken him to see the country's leading expert in child gender issues and he was now living a happy life. So many things had just been set off in my head; I could not believe what I was seeing. Thoughts, one after another, were crashing into each other through the murky confusion. There were links to more videos and I hurriedly clicked on the next. This one was an interview between US broadcaster Barbara Walters and a young girl called Jazz and her family. I was astonished at this little girl with so much self-assurance and her family with so much determination to do what needed to be done to allow her to be who she was. I fixated on these videos, playing them over and over again, drinking in every word they were saying of the time before their child's pain, the social backlash of their child's insistences, the journey to see medical experts, the first steps of social transition, the night and day changes to their child's mental state. So many things came at me all at once: there were children like this, supportive families, medical experts, specialist clinics, something called *gender dysphoria*... I brought up a new tab and initiated the most important search of my entire life.

Every word I read was as if it was written just for me. There was a *name* for the feelings I had fought for all my days, a real, actual name! At this, the gates on my emotional cavern burst open and I was overwhelmed with the raging torrent of repressed anguish and pain. So many memories were flooding back to me of all those times I sat alone with my textbooks, all those lies, all those hot summer days in thick hoodies, *that* train journey, *those* bra expeditions, the hours prodding my chest in front of the bathroom mirror. I did not realise until I was standing right in front of it that I had followed this newly linked chain of thoughts and feelings all the way to the back of my mind and to the door of that forbidden cage. I had to do it; I had to do it for any chance of a real happy authentic life. At last, I opened the door. And suddenly I was back standing on my parent's bed in front of the long mirror on their wardrobe door, crying in fright at what I had realised about who and what I was. I took a deep breath and sank back into the old and sagging student house sofa and mulled over the knowledge that had flowed out of that cage and washed over my consciousness, which armed with my new searched for information, had formed them into the words: *I was a boy. I am a man. I am transgender.*

◇━◇━◇

The feelings of self-love in that moment were so profound it is difficult to describe. It was as if I had become whole again after suffering a deep, unhealing wound. I cried and I cried some more and hugged myself from the inside out with the power of this extraordinary emotional release after all those years of confusion, melancholy and pain. I had never felt as alive as I did then; I felt as though I could have run a marathon or climbed the highest mountain, for I finally knew who I was. Furthermore, there were things to be done, treatments I could get to rid me of the parts I hated so much and to give me the body my mind craved to see. I was enveloped in such a great sense of calm, safe in the knowledge that for the first time in my whole life I could finally start to truly live.

Chapter 10

TRUST AND TRANSITION

HOLD YOUR HORSES

I hardly slept at all that night. There was too much to search, to read and to learn. The previously forbidden questions were queuing up in the front of my mind and I could hardly rampage through the Internet quickly enough. The fact that I could now do this wasn't lost on me and I sent a silent thank you to everyone who had made the Internet possible. As I did also to all those people who had put up websites and online support groups and as I rampaged further into educating myself on the history of the community to which I now knew I belonged, to all those who had campaigned and fought through so many unforgiving years to bring about the key changes in law and medicine that allowed me to know I *should* be safe and I *should* be able to make the changes I needed to make. What total comfort it was to know, through my first reading of the Equality Act (2010) that I had recourse if anyone tried to deny me employment or housing or the right to use the correct segregated facilities. What critical hope it gave me to know that the official line of the National Health Service (NHS) was that gender dysphoria was not a mental illness which needed conversion therapy, but rather a condition to be taken seriously and which had treatments available on this service to align the body with the internal sense of identity. My heart skipped several beats when I discovered the possibility of taking testosterone and of having a double mastectomy with chest masculinisation. Not every trans person chooses to have any medical treatment, but personally I knew I was willing to give everything I owned for that surgery, and how wonderful it was to know that the NHS understood this was a need and not a choice and would not make me pay.

These things were critical in steadying my nerves, which, as the supernova of euphoria that burst over me began to settle, had started to creep in. I had slowly realised this wasn't going to be the headlong rush into a golden future I had just hours before imagined it would be. This was going to be a difficult process full of many decisions. First, was I now able, at the age of 22, to withstand living my life outwardly as a member of two stigmatised minorities, one extremely heavily so? As an extension of this it also dawned on me I would have to tell my parents, my brother, my extended family and all my friends. Having come into my own truth was a massive, massive step, but it was not the end point of this issue. I ruminated for some days over the next steps I would have to take, including, in the first instance, the issue of whether I could actually take them. On one hand, I was absolutely desperate to do so; to move towards my goal with all the itching readiness of a race horse waiting for that door to open. But the realities of doing so were becoming clearer and more serious. This wasn't going to be as simple as my childhood fantasy character play or my occasional outings as Jake. Actually *transitioning* – being that boy or now young man I was and always had been in the real world – *was* going to involve a lot of the pain I had subconsciously feared.

There was a lot of transphobia to get over, both external and internal. Everything I had learned in my life, especially in my teenage experiences, about the people I was to become a visible member of, was not encouraging. I didn't want to be viewed as a freak according to the unconscious biases I still held. Because of this, as incredible as the emotional release had been to understand and be able to give a name to myself and what

I realised to be true of my experience of life, I found it hard to completely relinquish grasp of my membership in the safe majority. I'd recently begun to follow LGBT news outlets, such as Pink News, on Twitter and saw report after report of violence and discrimination towards trans people here and abroad. This told me that the ridicule I had known in my teenage years to be acceptable to spew at the LGBT – at my – community was alive and well despite the progress in protective legislation. The fight for equality was so far from over and I would have to become a member of the generation still fighting so hard for even simple respect from the media and the public. The negative feelings towards my own appearance, which I now knew were a product of gender dysphoria, were also playing on my mind. When I looked at myself all I could see was a girl. Maybe it was too late; maybe it wouldn't be possible to truly align my body with my true sense of self and in trying to do so I would just make myself a greater target and be even less likely to find and cultivate a meaningful relationship.

The idea of telling my parents was arguably the hardest issue I faced, as it is for a lot of people. And it was so even despite knowing they had previous awareness of the concept and having what I considered a complete guarantee they would not chuck me out of the house or excommunicate me because of it. For trans people, still to this day, I am acutely aware that is a pre-outing starting point to be seriously envied, and I know how lucky I was. I am also angry to think I should feel lucky for that – an expectation of familial safety should be a total given and I will not stop fighting until such a state is reached. But knowing it would be safe to tell them in that regard wasn't the only consideration. I knew they held a number of depressing stances on the whole concept of LGBT people and corresponding rights. And despite easy family gatherings with my gay cousin and her girlfriend and happily sitting through many a period television drama, all of which had of late contained a gay character suffering through terrible prejudice, they still made audible noises of derision and disgust at news items on gay couples. They were firmly against the idea of marriage equality. I was acutely aware that my parents and I stand at a two generation remove, a situation most others my age find with their grandparents. Whilst I am a Millennial, they are Baby Boomers and, in 2012, were over 65. They were also religious. These were the two demographics LGBT people seemed to be most nervous of. I knew for a fact both of these things were actively influencing their opinions.

However, what worried me the most was the example of my sister's transition and the comments I had filed away about the stress and difficulty for Dad and the undertones of disgust and selfishness I had picked up at the time, though I knew these feelings had receded greatly over the years since. But the memory of them made me nervous for the level of understanding and acceptance I could expect for my situation. The fact is, this was going to seriously challenge them and I spent quite a number of days carrying on the duties of my life whilst my head was going around in a tumble dryer of spinning thoughts. The idea of my parents being disappointed, disturbed and disgusted with me and the changes I had to make to be happy, even as they supported me financially and domestically all the same, was almost too much. Rejection doesn't have to be explosive, sometimes it can be subtle, a faint air of disapproval or a small underlying tension – these can be devastating too. It is important to note there is a difference between actions borne purely out of love and actions borne out of love, understanding and acceptance. I hoped for the latter but, from everything I knew, it was going to have to be a work in progress.

Furthermore, as yet another product of my stunted development, I found myself struggling with the idea that I was actually allowed to go ahead with my transition under my own steam. I found it difficult to grasp the idea that I and I alone was in charge of making these decisions – that one thing I didn't have to fear was my parents telling me 'no'. I didn't have to persuade them to let me do this, I was 22 years old and therefore a legal adult and I had been for four years, as shocking and bizarre as I considered that fact. I did not have to ask for permission from anyone. It probably sounds silly, but it took me some time to understand that my stance, when I finally did tell my parents, would be one of 'I am going to do this, I hope you can understand and support me,' rather than one of 'please let me do this'.

Shortly thereafter I hit the brick wall that is the state of the NHS Gender Identity Services. I had deliberately stayed away from researching the specifics of this until I had reached conclusions on some of the prior issues, but upon doing so was filled with worry I might actually have to give a lot of 'please let me do this' after all. I would need to be referred to a clinic and in order to get referred I would need to ask a GP. This didn't appear to be as straightforward as it sounded, according to many of the posts in support forums I had examined. It seemed there operated a kind of Russian roulette system across the country as to whether this was simple or complex and it all hinged on whether you were sat across from a GP that (a) knew anything about trans healthcare and (b) did not decide to block you due to personal prejudices. The support groups were littered with angry and heartbroken messages from people who had been fobbed off by their GPs or misinformed about the process or just bluntly told no, whilst being thoroughly misgendered. The most common tales were that of being misinformed by GPs harbouring outdated knowledge about the requirements for referral. Many people were being told they needed to have a psychological assessment as a prior condition to the GPs agreement. Some people had had to resort to moving medical practices just to find a GP that *could* or *would* help them. I realised it would be best to go into my consultation, when that moment finally came, armed with NHS England transgender protocols. I tried to think about what this conversation-cum-showdown might be like for me, but it worried me that I couldn't even envisage the doctor I would be asking, what with the fact it was simply a pot-luck affair at my university-oriented medical centre. Gone were the days of having *my* GP, as had been the case throughout my whole childhood; nowadays, with the system increasingly pressurised, it seemed you got in when you could with whoever you could.

The other issue which served to burst my bubble was that of the frankly unbelievable waiting times for even a first appointment at a gender identity clinic (GIC). I had not been so naive as to think transition would be an overnight process, but I was aware of the 18-week waiting time limit expected of NHS service referrals and the bottom dropped out of my stomach when I came across warnings all over support sites of the six month, year, two-year waits that people were experiencing. These times were discussed alongside assurances from NHS England that they were working on getting this down, but I was seeing from the Facebook groups I was now a part of that it had been in this state for some time and the rising levels of referrals from people who, like me, had found their way to personal understanding by virtue of increased social discourse, were now stressing the system to critical.

In light of this depressing knowledge, I was forced to reassess my road ahead. Even if I managed to get referred quickly to a GIC, the likely wait meant it was going to be a long time until I could expect to begin the transition process I wanted in earnest, and I had to think carefully about how long the whole thing was likely to take. After first assessment there was to be a second assessment, but there were likely to be three, four, five, even six months in between the two. And after that there was the fight to get your GP to agree to prescribe you the hormonal treatment directed by the GIC to which you were entitled. Many GPs were apparently against the idea, due to inadequate knowledge and training, and were refusing. After getting over that hurdle I would then have to wait a probable six months whilst on hormonal therapy before I could be seen by a surgeon and then join that waiting list. The whole thing looked to be a fight from start to finish and was going to involve every ounce of courage I had, as well as a seemingly endless supply of patience. I was going to be stuck in this hideous limbo for an indeterminate amount of time, which was likely to stretch on for years. I had also presumed I would have to be referred to the Sheffield clinic – Porterbrook, and I worried about the fact by the time they got to me I would have finished my studies and moved away to the North to my parents or who knows where, if I got a job, and wondered what difficulties this might create.

I also began thinking about the other prospect; what if NHS England did somehow manage to sort the waiting times out and I was seen within the time of my PhD? As ready as I felt for physical transition, I had learned the changes from testosterone can be quick and it would mean coming out to everyone else aside from my family – everyone I worked and lived with. I could feel my stomach knotting at the prospect. When I really thought about it, I didn't feel ready to come out in my current environment, to face the probing questions and possible ignorance of those around me or, worse – active hostility. To clarify, I worked at a university filled with lovely, incredibly smart people, but they came from many different backgrounds and many different countries. In consideration of this, one of the main problems of our trans-ignorant society, both here and in many other countries, is the often serious difficulty in determining whether you are likely to be safe and respected in any given environment. You need both in order to thrive and without knowing everyone you come into contact with on a regular basis in a reasonably close manner, you cannot hope to know their level of knowledge of what it even means to be transgender, never mind their knowledge of equality laws and how acceptable or not they might currently find it to mock the trans community.

As a case in point, I believe we've reached a state where every non-gay person either actually knows a gay person or knows someone who knows a gay person; you're never more than one remove away from awareness of a gay person in your personal sphere. Then, of course, there is the sphere of celebrities outside of that. And as a result we are now at a point where anyone who considers themselves to be a smart, decent and moral person and who would like the majority of others to consider the same, holds it as self-evident that being gay is an immutable characteristic. Following on from this they understand what being gay is and what it most definitely is not and see the obvious logic in the equality laws that have come forth. Companies are also falling over themselves to make sure they are seen to be gay inclusive, both for its own sake and for fear of losing custom. I'm not saying we now live in a gay utopia, it's far from that, but homophobia is now at the fringes or 'underneath' mainstream society, exactly where acceptance used to be, and our job now is to keep it there. In 2012 transphobia was still in largely the opposite situation, on the streets at least, and I knew I could have no such reasonable assurances, as gay people did, of a simple and peaceful outing among all the myriad people I came into contact with. I wouldn't have had any problem coming out as gay in my home or work environment and, as usual, operated under the assumption people were already presuming I was a lesbian based on my appearance and demeanour. But the potential run-in with transphobia meant I just did not feel I could come out.

During this time my studies were also becoming ever more intensive and my mind was now increasingly crowded with stresses and worries all vying for my attention. I couldn't spend the time that I needed engaged in personal research when I had a mountain of scientific papers to read and I was conscious of the side-eye I was getting from my supervisor for my lack of keeping up with this. Whilst there is probably never a perfectly opportune moment, the middle of a PhD is distinctly not the best time to be having a personal identity revolution. I was experiencing a level and type of stress I had never had before and, in the end, I decided to shelve moving forward with transition with all its potential of coming out, transphobia and medical fight stresses. I needed to focus on my work or I risked failing entirely in the one area I still hung my self-worth. This decision wasn't without risk itself; I would be saving myself from new potential stresses, but I would be stuck much longer than I would need to be with my old enemy, dysphoria. It wasn't an easy decision and it wouldn't be an easy road, but all things considered, right then I needed to stick with the devil I knew.

PULLING BACK THE VEIL

By 2013 I was spending untold hours alone in a basement room at a microscope behind a black curtain with only some condemned fruit fly larvae for company. These long hours trapped with my own mind were a serious test to my mental health. I was right about this not being an easy road; frustration was mounting inside me at the pain of holding myself back, which was whipping my dysphoria into an even greater intensity. I was finding it increasingly difficult to shower or even look at myself in the mirror without sinking in waves of self-disgust. I had tried to counteract this as best I could by taking some small steps towards aligning my body with my mind. Over the Christmas break, I had my hair cut back to the short style it had been before my teenage attempts at gender conformity. It was a kind of full-circle moment the first time I looked at myself after this. Oestrogen does not change the face in such a drastic way as testosterone and, though I now wore glasses, I could see much of the child who had stood crying in front of that wardrobe mirror. Only these new tears were not of fear, but rather a bittersweet mixture of sadness and happiness. If only it was possible to reset the rest of my body to the way in was then. By then I had realised some things were never going to be completely rectified, like the widening of my hips and the shortness of my height. A fat burning healthy lifestyle and testosterone-driven redistribution efforts, I was told by Internet research, would sort out my hips to a certain extent, but nothing was going to alter the shape my pelvis had now become.

Neither was I going to grow any taller. At 5 foot 3 inches (1.6 m), I was bang on the average height for a British woman, according to the Office of National Statistics, and that would not be changing. Curiously, I had been able to make a reasonable guess of exactly when I had stopped growing. As a teen I had suffered terribly from Osgood-Schlatter disease, which is an overuse issue affecting the growing shin bone (tibia) and patella tendon, which attaches to it from the knee. That tendon attachment was painfully inflamed and, as it was pulled by the thigh muscles, was causing the top of my growing tibia to shear away, creating a prominent bony callus and some very fetching knobbly knees. For several years the slightest knock against a solid object would cause the top of my shin to throb for hours, until one day when I was fifteen it collided spectacularly with a table leg and, while it hurt, it did not throb and I knew then that the growth plates had fused and I would grow no more. In all fairness I had never been overly bothered by my height, given my female presentation, not with everything else I had to contend with. That was until now, however, when I realised I would be plummeting down to distinctly below average for a British man and any thoughts of myself in the future as some tall specimen of manhood would need to be given a good reality check. It is hard, but you have to let go of the idea of that person you maybe could have been if you had been born with correct body chemistry. I tried to be gentle with myself here and let myself mourn in my own time for that image, so that I could work through my feelings and not shove them away into my cavern of emotional pain, as I had done for all those years.

That cavern had been burst open during my moments of self-realisation, but though the doors were now open, the painful feelings had largely drained back inside again. You don't get rid of years of emotional pain that easily. Here, I thought, was something I could try to deal with now as I waited out my transition limbo. Though it was going to be a slow process to clear them out for good and I wasn't entirely sure I could do it by myself, although I didn't expect to have much choice. Private counselling was for people not living on a studentship grant and getting it on the NHS, well... During my mental health crisis after my near-collapse on the tube, the idea of cognitive behavioural therapy had been floated about as a last resort if the anxiety medication wasn't sufficient and/or I wasn't able to heal my mind myself. As part of me wondered why this should be reserved for a last resort, I was told there was a lengthy wait for this drastically underfunded service. Given this, I was pleasantly surprised to discover the university had a free counselling service available to its students. I referred myself with some trepidation, mostly borne out of the prejudices I had been taught throughout my life about the reasons people would need counselling – addictions, eating disorders or abuse. In some ways I felt ashamed at going for what in the scheme of things I decided were minor problems compared to those issues. This kind of thinking is of course a result of the lack of priority our culture places on mental health and the idea that, unless you've been seriously traumatised beyond some sort of culturally set threshold, such as suffering an assault, then your trouble with it is simply a demonstration of your weakness as a person. Seemingly small issues as my own can actually have wide-ranging negative effects that feed physical stress, which people then try to deal with in every other way than addressing the mental source. Nobody wants to be thought of as weak.

So it was with some awkwardness that a month later I went in for my appointment. I planned to get help in the first instance with my train anxiety and then maybe broach the subject of what years of gender dysphoria had done to me. But I found the experience as difficult and embarrassing as I'd imagined, not least because I'd collapsed into tears after the counsellor asked me if I was happy. I'd then spent a few excruciatingly self-conscious minutes pulling back in my emotions and wiping the tears off my face with an old tissue as she sat silently and perfectly still across from me. I felt pathetic and judged, not at all at ease, in what felt to me to be a clinical atmosphere. I got through the rest of the session in which she informed me I was likely suffering from post-traumatic stress disorder (PTSD) from my train experience and showed me some breathing exercises I could do to deal with it in the moment. I found it hard to accept I had PTSD, surely that was experienced by returning soldiers or crime victims, what right did I have to claim it? But I had to agree the emotions and behaviours I experienced when alone on a train fit the broad description. At the end of the session she gave me the option of returning for a set block of sessions to further work on this problem, but, after I'd gone away to think about it, I decided not to pursue it.

I did not feel like I could relate to this woman enough to trust her with my feelings, nor did I want to try again with someone else given how unpleasant I'd found the whole experience. So I decided to shelve attempts to work out my emotional cavern in this way, at least for now.

REVELATIONS

I was upset my attempt at counselling had gone badly, I wanted so much to tell someone about how I felt, to get it out there in the real world, to relieve some of the pressure of holding back from transition. I needed to start telling people. But I wasn't yet up to telling my family, I was far too emotionally unstable for that and I knew if they put up any resistance to the notion I would probably just collapse in on myself as a sobbing mess. The first people I would tell had to be those whose reactions were guaranteed to be total acceptance. I wanted to tell Kat 'n' Dave but, to my sadness, our lives were taking us in different directions and we'd rather fallen out of regular contact due to a combination of geographical spread and lack of time and money to visit each other. Then there was the issue of their inexplicable failure to maintain the same phone number for any period of time (think of a way to destroy or lose a phone and Kat will have done it) and they were both poor users of social media. This didn't matter in the grand scheme of things, our bonds of friendship are very deep and not the sort that require regular contact to maintain. But it made it difficult to tell them in that moment. Additionally, I found the idea of telling people who'd known me right from the very earliest days to be harder than I expected, even though I knew their reactions would be acceptance with open arms. Something about our extensive shared past made it hard for me, like I'd be altering the memory of those three kids who'd done so much together.

I settled on telling the MedGen girls. Most of them were planning to meet in London on Friday 12 July, on the night I had arranged with Katy to go to the midnight matinee of *A Midsummer Night's Dream* at The Globe. This was to be for my birthday celebration, as I was determined that this year I'd actually do something instead of hiding away in my room depressed at the state my life had been in for yet another year. Going down to London meant combining a trip to see the MedGen girls as, aside from Katy, many of them worked in and around London too. We were to have dinner at an Italian restaurant not too far from St Pancras station and I planned to tell them then. On the train down, I tried desperately to rehearse the words I would say until I knew I would be word perfect, but I couldn't concentrate for mounting anxiety over being on a train in the heat. That summer saw a couple of weeks where large swathes of the country were in the grip of a serious heatwave. For many years just the term 'heatwave' had been enough to raise my blood pressure and knot my stomach. It meant long days trying to stay inside away from any situation which would make it difficult to hide the lumps on my chest. In 2003, for example, I had spent many days just lying on a mattress in front of the air conditioning unit in my room, reading and hating everything.

If I thought it was hot in Sheffield, it was nothing compared to the furnace I entered when we arrived at St Pancras. Despite the lovely air conditioning of the train, it had taken a lot from me to make it through that journey, in which I fought hard to employ the coping tactics the university counsellor had shown me. Fortunately I was better dressed than on that previous occasion, having recently discovered that I was able to present a passable socially acceptable breast shape with the crop tops covered by a button-up shirt (so long as the shirt had pockets over both sides of the upper chest). Nevertheless, it was a huge relief to be enveloped into the company of the MedGen girls and dive into the cool sanctuary of the restaurant. I had told them in advance I had something I wanted to say to them and it wasn't long after we'd ordered when they asked me to spill the beans. This was it, the big moment of my first outing.

But my brain was suddenly a mass of panic, I felt unprepared on what I wanted to say, not having been able to fully rehearse. The words were fading away as I chased them and looking at the table of expectant and increasingly concerned faces, I was suddenly overwhelmed by the fact that 'what is said cannot be unsaid'. This information was going to upend how they viewed me and, as much as I wanted the way they viewed me to change, I just didn't want any of the shock or the struggles to adjust that would likely ensue. In that moment I was also rudely stabbed by the sudden fear of transphobia, a thing so pervasive, so a part of normal discourse that I lost the grip I'd had on the certainty my friends did not harbour it. All this conspired to slam down a mental block, which cut off my ability to speak. I was psychologically choking. I just sat there opening and closing my jaw, but I could make no sounds come out of my vocal chords and all I could think was *'How extraordinary'*. My friends were now very concerned and had taken my struggle to speak as a sign what I had to say was really very alarming. 'Are you seriously ill?' they asked. I managed to regain my speech to allay those worries, but I knew I wasn't going to be able to get out the news I had intended to give. I ended my efforts with profuse apologies and promises to tell them soon, maybe one by one, then there would perhaps be less pressure.

Katy and I departed and made our way to The Globe to spend the night watching the best rendition of *A Midsummer Night's Dream* I've ever seen, played out as it was under the open sky on what was literally a mind-warping midsummer night. Afterwards, we tried to catch some sleep in the youth hostel close to St Paul's cathedral. But, in the heat trap of central London, the temperature refused to appreciably decline, even in the dead of night, and the lack of air conditioning in the room meant we had to have the window open. The ensuing regular bongs of the bells drove me to despair and to rather ashamedly wishing the whole thing *had* been demolished in the Blitz. We gave up on sleep early and set out into the weirdly quiet streets and into sunshine already intent on making this day just as scorching as the last. Eventually, we took refuge in an air conditioned O'Neill's close to St Pancras for some breakfast. In between bongs, I had spent a lot of time in the night rehashing my failed coming out and resolved opting for the one-to-one approach was the best way to go. And here I was sitting one-to-one with Katy while we waited for our food.

The situation wasn't as imposing as the previous night and I had managed to banish the fears of latent transphobia in my friends. I wasn't going to let such thoughts override my instincts and my knowledge. And so I took a deep breath, ignored my racing pulse and told her, simply and directly, without much of the big speech I had tried to prepare. 'The thing is…' I said, forcibly pushing through the lump forming in my throat. 'I've finally realised what's been wrong with me all my life. It turns out I'm transgender. I'm not a girl, I'm a boy.' Her eyes widened slightly and her face went into that expression halfway between shock and sudden understanding. She had tears in her eyes as I explained how it was the real reason she'd only known me ensconced in a hoodie rather than my believing them to be the height of some fashion trend. Something had clearly just made sense to her about my apparent difference and sadness, which I think had always confounded and concerned her and she did an unbelievably good job of controlling her own emotions to give me coherent words of encouragement in return. 'I'm so happy for you!' she said with a beaming smile and I knew she was. I felt myself physically and mentally relaxing in that moment and awash with the same kind of euphoric feeling I'd had when I came out to myself. It was a good idea to have come out like this in the first instance, with a guarantee of acceptance and with someone who did not need to have the basics of what it means to be trans explained to them, so that I could focus on controlling my frantic emotions in that most surreal of moments instead of the added ask of playing the teacher.

It certainly was surreal to think I was now living in a world where the truth of my identity was out there beyond the confines of my own head, that it was known and accepted by another person. Slumped exhausted on the train home, I felt so proud of the huge step of progress I had taken and the way it seemed to make the path ahead come into better focus in my mind. Something I had been struggling with for a while was the issue of my name. There was no question: it was changing.

I'd never liked it and it was far too culturally female for me to want to keep it. My first thought had been Jake, my secret and sometimes not-so-secret childhood name. It felt right in a lot of ways, parallel universe me wasn't so parallel after all. But sadly it was also bound up in the internalised transphobia and dysphoria-induced pain of my teenage years and in the end I acknowledged the feeling it had been tarnished for me in that way. I cast the net wide for a new name.

It turns out there are an awful lot of names in the world and the prospect of naming myself was actually as daunting as it was exciting. What would you call yourself if you could call yourself anything? I managed to narrow it down a considerable extent with the conclusion I wanted an uncommon name, a desire probably at least partly driven by the fact that, throughout my life, I had always been one of two or more with my first name in school or clubs. I also knew I gravitated towards names that were slightly older and out of fashion, which was perhaps a product of the quiet passion I held for the roaring 1920s and '30s. After trawling through lists on baby name websites, I was reminded of the name Caspar, which I had first come across as a child with the film *Casper* (the friendly ghost). I liked it as much now as I did then, but I was hesitant about whether there wasn't a little too much association with the cute cartoon ghost, especially among people my age. It took until the new clarity I felt after my first coming out to make a firm decision in favour of the name. I liked it and felt a comfortableness with it and an extraordinary sense of personal confidence and pride whenever I stood in front of the mirror and said it out loud or pretended as though I was introducing myself to someone.

It was only a few weeks later when I came out again. I was growing and relaxing into my true identity with each passing day and was chomping at the bit to build on the momentum created by that critical first experience, especially in lieu of being able to move forward with the physical changes I needed. It was August and I was down in the South with my parents, house sitting for my brother Neil while his family were off on holiday, which gave us a good base to visit James and see many family friends my parents hadn't seen since their move North. I took the opportunity to go to lunch with Gemma, who lived not too far away in Uxbridge. Having already done it once, the nerves were easier to check and my emotions were not sloshing about quite so rapidly. I kept to my strategy of coming out with it simply, with only a small preamble about my being serious with this information and reminding her of the melancholic air she was aware surrounded me to contextualise it for her. 'The thing is, Gemma…' I said, trying not to fiddle nervously with my cutlery. 'I've figured out the reason I've always seemed different or depressed and…it's because I'm actually transgender.' Her eyes widened a lot and she exclaimed, 'Really!' It was clear this wasn't high on the list of things she had expected me to say and there was a moment where I could see she was casting around for how to phrase her response.

For the first time I felt a bit worried about the position I'd just put my friend in. I had not spent too much time previously in thinking about how it would be to hear this information, rather, all my focus had been on what it would be like for me to say the words and making sure I prepared myself for every type of response. But, as it was happening, I realised it can be quite scary for the other person to be blindsided into being entrusted with this information and faced with the requirement of producing an immediate response. A response they know is important to get right given the very personal information shared and the vulnerable state you've just placed yourself in. I thought back to the only time I'd ever been come out to in person, when a friend from my undergrad course said to me one day, as we hung out in my room watching a tennis match, that he wanted me to know he was gay and hoped I was alright with it. I had been so unprepared for that news in that moment, even though I had vaguely wondered throughout the year I'd known him that I froze and spent long enough in silence to make it slightly awkward, as I tried to make sure I constructed exactly the right things to let him know it was totally fine. I think, just like coming out, the more times you experience being on the receiving end, the more you're able to get over the unpreparedness you might have felt to hear it at that particular moment. In terms of people coming out as gay, these days most people are fully aware of the gay people in their lives and of many celebrities too – it's part of normal discourse. They have also probably seen coming out scenes either as part of television/film or on YouTube, which gives them a proxy experience even if they've never been in that position in real life. Nowadays, I know that if anyone were to come out to me about their sexuality, I wouldn't even blink and the words would flow simply.

However, it's true now, and it was even truer in 2013, that few people know a trans person, or have seen one on any media, coming out or otherwise. It is decidedly not the same thing as hearing someone is gay – the implications are totally different. All this I thought about on the way home, but back in the restaurant Gemma found her wonderful words of encouragement and of gladness that I was on the path to happiness and I was once again aglow with euphoria. She listened with great interest as I excitedly rushed to tell her about the medical and social transition I intended to go through. It was another good experience but, as I reflected on the journey back to Neil's house, I thought it might be worth exploring other ways of telling people which allowed for more time to let the information sink in.

PUB QUIZ IN THE PEAK DISTRICT

2014 was characterised as the year of the 'trans tipping point' (Steinmetz 2015), where public awareness of trans people and trans issues seemed to rise massively. Trans activists were appearing more in all types of media and trans characters, some played by trans actors, were in major shows. There was a definite air that trans people, at least from a binary perspective, had broken into the mainstream determined not to accept anything short of full equality. Although, ensconced within my basement microscope room, I felt like this was a battle being waged at a certain remove from myself. The trans people dominating media attention and the awareness conversations and debates going on around them were trans women, such as Laverne Cox. It seemed practically every media piece was revolving around the visibility and acceptance of trans women as if they were a new discovery and it never really seemed like the world was reaching the same awareness of trans men. We were a side line, a footnote, or a one sentence tag-on to the main thrust of the conversation. I had also made the decision not to watch *Orange is the New Black* for the same reasons I had been consciously keeping away from big shows like *Game of Thrones*. I knew how prone I was to getting obsessed with things like that and I was in the critical third year of my PhD and up to my eyeballs in work and scientific papers. I couldn't afford to get sucked into binge-watching. But the rise in trans awareness was such that the trickle-down effect was wide ranging, and even with my head almost buried under biomedical science I felt buoyed by the general development of the message that transphobia is disgusting. I was more hopeful than ever before that I would never experience transphobia born of ignorance or malice, both of which I had so far avoided in my one-foot-out-of-the-closet state.

Kat had also made a rare appearance on social media to tell the world how obsessed she was with *Orange is the New Black* and, in a microscope break, I grabbed the opportunity to tell her in writing over Facebook Messenger. It was definitely a lot easier to produce a coherent statement and say things I wanted to say, which otherwise I might have lost in the moment or chickened out of saying. Some people might think it's a cop-out to do it this way so you don't have to face their reaction straight up, but I don't view it like that, a lot of people appreciate being given that time to get over whatever shock they might feel and organise their best response. Though, Kat, who by this point was living her own authentic life in Brighton as an out lesbian and as a drag king, was the sort of person who wouldn't have been blindsided at all with this information and, indeed, was her completely accepting and excited self at the news. I did wish I could have told her in person, but this was the easiest way at the time and it gave me a chance to see what it was like to come out this way. Perhaps the only downsides are not experiencing that human connection, which is at its greatest with physical company and the possibility that any written response they give you may not be a true reflection of their actual feelings, something you might be able to pick up face to face in non-verbal cues.

Around this time, I was increasingly occupied with the prospect of when and how to tell my parents. It had been over a year since my initial wrestle with this issue and back then it had largely focused on whether I could ever do it. I had concluded I simply must, however hard it might be, but since then, as the time I must do it inched ever closer, my resolve wobbled constantly and more than once I felt the urge to sequester this information away and retreat from transition altogether. How could I tell them this? The confidence I had gained for my comings out so far was useful, but this was going to be an altogether different situation, because they were my parents, the people who had known me longer than anyone else as the person I was presumed to be and were the people most invested in the existence of that person. I had seen accounts from some parents of trans people who had described the feeling as a real grief, a type of mourning as if for the death of that child. But their child was still alive and so they were faced with a sort of living death – losing the child they had, while the child 'became someone else'. Whilst I knew it wasn't true that I was becoming someone else, rather, just outwardly showing who I had always been, I understood the thoughts these parents had been trying to express. In a similar way I was going through this myself. For over two decades I had been presenting as this person and, even though it had never felt right or truly who I was, I was used to that presentation and being viewed as that person. No matter how much we hate something, we seem to have this strange ability to be sad at the prospect of losing what is so familiar.

All these feelings of worry for this step I would ultimately have to take was taking a heavy toll on my mental health and was severely impacting my ability to cope with the other stressors in my life, such as waiting out for physical transition and racing the ticking clock counting down the time I had left to complete the necessary experiments for my PhD. I think I hid it well, but I was frequently on the verge of tears amid fears I was circling down into that pit of depression from which some people never return. I had seen the statistics about trans suicide attempt rates, which had simply scared me out of my wits. It was almost a 50–50 (Strudwick 2014) and a huge factor on what side of the line you came down on appeared to be whether you had familial acceptance and support. I'd never seriously thought I would be in any danger of being a part of that terrible statistic, but now my mental health was being pulled apart at the seams by the grabbing hands of so many extremely serious stressors I was terrified that one day it would just break completely and push me into a hitherto unknown sense of oblivion.

I had to tell my parents. I had to resolve this issue, which there simply wasn't any way of getting around. To move forward with physical transition I knew you had to be socially prepared and if I was going to do it within the next few years I would need the help of my parents. As I mentioned at the beginning of this chapter, I was as sure as you can be, without actually having taken the plunge, that my parents were not going to bluntly reject me and throw me out of their lives. I thanked all my lucky stars for that. If I didn't have that assurance I simply don't know if I would have been able to do it and then what would have become of me? But, as I also mentioned, I had serious worries about the level and type of support I was going to get. Would they operate purely out of parental love as in 'We disagree wholly with you saying you're transgender and everything you plan to do, but we love you so we'll support you financially and domestically through it'? Or was it going to be combined with acceptance and understanding? I was convinced I would get at least the first option. The fight to get to the second option was probably going to hurt a great deal, but I was backed into a corner by stress and making headway here was my only plan. I thought it was best to go with a written coming out. There was simply no way I was in a mental state capable of getting me through any attempt to tell them face to face.

My private counsellor agreed. I had been seeing her for a few months after struggling to sleep for the endless carousel of stresses going around and around in my head. She specifically stated she was LGBT friendly and had experience dealing with issues arising from that, which had put paid to some of the worries I'd had after my first attempt. The need to talk to someone who might understand was becoming paramount and also served to drive me into seeking and paying for private therapy, as my physical health began to suffer the effects of stress. The counsellor was separate from the university and I could keep it risk-free in that regard and so, despite the cost, I began pouring my heart out to this kindly middle-aged lady in a small room at the back of her house. Of course what I really wished was that she wasn't just an LGBT-friendly councillor, but a member of a GIC care team and this was marking the beginning of my physical transition. However, in lieu of that, being able to use someone as a sounding board and have thoughts returned to me was unbelievably helpful at loosening the pressure valve on my mind. It was there that I realised conversing with yourself is only so helpful and that much can be said for speaking it out to another person, even if they can't offer you all you are hoping for in return.

I worked for three weeks on my letter, making sure it not only told them of my truth but contextualised it for them and set forth the seriousness of my conviction, the right I had to make it and the fact this was a recognised condition and most definitely not a mental disorder. The only thing left to do was send it. Before I could do so Easter was upon us and that meant the physical arrival of my parents and James for a long weekend stay with the caravan in the nearby Peak District. Even though I had lived nearby for nearly three years, I had never actually ventured into the Peaks, despite several social invitations, which I had turned down for fear of walking myself into the need to remove an item of breast-hiding material. We had a good day going for a short walk in the forest beside a dam, which was followed by a bad night listening to Dad snore his head off with no possibility of escape in that tin can. As a result I was already tired and irritable for the second day of our gathering and by the time we went for dinner at the lovely pub where I'd arranged my lab's most recent Christmas dinner, I was really quite exhausted. This fact was distinctly not helping my fight to keep the burden of my growing secret from overwhelming my emotions, a fight made inordinately harder by being in James's presence. All my old jealousies were alive and kicking, whipping up my dysphoria into a frenzy.

Unfortunately James and Dad were in a debating mood. James, who is interested in philosophy, loves a good debate and in my opinion is very skilled at it, he pivots wells and uses just enough aggression and volume to hammer points home. But I was in no mood or in any fit state to be even peripherally involved. Sadly, I would have no such luck. The debating started on other topics, but the subject of my apparent listlessness in life was soon dragged into it, probably because I was sat there so obviously shadowed by a moody introspection. I was immediately defensive, like an injured animal being harassed by well-meaning rescuers. I can longer remember what was said, probably because of the emotional outburst that followed, but I know I tried to explain myself whilst giving absolutely nothing away, a tactic that did not serve me well at all. They took my vagueness and refusal to be drawn on any point as a sign I was just being ridiculous. I was also irritated by this seeming demand that I should have to mount a defence for my behaviour: that's not a good thing to do to someone gripped by depression. The exchange became more heated and began morphing into other topics as James's points inched closer to the line. He was so adamant in his opinions and whilst I can no longer remember what they were, they were such that alarm bells went off in my head and I was suddenly gripped by a terror that he was not going to be as receptive as I had hoped to the information I had to share. The thought of him trying to debate me over my identity and thus attempt to debate me out of it, was more than I could deal with. In my state I would be no match for him in that arena. The extreme emotions of anger and frustration of being sucked into justifying my identity whilst simultaneously trying to assert the fact I was not required to justify it to anyone, would very likely paralyse my capacity for coherent thoughts.

In the face of this future prospect, I lost the fight against my emotions and these new fears were engulfed into the tidal waves of anguish which burst forth from just below my surface. Fortunately, we had reached the end of our meal and I was able to rush unceremoniously from the restaurant and collapse into ugly sobbing against the side of the car. It was an uncomfortable journey of silence back to the caravan in which I hid myself under both my hoods. Once there, Dad tried to soothe my distress in an effort to smooth over this interruption to our happy family gathering, but by now I was so defenceless against the outpouring of my emotions that at the first sign of tenderness I collapsed completely into a sobbing, wracked shell of a person. I was full up; I had reached the absolute end of my capacity to cope – with dysphoria, with jealousy, with my secrets, with everything. 'I've got something I have to tell you,' I managed to get out against his shoulder. 'Well, let's have it then,' he said softly, aware that this really was something real. 'I've written you a letter,' I croaked. 'I look forward to reading it,' he replied, stroking my back. I asked to be take back to my student house, I didn't want to be in their presence right then and I needed a good night's sleep and some alone time to try and patch myself up again.

A couple of weeks later I sat at my laptop and hovered the cursor over the send button of the email containing my coming out letter. Things were simply not going to get better until I took this plunge. The future, *my future,* lay in this. I clicked send. After cycling to work I sent Dad a text to inform him to check his inbox and then tried my best to get some work done, dreading what might be taking place in a house 150 miles North. A couple of hours later my pocket buzzed signalling the arrival of a text marking the first contact between myself and my parents in the post coming out world. I left my work and locked myself in a toilet cubicle. Sitting down on the closed lid, I pulled up the text, pushing through the impulse to stop and stay in the safety of that Schrödinger paradox: dead and alive, accepted and rejected. The text was short, 'Read your letter. It was brave of you to send it. You're not alone anymore. Will talk more later. We love you.' Accepted. Well, option 1 accepted at least, which was a guarantee of love and domestic support. It was unclear if option 2 had been declared, but I didn't worry myself over that right then. This was enough for now and I let myself quietly cry out the anxiety and tension which had kept me up half the night.

The 'later' of the text would not come for a couple of months, until the four of us had convened up North for a summer break. I was excited and terrified. Could I control my emotions during the inevitable conversation? Could I keep a hold of my points? My big fear was that they would try to throw their religion at me as a justification for withholding option 2 – full support and true acceptance. I am an atheist for want of actual objective evidence and this is an area in which my parents and I have clashed a number of times. I made no attempts to prompt The Conversation; I felt it had to be them. Only they knew if they were ready and I didn't want to push it, though there was the definite shadow of the elephant in the room. It didn't last long, however, for it was only on the second morning that Mum, who does not count subtlety among her many gifts, instigated The Conversation by telling me how difficult they were finding it and then she brought around the subject of their religious beliefs. I was defensive but she doubled down and it grew more and more heated. I could not do it; I could not contain my emotions. I knew it was going to be hard, but not like this. I ran to my room overcome with tears. Option 2 was receding into the distance even as I reached for it and I began to lose hope they would ever make it to acceptance and understanding. 'The year of the trans tipping point' – that seemed like nothing but empty words as I cried into my pillow. I briefly thought about leaving, getting a taxi and buying a train ticket back to Sheffield, but it quickly dawned on me that I could not afford the monstrous fare of such a last minute ticket. I was trapped in this situation with people who it appeared to me were determined to use their religion to invalidate my identity. The anger was immense and I vowed not to speak to my mother for the time being; if she wasn't going to accept me for who I was then I wasn't going to speak to her.

We spent what was meant to be a happy family day going around Chillingham Castle, one of the many castles in the area. It is apparently haunted and as we went round I certainly felt haunted, if only by The Conversation that morning and by my mother, who I tried to get away from at every opportunity. That night I sat in my room stewing in my anger and sadness. There was a knock at the door. Dad came in and sat opposite me on the bed. He was trying to be conciliatory and I tried hard to pull back from my anger and see how this must be from their perspective. They were faced with losing the child they though they'd always had, who was set on embarking through a series of medical changes, of which despite my including information in my letter, they knew very little. In short, they were being driven by grief and fear. Mum came in and I tried very hard not to let anger overwhelm me. We had to try and resolve this; it would only get worse if we did not.

But almost immediately the religious objections came down again. I find these kinds of objections to be the worst to deal with, far worse than just outright hatred – at least with them you know exactly where you are. But religious objections are often said with a smile and sugar-coated with protestations that they are being said out of love and for your own good and you're told you must respect it. Of course I believe in religious freedom and respect, but it is extremely difficult being told to respect people's religious beliefs when those beliefs belittle your existence, say that you simply don't exist, no matter how nicely they say it or how sincerely they believe it. I did not and I still have no interest in respecting those specific beliefs which so brazenly try to take away my personal dignity. My parents were trying to argue that I didn't exist because 'God made men and women.' I fought back furiously with all the coherency left in me. I told them everything I knew about trans history, about the suicide statistics, about all the medical data on gender dysphoria and its appropriate treatment. I put my stake in the ground and through tears I told them I realised how hard this was for them, but this was really what I was and if I did not do this they might lose me altogether. Eventually, they seemed to understand to a certain degree. I know I'm lucky, I know many people, some kids just fourteen or fifteen, have at this point being picked up by the scruff of their neck and thrown out of the front door. It was the most emotionally draining conversation of my entire life, but I was glad to come out of it assured of the parental love and domestic/financial support I needed to make it through the road ahead. Total acceptance and understanding so early on was always a pipe dream, but, as ever, tomorrow was a new day.

◇━○━━━○━◇

I often wonder how I managed to get through those couple of years between personal understanding and coming out to my parents. It was a time which I hope marks the most stressed I will be ever be, in which my daily existence was a carefully balanced equilibrium of work worries and gender-related fears. I was close to total meltdown on more than one occasion but, by survival instinct or luck or both, managed to ease the pressure in my mind just enough to keep myself going.

Becoming who I was with the physical and social changes I needed to make was not going to be easy, quick or simple and the unfolding reality of that was a bitter pill to swallow. Deciding to wait was an enormously hard decision, but in hindsight I needed that extra time to get my head ready to face everything that would follow. If I had been fortunate enough to live a world free of transphobia, or even just free of blatant transphobia, perhaps it would have been a quicker, simpler process, but I'm proud of myself for taking that first leap to come out and for making it through telling my parents – arguably the scariest thing of all.

Standing up for myself during The Conversation marked a point in my personal development in which I knew I could handle everything else that needed to be done. I would meet the challenges of patience and frustration, which awaited me in the next chapter of my life head on and with a newly invigorated fierce determination.

Chapter 11

WALKING THE RIGHT PATH

DOWNSTAIRS DECISIONS

I returned to Sheffield exhausted from the emotions of the holiday at home up North, but relieved to have made it through to the other side of that momentous showdown. I was glad I lived away during this time, having that physical space between us allowed for my parents to process this change and begin to go through the grieving they needed to go through in their own time. I needed to be alone too. The frustration and stress from waiting to transition had begun to fill the stress vacancy in my mind previously held by the fear of telling my parents and I was prone to outbursts of irritability, which would have been more difficult to cope with in closer proximity to family.

I did my best to combat this frustration by seeing what else could be done in the meantime to alleviate my dysphoria. Binding – the use of a specialist garment to flatten the chest – was a subject I was most interested in. I would not be able to do it at work or in daily life in Sheffield without inviting comment, but in the presence of those people I had told it might be a wonderfully freeing experience. I had my misgivings, however, given that I had never been able to wear even a loose bra without The Rage bubbling up to the boil. How could I hope to wear something that was very likely to be even tighter? Still, the lure of seeing and being able to walk around with a flat chest, to be relieved even for a couple of hours of that most exquisitely painful mental distress, was hard to ignore. I made sure I did the proper research and did not return to any teenage notions of wrapping elasticated bandages around my torso, which is a dangerous practice that restricts breathing and damages muscles. Blog posts and videos by other trans masculine people had made it clear the community had developed guidelines for binding to ensure a safe and responsible practice. I was most intrigued to discover the existence of several companies, Underworks and GC2B, who made specialist binders designed for the purpose and that these products were used comfortably by many people up to a recommended maximum of eight hours a day. I took care to measure myself properly and eagerly awaited the arrival of my binder.

However, it was pretty clear to me almost straightaway that I was simply not going to be able to deal with the tightness, or the fact the material was quite thick, which would cancel out any of the cooling effect in the summer heat I might have gained by dispensing with a lump-covering hoodie. Indeed, try as I might, I could not get away from the anger created by the central notion that I would have to put up with these discomforts because I was trying to deal with the breasts that were upon me. These facts combined to actually make The Rage worse. The potential benefits were also disappointing, not that I was very surprised. The laws of physics are immovable and thus there is only so flat you can make things that are so large. Despite this, I couldn't give up on the possibility of being rid of this dysphoria and ended up going through about five other binders at considerable cost, but I was unable to find one that did anything to alleviate The Rage in my mind to make it worthwhile. I was quite disheartened by this as I sat back down on my bed opposite the mirrored sliding doors of my wardrobe. I would have to be stuck with dealing with this dysphoria without any rest bite until that magical future time in which I could have them cut off like I'd always dreamed. For a time it was difficult to wrestle with jealousy towards trans guys with smaller chests, whom I had sought out on social media and YouTube, for whom binding and the results of it were arguably easier and better. I didn't want to feel like that though, I had enough to deal with in my head, and so I consciously pulled away from engaging in anything to do with other pre-top surgery trans masculine people as a defence mechanism.

Paradoxically, however, I began to cast about for people I could look to who had made the physical changes I needed for myself. I wanted role models of what life was like for a trans man who had taken the transitional path that I needed to take. How successful has it been for them? There are now, and certainly were then, far fewer visible trans men than trans women, a fact which always made me sad. The 'trans tipping point' conversations were still going on but were still largely about trans women, although expanding ever more into the topic of trans children. But, even there, it was usually trans girls in the spotlight or having it thrust upon them by being forced to fight for equal access rights. However, a German friend, who was obsessed with their version of the television show *Strictly Come Dancing*, made me aware of a man by the name of Balian Buschbaum who had been on the show and who was once an Olympic women's pole-vaulter before transitioning.

He'd had all the possible surgeries as well as hormonal therapy and had since become a motivational speaker and life coach. I was so intrigued by him, this example of someone like me who had been through the things I wanted to go through and one that I wasn't sure was right for me – bottom surgery. Most interestingly, he'd written a book (Buschbaum 2010) detailing his transitional experiences and I found myself desperate to read it, to learn from and connect in that way with another trans man. Annoyingly, however, I couldn't get hold of an English version and in the end went as far as buying a Kindle Paperwhite just so I could use the translation function and was finally able to read it translated page by translated page. He'd had a different life path to me; he'd identified as a lesbian for want of self-awareness, had been a professional sportsman and had dysphoria heavily encompassing his genitals as well as his chest and other areas. I read his account of that dysphoria and the surgical steps he took to alleviate it with the most interest. Was bottom surgery right for me? The more I read, the more I realised it was not. What dysphoria I had surrounding my genitals was mild and because of that the risks of that surgery he detailed did not seem worth it to me. Neither did the removal of the internal structures like the womb. If it was to end up silenced then, much like the appendix, I was happy to allow it to remain out of sight and out of mind. But I thought long and hard about it in the quiet of my room and made a list of the possible for and against arguments. From that I concluded I really didn't care enough about not having a penis to put my body through the surgery. If a doctor could wave a magic wand and furnish me with one then sure, but failing that I wasn't particularly fussed. This wasn't the last word on it of course. I could and in fact would very likely be asked to examine it further when I made it to a GIC. But, for now, I was satisfied in my conclusion.

Aside from his having had that surgery, looking through his pictures on social media, I realised I was also drawn to Balian for how masculine he looked according to the stereotypical ideal. I was very consciously aware of that and it wasn't without internal conflict. I felt a little guilty about the desire I harboured to make my external appearance be this stereotypical notion of physical masculinity, perhaps spurred by a worry that I was just falling unwittingly into continuing the damaging conceptions of what a man is 'supposed' to be. But the more I checked myself, the more thoroughly I knew that my gender identity and expression just happened to align with what was considered stereotypically masculine and there wasn't anything I could do about it, nor should it make me feel guilty – that was just who I was. I felt assured in this in that I wasn't going to have bottom surgery because I didn't feel the need for it *and* because I wasn't about to have serious surgery just to conform my body to anyone else's stereotypical view of what a man's body should look like.

By now it was early 2015 and a serious situation was growing closer on the horizon, which would force a demonstration of my gender identity and expression. Wonderfully, Gemma had got engaged to her boyfriend, Tom, the previous year and, a month before her wedding, was embarking on an outrageous hen party weekend cruise to Belgium. The thought had briefly flitted through my mind that I ought not to be going on a hen party in case it undermined my gender identity in other people's eyes, but I dismissed that bias immediately. I was good friends with the bride and that is all the criteria necessary to go on her hen party, I wasn't going to miss it because of some dated hang-up. The only problem was that one of the nights was to be a strictly black tie affair. My stomach had dropped when I read that on the list of information for the cruise. The binary choice was clear: tuxedo or evening dress. Images from my disastrous dress-wearing memories paraded rudely across my mind as I pondered what to do. I couldn't do that to myself again, not now, not when I'd already confided in Gemma about the truth of who I was and with my dysphoria so highly strung. It would have to be a tuxedo. Well, that was most definitely what I wanted; for years I had nursed the desire to wear a tuxedo and to be considered a man whilst I was doing it. I had done my best throughout those years to wear suits and shirts to formal gatherings, but it was always in the knowledge that I was seen as a girl (again with the butch lesbian assumption) in a shirt and waistcoat and the trousers were almost always those from a woman's suit outfit. I had never been to a proper black tie night before in which the rules are not just formal attire but even more heavily overlaid with a gendered binary expectation: tuxedos for the men and evening dresses for the women.

Furthermore, there were going to be about 2000 people on this ship and maybe fifteen that I knew. In other words, it was not the sort of 'friendly' environment in which one might feel secure in breaking such a traditional statement of gender divide. What if I didn't pass? Which I almost certainly wouldn't given my chest binding failure. The statistics about hate crime and discrimination I'd been learning also punctuated into my deliberations and made me extremely nervous. What if I not only failed to pass but was barred from entering the restaurant for failure to conform to the rules of dress? It would be against equality laws most probably, but in so protesting I'd have to make a scene and further out myself. And what if they still refused and it was to be one of those cases where you are forced to back down in the moment and complain to the parent company thereafter? I embarrass easily and had no desire to create an issue on Gemma's hen party. But the alternative wasn't an alternative. It was tuxedo or don't go. I could feel myself being pulled by all those years of insecurity and fear into the 'don't go' option, but I fought against it hard. *'If you are going to be a trans person in this world, you are going to have to be brave and courageous and strong in the face of fear,'* I told myself firmly. I had already come a long way and been forced to stand firm for who I was, this was just the next step. And I wouldn't be totally alone in taking it; most of the MedGen girls would be there (bar Katy and Anne who had to work) as well as Gemma's lioness of a mum whom I'd met several times. I was going and I was going in a tuxedo come what may.

The first thing I had to do was out myself to another of the MedGen girls, Jess, with whom I was sharing a cabin. Having gone through several such experiences, I was now leaning hard towards doing so in writing for all future situations, but I had not known or even considered in advance who I would be sharing with and realised far too late that it might be something I'd need to do. I didn't *have* to do it, but it was hard to imagine Jess not commenting on my wearing a tuxedo as we got ready, and I was gripped with the desire for her to know that I was wearing it as a man, not as a woman, and so I told her in the late afternoon as we rested in our cabin. It was the most awkward of my face-to-face conversations, she had most definitely not expected those words to come out of my mouth and was more visibly taken aback than I had experienced before. As a result, the conversation was brief and we deliberately moved on to other topics to skirt over the vague air of awkwardness. It wasn't that she took it badly, more that she really didn't know what to say or do and I kicked myself for having not told all the MedGen girls over Facebook Messenger beforehand. In light of this I decided not to press ahead and tell the other members of the party, who included a number of girls I'd never met before, the partners of Tom's male friends, who were on his simultaneous stag event.

Thus it was with a fairly large amount of trepidation that I headed with Jess out of our cabin and to the bar to meet up with the others before attempting to navigate to our allotted restaurant. Jess and I had got over the awkwardness and had much fun getting ready, in which I spent as much time as possible focusing on her outfit rather than giving myself a chance to become victim to the circling dysphoria trying to tell me I just looked like a woman in a suit and who the hell was I kidding? As usual I'd bought an overly large shirt so as to better hide the breasts and was most pleased with this and the extra rigidness of the proper tuxedo jacket I'd acquired, which I thought provided good cover. The walk to the bar was frightening and infused with paranoia. As ever, when you feel you have something to hide, I was conscious of every pair of eyes and searched every face for any trace that the owner of it was scrutinising my appearance for arousing a suspicion about my gender. But there were no obvious signs as we made it through the first corridor and down the first set of stairs. Men in tuxedos and women in evening dresses were wandering around everywhere, but there were still no clear looks of disturbance at my appearance. I tried to relax but realised my heart was pounding and I did my best to execute a set of cleansing breaths. *'Confidence is half the battle,'* I reminded myself.

The walk was only the first test, however. All afternoon everyone else had been excitedly giving each other the lowdown on what their evening outfit was, swapping details on dress cuts, colours and materials, while I stayed quiet and deflected any enquiries. And so it was without any direct warning that I rocked up to where some of the girls were already sitting, feelings simultaneously exhilarated and terrified in my full-on tuxedo. They were surprised, for sure, with wide eyes and slightly open mouths, but it was with relief I felt them quickly make it over that and embrace my clothing choice without any concern. In the few hours they had known me it had been clear I wasn't feminine and this looked simply to be an odd but no big deal extension of that. This acceptance meant a lot to me and my exhilaration grew to outweigh the terror. Soon after, Gemma arrived in a blue gown with her pink 'bride to be' sash making her remind me strongly of a young Queen Victoria. As soon as she saw me she threw her arms around me exclaiming, 'You look fantastic!' My exhilaration skyrocketed, for she knew the real deal behind this important moment and I couldn't help but beam from ear to ear.

The role clothing plays in shaping how we feel about and how we express ourselves was brought into sharp relief that night. This was the first time since I enjoyed the androgyny of childhood that I had sloughed off most of the costume of that other person I was supposed to be in the eyes of the world and was simply my real true self in personality as well as in external looks. Though the majority of the rest of our party was under the impression I was a woman in a tuxedo, it didn't matter as much as I had expected. That was crowded out by the completely joyous reconnection with myself in this external sphere. A feeling further compounded by the fact the waiters and other passengers all appeared to view me as male, allowing me to lose most of the rampant paranoia of earlier. I realised people revelling with friends in their own bubbles weren't looking at me that closely and, when they did, they simply saw what they expected to see of someone in a tuxedo. Thus I threw myself into the merriment in a way I had not done for a very long time, largely free of crippling dysphoria and the pain of false portrayal.

However, halfway through the meal I noticed I needed the toilet. I rose to leave the table but as I stood vertical, had the sudden blood-draining realisation that I had placed myself in a precarious position. I was wearing a tuxedo and was being correctly gendered; so perhaps I ought not to be wandering into the women's toilet. But my nerves bristled under the fear of being read as female and 'caught' in the men's. *'Oh God, Oh God, Oh God, what do I do, what do I do?!'* I panicked, trying to walk slowly through the crowded restaurant to give me more time to come up with a plan. But I was still paralysed by indecision as I reached the entrance where the toilets were situated. It was only upon catching sight of the long queue extending out of the women's toilet that my decision was suddenly made. There was no way I was standing in that queue dressed like this, it would be the passport to a huge scene being made if ever I saw one. So I pulled the sides of my jacket further over my chest and walked as confidently as I could straight through the opposite door, hoping it wasn't at all obvious that my heart was in my mouth. There was no else in there and I thanked all my lucky stars. It had been over a decade since I'd last hurried past a row of urinals into the one and only cubicle and I was in and out of it faster than Usain Bolt can run a hundred metres, but I had survived unscathed through my first transition period visit to the correct toilets. I sat back down feeling even more buoyed and jubilant, though still partly disbelieving of the fact I was actually out there doing this.

I stayed with the group only for a few hours after dinner before making my excuses and returning to the safety of the cabin. I'm not a late-night party animal and was feeling considerably exhausted from the emotional rollercoaster of the evening's events. I moved to take my jacket off but caught sight of my reflection in the floor length mirror. The funny thing was it really was *me* staring back. I stood still for a moment, just staring in quiet joy at the person looking me in the eyes. This was the person I had shown to the world that night: my true self. I had been brave and strong and I had survived. Instinctively, I moved closer to the mirror as if trying to drink in my reflection so as to keep in my memory for those times ahead when I might not be able to be so open. Then I realised I live in the twenty-first century and took out my phone to snap a selfie, perfectly preserving that image for all time.

BROTHERS AND BABIES

July 2015, slap bang in the middle of the most intense period of work in the whole of my life. I had until September to finish writing and submit my thesis, the culmination of three years hard work. But in the midst of this I was gripped with the desire to write something else as well. There was still one important person I was yet to tell about the truth of who I was: James. I had deliberately put off this step for the longest possible time, punting it way out beyond the crucial showdown with my parents, I could not have dealt with telling them all at the same time. Sibling relationships are different to parental relationships of course, but I found it just as daunting. He had also known me for all my life after all and had grown up with me; this was going to be such a big change for him. I was also very worried about the possibility of him, in his struggle to understand, trying to debate me over and out of my identity as I had feared over that meal in the Peak District. Additionally, although he was a loving and kind person, he had grown to be a 'masculine man' with, in my opinion, a narrow view of what it means to be a man: football watching, beer drinking and karate practising. I wasn't sure how much faith I could have in him as a fellow Millennial, as someone of the most current and meant to be most open generation, for he was not the type whose interests or experiences had taken him on any enlightening journey when it came to LGBT issues. As far as I could tell, his learned biases from our earliest decade remained largely unchanged.

The need to tell him had also been made more pressing by the unexpected news that James and his girlfriend, Charlotte, were having a baby. It had been at our Easter gathering that I was handed what appeared to be an Easter card, but which contained the words telling me a baby was on the way. As soon as that information registered, a tsunami of emotion swept over me, with tears flowing out of my eyes before I even knew it was happening. For I had found myself in that moment released from another of the difficult considerations a trans person who needs medical intervention must face:

the loss of fertility. Though I had always been appalled at the idea of being pregnant, I had harboured some hope of having my own child through surrogacy. But now, even this possibility was quickly fading.

It is hard for a lot of people to have to accept the knowledge that the hormone treatment we need to be truly ourselves and at peace in our lives will massively impact any chance we have of creating new ones. It doesn't have to be this way of course, but gamete storage, which is recommended before the start of hormone therapy, is not available on the NHS for trans people and the private costs are usually prohibitively high. I could not afford it and saving up would take years, which I had the gravest of doubts my mental health could cope with, and I wasn't willing to take that risk. At any rate, I had discovered chances of live birth from cryopreserved oocytes aren't very high (Human Fertilisation and Embryology Authority 2018).

This was not and could not be an issue which prevented me from having the hormonal treatment I needed to have for the sake of my own life, but that knowledge didn't make it any less painful or easier to let go. As someone whose interest in genetics had driven them all the way through a PhD, the fact that having a biological child of my own would now be an even more drastically reduced possibility was proving hard to accept. Though I knew it wasn't impossible, and trans men have successfully given birth after some years on hormones, the evidence does suggest the chances are on a sliding scale. Then, of course, there is the usual ticking clock and I was already 25. But I also had further considerations as someone who could never cope with being pregnant; I would need a surrogate, I would need to come off hormones at the risk of serious dysphoria, pay for and go through the cycle of egg retrieval and I would have to hope they were still alright. It would be a long time before I would realistically be in that kind of social and financial situation, perhaps too long. Overall, my chances of a biological child looked to be very slim indeed.

I had tried to run thought experiments on the issue, hoping to resolve my sadness and come to better terms with it.

Was biology really that important to me? What about the possibility of James having children? That was probably going to be it for my chances of being involved in the raising of a biologically related child. Of course I already had a niece and multiple nephews, but I was all of six years older than my eldest nephew and thus had never had that real relationship as an additional role model which adult aunts and uncles create. But it would be different now with James's children; I would be involved as an adult right from the start with a child who would be as closely related to me as was possible without being my own. Was that enough to resolve my sadness at the probable loss of my own children? It was only in the moment when the words from that card sunk into my brain when I knew the answer was *yes*. For me, the few words on that card had suddenly propelled these wonderings into a reality and without any warning I had a baby to uncle and it was so much more than enough.

Outside my head however, I was being hugged into the chest of the father-to-be whilst he told me that I was going to be an awesome aunty. I needed to tell him and it needed to be soon. Back at my desk in Sheffield I began to think seriously about how to go about it. Having been through it with my parents, I knew my letter needed to be improved, it needed quite a bit more detail about what transition actually involves and much more information about what is known about why people are trans. If he was going to be tempted to debate me over this then I was going to be sure to get in there first with real data. I also thought it might be helpful to include some accounts of how other siblings of trans people had taken the news and worked through their feelings because I knew he was unlikely to search for it himself or even know where to look. In the end it ballooned out so much that I decided to split it into sections and create a full-on coming out folder, which I sent to him with much trepidation. It's quite disconcerting to know you have the power to change someone's life and I kept wondering what it would be like to see that post come through the door and have your whole perception of a person upended in a moment. Though there was a possibility he already knew either completely or partially. I hadn't explicitly banned my parents from telling him and I knew how Mum has no filter. He had also been there in the Peak District and was sat downstairs alone for the whole evening the three of us were having The Conversation in my room. He must have known something was happening.

I think it was Charlotte who first texted me about its arrival. She thanked me for sending it and said they were going to take some time to read it and get back to me. I didn't detect much surprise when James and I had a text conversation over it, although having it made so clear as a thing that was actually going to be happening was hard for him. He seemed a little bewildered but supportive of my quest for happiness. He did make some enquiries into how I knew/how I was so sure, but did not mount an all-out argument as I had feared and I hoped my folder of information had been of use in that regard. He did however decide to write his own letter in response, which I encouraged as a way to organise his thoughts and feelings. When it arrived I saw he had entitled it 'Newton's third law' because as much as he likes to pretend otherwise he is as much of a nerd as I am and because Newton's third law states that 'For every action, there is an equal and opposite reaction.' I had expected an 'equal' response, but the 'opposite' part scared me. His letter did confirm the presence of some disagreeable perceptions and beliefs, but there were no positions that I felt were so immovable as to be a problem. It also confirmed how hard and sad he was finding it, but with assured tones of support and hope for my happiness. For him, I believed the actual pre-transition period would be the hardest, to see those changes happening, but once it was done he would find it simpler to understand and accept fully. For his part, though he couldn't bring himself to call me his brother, he made effort to stop calling me his sister and instead referred to me as his sibling, which was something. It was another relief moment to know I had got this hurdle over with and that road, though bumpy, was not blocked. I was right to ultimately have faith in his loving and kind nature to win out against all else. For whatever he understood and didn't yet understand about me as a trans person, he cared most of all about my happiness, which had deeply vexed him over the years, on one occasion as a teenager prompting him to buy me an unsolicited Nintendo Wii to try and pull me out of a depressive state. I knew that in the end he could deal with whatever it was I needed to do to be happy and that was really all that mattered.

INTO THE BREACH

By this point I had successfully submitted my thesis and returned home to the North. Though, after a brief recuperating trip to burn off some skin in Tenerife, we were rushing down South to the same maternity wing in which James and I were born to welcome the arrival of my nephew. After holding him for the first time, I bequeathed him with the appropriate nickname of 'Squishy' after the tiny jellyfish in *Finding Nemo*, for he really was the squishiest and cutest thing I'd ever seen in my whole life. I remember the first time Squishy looked me in the eye and, whilst I fell further in love, I couldn't help thinking that by the time he was old enough to remember such moments, this would not be the face he looks up at. I hoped vehemently that by the time he was old enough to create memories that would stay for the rest of his life then I would be visible permanently as the person I really was.

It was time to go to my GP. The only problem was I didn't even have a GP since I had just moved to live permanently in the North. I asked Mum, who had seen quite a few of the doctors at the local practice, to recommend the one she thought was likely to be the most open and knowledgeable about trans issues. She suggested the youngest female doctor, who she said had a lovely and open manner. I was hopeful her intuition would prove correct but, even so, my expectation of a possible showdown had not diminished in the years since my initial consideration of this very moment and I duly filled my bag with World Professional Association for Transgender Health

(WPATH) Standards of Care (WPATH 2018) and information about the Northern Region Gender Dysphoria Service to which I was asking for a referral. I tried to practise what I would say because I could feel myself getting increasingly nervous to a degree I'd not experienced since my first face-to-face outing and in this of all moments I did not want to suffer a possible relapse of the psychological choking I'd had then. There were in fact two issues I needed to discuss with this GP, the second one being the unbelievable riots I was suffering in my digestive system. The gut and the brain are more connected than most people have cared to realise, but I knew on some instinctive level that the progressively debilitating intestinal battles I faced daily were a direct product of the intense stress I had been living under for almost four years.

I sat in the GP waiting room thinking about all those times I'd sat in GP waiting rooms thinking about the moment I'd be sat in a GP waiting room about to go in for this, the most important discussion of my life up to that point. Suddenly, I was brought out of my thought cycle by the piercing interjection of the electronic message board, which displayed my old but still-in-use name for all the assembled people to see. As usual, I got up quickly and without looking around, moved as fast as possible down to the corridor leading into the treatment rooms. I had no interest in acknowledging the looks of surprise, confusion and disgust that arise in people who see a person they take to be one gender respond to the call for a person with a title and name distinctly reserved for another. The GP was, as Mum had said, young and smiley and with a good air of approachability. But my nerves were coming and I could feel the lump of anxiety forming in my throat. I sat down on the edge of the seat as she asked what she could do for me. I steeled all of my courage as my survival instinct as much as anything else forced the words from my mouth, 'Well, there are a couple of things. The first is that I'm transgender and I would like to be referred to the Northern Region Gender Dysphoria Service,' I managed to get out just before my voice cracked entirely. I sat looking at her, one hand on my bag full of papers, awaiting her reply as I rapidly tried to *swallow swallow swallow* in a futile attempt to stop feeling like I was being choked by my own neck muscles.

But she didn't even blink and her smile remained in place. 'OK,' she said in her still cheery voice. 'I've referred someone before,' she mused, turning to her computer and beginning to type, 'What hospital is it again...?' 'Walkergate Park,' I filled in, the hand on my bag slowly relaxing away. 'I'm not sure what the waiting list is, but it's probably quite a bit,' she said turning back to me with an apologetic expression. 'I know,' I said quickly. I didn't want her to think I was naive or that it was her fault, she was being everything I had desperately hoped for: knowledgable, open and cooperative. I had hit the jackpot; this wasn't even the first time she had done this! In my tiny, semi-rural Northumberland town, I did not think I even had a chance of finding such a GP, especially not since the horror stories continued to build up online. I felt a big rush of relief as she tapped away on her keyboard and the lump in my throat finally cleared.

As for my other issue, she diagnosed me with irritable bowel syndrome (IBS). I wasn't at all surprised, but I was scared as IBS is one of those conditions with 'no specific origin' and thus no specific treatment. It is often psychological, a product of stress. However, food intolerances can be a cause and so she recommended I try a stringent exclusion diet to rule out that as the reason. It was called the FODMAP diet (fermentable, oligosaccharides, disaccharides, monosaccharides and polyols). Going down the list of banned foods it was hard to see what there was I could actually eat. It wouldn't be that way forever of course; if my abdominal riots were caused by an intolerance then it wasn't likely to be all of them, but it was a hard and expensive couple of weeks trying to stick to things like cardboard bread. Though I did hope desperately that I actually had an intolerance (so long as it wasn't gluten, which I realised was extremely important to me!), for then there was a relatively simple fix to this painful condition. No such luck: the riots continued. In the end, as I stuffed my face with the glory that is a freshly baked slice of bread with butter, I accepted my IBS was clearly a product of the stress and mental anguish I had been living under for far too long and there would be no quick fix. *'I should feel lucky this is all I have,'* I thought grimly, reaching for more bread. Other people don't get off so lightly with the psychological torment of this limbo state of transition. Other people have died on the waiting list.

On 15 November 2015 I received the letter telling me I was on the waiting list for a first appointment at the GIC. Though they were very sorry that the waiting list was 'many months' long. The word from the Newcastle trans support group I had made tentative steps at joining was that 'many' actually stood for 12–18 and was going in the wrong direction. I needed support to make it through these months and so did my parents if they were going to make any more progress. The Newcastle support group had a Facebook page but also met face to face in a building within a side street off from Eldon Square. I didn't know Newcastle at all and it only compounded my fear of the evening ahead, walking through unfamiliar streets on a dark and cold November night and then into a nondescript building. As we waited for the lift up to the right floor, I thought about all the isolated trans people from decades gone by who had also found their way into side streets and plain buildings, hoping they weren't spotted by the wrong people and that a warm welcome awaited them from the first people they'd ever met who were like them. I felt very thankful that advances in technology and society meant that in my time I knew in advance who at least some of the people at the meeting were and had already talked to them online and that our meeting in a deserted side street was not so much a function of a critical need to hide our gathering from the world.

There were quite a few people there because the writer of the BBC 2 television trans comedy show *Boy Meets Girl*, which was set in the area, was going to be there to discuss the show and hear community thoughts on it. My parents went into the little kitchen to fortify themselves with a cup of tea and I sat down trying not to stare at the trans people all around me, especially not the person sitting right in front of me. He was called Lucas, I discovered, and he was the first trans masculine person I had ever seen in real life. He seemed around my age and had bright green hair and was already on testosterone. Looking around I saw people across the whole spectrum and in various stages of transitioning. Men, women, non-binary people, young and old and of many different sexualities all assembled together. It was hard not to feel very young and inexperienced and incredibly conscious that this was not a group of people my parents had ever been in before either and the only thing that would ever have brought them into such a sphere was me.

The meeting began well with questions and answers about how the series first came about, but there was one trans woman there who began interrupting the questions and criticisms being given, particularly by some other trans women, and started careering off into rants about how their opinions were wrong. She did this multiple times and the atmosphere grew more and more heated. This wasn't what I had expected; in-fighting was not on my radar. When so many external forces are united against a small group of outsiders, the least I expected was for that small group to be united in their views and goals. I learnt very quickly how ridiculously naive that was. Of course trans people are diverse in many ways, same as every other group, and there exist a number of conflicting views about how activism should be conducted and what constitutes good or bad representation. But this particular individual was becoming more and more irate, more and more antagonistic, derailing the whole purpose of the meeting. Eventually the facilitator asked her to leave, but she refused and the police were called. All the while I sat near the back with Mum and Dad on either side, slowly sinking into my seat in horror. If this was the community then I wasn't sure I wanted or was strong enough to be a part of it. In my eyes there seemed to be a lot of anger in this individual and I think I saw for the first time an example of what fighting against never-ending transphobia can end up doing to a person. But what were my parents thinking? Where they were in their process of coming to terms with my transition, it had taken a lot of for them to decide to come to this meeting, to go so far out of their comfort zone. I worried that their acceptance and understanding hung by a thread and this disruptive display might turn out to force them into a backward step.

Thankfully, after the police had come and gone, the meeting returned to the topic at hand and then segued into coffee and chat. All the people who remained were very open and many made a point of coming over to talk to me as an obvious new face, including Lucas, who I was most anxious to ask about how he was finding the hormonal therapy. Though everyone's experience is different, there is something very tangible about being able to speak to someone like you in real life, there is nothing more profound to tell you how not alone you are then by sitting and looking into the eyes of another you know understands the feelings you had to keep to yourself for so long.

Another thing that had happened at this meeting was the momentous first use of my name out loud and in the presence of my parents. I had told them in the letter what name I had chosen for myself and we had discussed it long enough during The Conversation for me to know it wouldn't have featured in their own considerations, although they didn't hate it. But I had been firm on it, having connected strongly with the name already. I had lived with their choice for a quarter of a century; it was now time for me to live with my own. As the meeting quietened down for the start, the facilitator, perhaps conscious of new faces, suggested we go around the room and say our names and a little bit about ourselves. I tensed slightly for I had not yet made any formal attempts at social transition with the use of name and pronouns and I wasn't sure if my parents were ready to hear it. In truth, I had been putting this off partly because I was so worried about how they'd cope with that step. Dad had even stated a few months prior that he couldn't do it and I'd just have to change them in my head after every time he spoke about me. But the time was coming and as I looked around at all the people giving their true names, my courage grew and so when it was my turn I went for it. Perhaps it would be good for my parents to start hearing it and have the experience of hearing others address me by it. Later on, during the coffee and chat, Mum and Dad each had an emotional moment, partly in response to this and partly as a function of having realised truly how real and serious I was about this and what it involved. Overall, it was a good end to a tumultuous evening in which all three of us gained important knowledge and understanding.

SOCIAL BUTTERFLY

I didn't insist on a name and pronoun change straightaway however. I had my PhD viva to prepare for and then almost straight after that was Christmas, which was being held at James and Charlotte's house down South. Her family were also going to be there, people who I hadn't spent a great deal of time with previously. I wasn't ready for the possible awkwardness and probable multiple accidental misnaming and misgendering situations. I felt very self-conscious of not passing but expecting others, most with literally no knowledge or experience of trans issues or people, to get my name and pronouns right. It is such an awkward time and I wished very much to fast-forward through it to the time when people no longer had to remember that my name had changed and it all just came off their tongue naturally.

My trepidation of this awkward side of social transition dragged on well into the new year as I did my best to wait out the indeterminate number of months for the magical time a letter addressed to me stamped with 'Private and Confidential' would drop through the letterbox. The months went on and on and still I had not made that vital change, except when in the presence of the other trans guys I was getting to know at the sporadic trans masculine oriented meetings I would go to at the centre in Newcastle. Eventually, the irritation of still hearing my old name and of the endless instances of 'she' and 'her' drove me to take the plunge and set about formally changing my name. But there was no 'how to' manual for figuring out how to go about all the changes to documents a trans person might need to take and if it wasn't for some of the other guys at the Newcastle meetings I probably would have ended up paying a solicitor to certify my deed poll. However they told me there was no legal requirement to use the Government's convoluted method and making one yourself with the aid of the website www.freedeedpoll.org.uk would suffice. I put my old details and new details into the template and watched as my deed poll was made. I printed it off on fancy paper, as I had been advised to do because official document administering departments like a nice bit of quality paper. I needed two witnesses for my deed poll and ended up press-ganging several of Dad's friends who were in easy reach into doing it, friends who I had allowed my parents to begin to tell.

It was now August and my parent's massive thirtieth anniversary garden party (which Mum had been planning for an entire year) was rapidly coming up. I wanted to have socially transitioned by that day for both my own sanity and for that of my family, who I was becoming more conscious were finding this cliff-edge half-out half-in situation to be a hindrance to helping them come to terms with the fact I was trans. It was every bit as bumpy as I expected it to be. Mum and Dad did their very best with the name but were maddeningly inconsistent with pronouns. For my part, I oscillated unhelpfully between trying to give them the space to correct their own mistakes and roughly lambasting them for getting it wrong. The tension between trying to back off and let them get over this awkward change in the time they needed and my rapidly increasing desire to never again be addressed in the wrong way led on several occasions to either Dad or I storming off in a huff. Gradually however, everyone got over the oddity of using and hearing the different name and pronouns and I grew to relax at the increasingly rare misgendering safe in the knowledge that they weren't doing it for want of trying.

By the day of the party I had also written and sent off an abridged version of the intensive letter I had sent to James to most other members of my extended family. I was nervous for this stage, but not as much as I could have been were I not basking in the high of social transition and if I didn't know from the way they had come to accept my sister's transition and my gay cousin that there was no rampant LGBTphobia in either side of my extended family. Thankfully, feedback from everyone was good; nobody was really very shocked, given time to reflect on the manner in which I had always lived my life. Similarly, I finally set about changing my social media, perhaps the strongest statement of all in this modern world that I was ready to be seen. Along with the change of profile name, I published the shortened version of my letter on Facebook to reach all the rest of the friends I had picked up along the path of my life. Everyone was wonderful and again not particularly surprised, most having in their own ways grown in their lives to shake off the negativities still hung on the LGBT community during our 1990s childhoods. I wasn't afraid to take that last step, the younger generations have much more of a capacity to 'just get it' so they say, nobody unfriended me and the congratulations came pouring in.

But I was surprised by the almost totally positive reactions of other generations around me, namely the myriad social groups of my parents, people who were overwhelmingly 60+. I left it to my parents to tell their friends, including the other members of our Thursday night pub quiz team. Nobody made a big deal out of it and everyone was kind and accepting in a way I can't really imagine happening twenty or even ten years ago. Maybe the increased trans visibility had had an effect even up here in the North East coastal wilds. Certainly the decades-long efforts of activists had done something to change the social environment to make it safe to have faith in the people around you, at least those who are friends, and I couldn't help but feel so thankful for the decades of effort put in by countless others from before I was even born.

NO MORE TIME TO LOSE

By my 27th birthday in July my patience and capacity to wait for treatment had run out. The press were now routinely throwing out stories of the crushing pressure all over the NHS, which although it felt like the NHS had been said to be on the brink of collapse for what felt like literally all of my life, apparently now it wasn't hyperbole. In addition, LGBT-specific publications were sounding the alarm over and over about the continuing crisis in GIC waiting times, which were spiralling out of control. My heart would sink every single time I heard one of these stories and my digestive woes reached new heights. Furthermore, having turned 27 I was feeling the first nagging pulls of worry about the way my time on Earth appeared to be slipping through my fingers. Left, right and centre my friends were getting married, pregnant, promoted and on the property ladder. Though I took comfort in the fact that, for my generation at least, the last of those things is proving difficult for a lot of people, I could not escape from the fact I was being held back from even attempting to engage in any of this 'adulting' by the fact I was trans and in a limbo state of transition.

I wasn't in limbo over anything else; I knew what I wanted to do with my life. I wanted to go into teaching, something I'd wanted to do even before my PhD, and if I wasn't living solely on academic accomplishment and I'd been in the habit of listening to my own mind I probably would have done so then. However, I wasn't sorry for the way things had turned out in that regard, I think I needed to reach the rock bottom of the state of my life to get to the moment of self-realisation. Who knows how much longer I would have clung to my half-life without that. But now I was between careers, I wanted to have completed the transitional steps I needed to undergo before entering into anything else that could possibly introduce any level of new stress into my life. I simply didn't have enough space in my mind to absorb anything so much as a mild bit of new stress. Thus, I wasn't willing to start a teacher training course before being considerably through hormonal therapy and having had top surgery. I wanted to be able to give my whole concentration to it and not struggle through the training as I had done my PhD with half my brain permanently siphoned off to exhaustedly engage in battling dysphoria.

My frustration over this 'limbo life' and my anger about it rose exponentially to the point where it exceeded my coping threshold. In my desperation, my resolve to wait for the NHS finally broke and I knew I would spend every last penny I had to my name if it meant being able to be rid of this dysphoria and to get on with my life at last. Since July I had been working as a lifeguard at the local swimming pool to earn money. I set about saving every last penny I could to go into my private treatment fund, which was substantially helped by not having to pay rent to my parents. They knew the situation and if they had any hope of getting me out of the nest for good then they accepted to carry me this while longer. I know how lucky I am to have parents who could and would do this for me, but it still made me feel awful if I dwelled on it. There comes a time in every grown-up child's life when getting free stuff off your parents is no longer a 'win'. I wanted the self-respect of being able to pay for my own self, but during this time it was a constant tug-of-war between that self-respect and the desperate desire to have enough for private treatment so I could at last begin to live my life.

I liked my job at the swimming pool. Though being a lifeguard is a serious position, one hopes the actual practice of it will consist of sitting in a chair and watching people swim. And so it proved for me in this small rectangular pool with no additional hazards and on many a cold winter night my eyes were taxed with keeping tabs on no more than two or three people giving a creative rendition of breaststroke. It was about as much stress as I could deal with. I was an oddity at the pool, however. My colleagues and anyone else who found out about my age and my having a PhD would express shock and confusion over why I had wanted and taken this job most commonly filled by older teenagers and students. I had told them I wanted to earn money to learn to drive (which was true) and to save up for teacher training (which was also true), but this led to sporadic questioning over when I was going to be moving on that grew more earnest as time went on.

Finally, by September, I thought I had enough to commit to private hormone treatment. There were three options to this I could see from my research, two in London and one in Edinburgh. Being in Newcastle I went for the latter and over three picturesque drives had my first engagement with trans healthcare. It had been simply marvellous and mentally relaxing to sit across from a doctor who I knew understood and who was going to do something to help me. I'd had to have a psychological assessment of course, it's required even in the private pathway, though getting over the affront of that I found the experience not as rude or personally intrusive as I had imagined, for which I was thankful. Finally on 17 October 2016 I received my first injection of testosterone. It was a long injection into the top of my backside and I could feel it going in, a sensation which far from being disturbing was actually unbelievably liberating and finally understood what is meant by the concept of painful pleasure. I had a small moment to myself as I lay face down on the examination table with the top of my backside exposed listening to the doctor readying the needle. I had made it, I had finally clawed my way back to that fork in the road and, although I now bore the marks of that false turn, I was at long last about to embark down the right path. I felt like I floated home on cloud nine and went to bed that night eagerly anticipating the changes to come.

UNDER CONSTRUCTION

And just like that, the riots in my intestines stopped dead. Literally overnight it went from about a nine out of ten to a one. Never in my life had I witnessed a physical change so profound and experienced to such a degree the true power of the mind on the body. Nothing had even happened to me yet, but just the mere knowledge I was now on the right physical path had been enough to lift that psychological torment and all the additional pains that came with it. It was as if I had been like a horrifically tightened coil straining under the pressure and suddenly I had unwound. I say nothing had happened, but I had woken up with a mildly sore throat and urine that smelled weirdly of cress (from the oil in the injection). I was a bit worried about the throat until I realised I had no actual symptoms of cold and it was more likely the testosterone getting to work on my voice box. My voice itself excitedly began to lower within a few weeks, at least to my perception. Blissfully, it took just a month for my periods to stop and for those internal structures to 'quietly go to sleep' in the words of my doctor. To know I had stepped off that endless carousel of anguish was a particularly peaceful moment and was the best Christmas present I received that year. If all adult humans are to a certain extent run by our hormones, then to know in that clearest of ways that there had been a change of management was totally and utterly joyous.

I tried not to obsessively look for changes, it's a marathon not a sprint, but I couldn't help the new-found interest I had in looking in the mirror and to realise how my attitude towards physical change was now the total opposite to first time around. I started caring more about my appearance, like the state of my hair, and noticed for the first time things Mum had been telling me for ages about the dryness of my skin. Testosterone helped with that, of course, though I was glad to be spared the worst excesses of acne. One thing I had been quite worried about was any further increase in appetite, especially after recalling how, when James was a teenager, 'having a biscuit' meant eating the entire packet. But actually my appetite seemed to decrease with the extraordinary calming of my IBS and I was able to make a concerted effort to deviate from the 'safe' foods I had routinely eaten before and to make more headway in learning to cook. In this way I lost over a stone, which went some way to ridding me of hips. I also noticed, one morning after a shower, that there was now actual definition in the muscles between my arms and shoulders and looking down, also in the joins between my quads and knees! This coincided with the joy at discovering, as a lazy person, the amount of shopping bags I could carry in from the car in one trip had increased by 50 percent and I rapidly moved through weights in the gym.

I do not think it changed my personality in any way, however, merely allowing to come to the fore that which I had previously suppressed and simply served to furnish me with new self-esteem, which manifested in more personal assertiveness. Some people wonder and worry about whether they'll become more aggressive or obnoxious and turn into some sort of clone of Kevin from 'Kevin and Perry', comedian Harry Enfield's exaggerated stereotype of male puberty. But this wasn't exactly like going through puberty the first time, my brain had already done its drastic restructuring associated with that and I'd lived some semblance of adult life, so it's not quite the same experience. Being an adult in puberty is entirely its own experience. For example, I discovered the interesting phenomenon that is the way, if you're over 25, social female to male (FTM) transition knocks about a decade off your presumed age. The fact is if you present as male and you're 5 foot 3 inches (1.6 m), have a high(ish) voice and a completely smooth face then people generally decide you can't be more than fifteen, no matter how many times you try to tell them you're not even at university anymore. Suddenly, I found myself being asked for ID to buy paracetamol, for which you need to be sixteen, and on my pre-Christmas trip into London to see the MedGen girls I was offered a child ticket for the train. I flatter myself I retain a fabulously youthful appearance but this was getting ridiculous. It was really odd to be interacted with like this, like I was a teenager who should be viewed with general teenage suspicion or with a reduced expectation of responsibility. On some occasions, when being spoken to by cashiers in shops or people in authority, I felt irritatingly patronised and quite a bit like saying, 'Excuse me, but I'm actually sliding towards 30! I may even be older than you!' I don't remember feeling like that when I really was a teenager and wondered whether that was simply a perception thing at the time or whether this marked a difference in the way people treat teenage boys as opposed to the girl I had presented then.

Another thing that can come into play during transition is the acquisition of male privilege. As a young child I had experienced both female lack of privilege and male privilege, sometimes within minutes of each other depending on how individual people perceived my gender. But as I grew to become entirely stereotypically masculine in my presentation I feel I escaped the worst excesses of patriarchal patronisation and the dangers of being a young woman in this world. I still remember the shock when, after a night out at the point where the MedGen girls were parting ways, Kelly said to everyone, 'Make sure to text when you get in.' I remember thinking for a split second, 'But why?', before I realised it was to let each other know we had all made it home safely. Since I rarely went out on nights out I wondered if this was something they always did. I walked home thinking like I'd never done before about the cautious way in which girls are forced to live their lives and how these restrictions applied and didn't apply to me because of my expression. The most serious thing of that nature that had ever happened to me was the time at the children's holiday club up at the leisure centre when I was around seven where a boy of maybe thirteen had made a point of groping my bum whenever he passed me. I had not known how to protect myself and I'd never told anyone it was the reason I refused to go back. But nothing anywhere close to this had occurred to me since I became outwardly masculine and my only experience of things like cat-calling was when it was directed at Katy during our walk that day to the Boys' Grammar. I was outwardly shocked and inwardly furious at the perpetrator, but Katy looked annoyed yet resolute to ignore it and I could tell this wasn't the first time it had happened. Neither had I ever felt like I'd been shut down in meetings or otherwise passed over or patronised because of my apparent gender. I still wonder whether this was real or whether I was merely blind to it. Yet, as I starting gaining a deeper voice and some musculature, I noticed several things that appeared to be my first tastes of explicit male privilege the likes of which I had not previously experienced. At the swimming pool groups of problematic teenage boys would actually heed my warnings the first time instead of fixing me with a manic smile and continuing on with their attempts to crack their heads open on the side. I grew very quickly to enjoy this new found respect and power. I did not however enjoy the way it made me appear a threat to girls who stood at the bus stop. Once after I sat down next to a girl in the shelter she got straight up and went to stand facing me under the light of the lamp post whilst giving me regular glances. I don't know if she did indeed feel worried about my presence but it certainly felt that way to me. I've yet to enter the world of work fully after having transitioned but I am determined to be on alert for male privilege. I have no interest in using it to my advantage and feel the importance of being one of those people well placed to shine a rare perspective on it. I will not be letting it slide.

Starting hormone therapy also means you find yourself in greater contact with medical services than you may have been in previously. In the beginning, especially, you need to have bloods checked fairly frequently to make sure your body is dealing with it fine and to check your levels of testosterone over the course of time so as to work out the best timespan between injections. I had been fortunate enough to secure shared care with my NHS GP and the private clinic, in which the GP agrees to prescribe with the bloods checked by the specialist at the clinic. GPs don't have to work with private clinics but this is how it works with NHS gender clinics also, although, even with that, many GPs are still refusing to have anything to do with the treatment, citing lack of training. I had been fortunate again to find a GP who was willing to carry out the duties of care GPs are supposed to provide to trans patients after I'd had a moment of panic when my jackpot GP left the practice. I wished I could keep her for the rest of my life and never have to fear that walk down to the treatment rooms wondering if I'll have to start from scratch explaining what being trans is and what my healthcare needs are.

I picked another at random, hoping I'd be lucky a second time and wonderfully I was. She was older, which I didn't mind because it usually denotes more experience, but from the look on her face it was clear immediately she'd never dealt with a trans person ever before. Thankfully she was very willing to learn and so began a sort of team effort in which I was more a collaborative partner than a patient passively sitting there being told what I needed and what was going to be done regarding my care. You have to be proactive as a trans person accessing healthcare, there is no other way. Oftentimes you may find yourself as an intermediary between your GP and the specialist clinic, particularly if the GIC is struggling with its lines of communication. You have to be organised too, as between you and your GP you are probably going to be the person who has the best handle on what tests and injections you need and when. Several times there have been trainee GPs at the practice and I have made a point of being a case for them to study. I'd sit there thinking, here's a case you'll probably barely touch on at medical school, but it's likely to come at you with a certain regularity as the social stigma is torn even further down and you need to be ready.

I've been very fortunate with my GP practice, the doctors, nurses and reception staff and sometimes I can't even get over how easy it's been for me given the almost daily postings of health professional woes by members of the thousands strong online support community I am a part of, it still seems to be a Russian roulette. The only issues I've had were in getting my name and title completely changed over on all the systems. I'll never forget the moment I sat idly in the waiting room only to look up at the loud beep to see MISS CASPAR BALDWIN, ROOM 6, written in big red electronic letters for all the waiting room to see. I actually had that moment of finding myself spontaneously leaping clean out of my seat in panic and running over to the desk with my heart thumping in my throat. Having sorted that out, I went over the road to the pharmacy to pick up a prescription only to find the label printed with 'Mrs Caspar Baldwin'. In both instances the staff were wonderfully helpful but that should not be happening. Despite what some press might say, the NHS is not bending over backwards to accommodate trans people. In reality the systems are not very well able to deal with the concept of even binary trans people and you have to be proactive again with making sure you don't end up losing all your medical records when your gender marker is changed and that you do in fact remain on the right cancer screening programs.

Changing my name and title at the bank proved to be a good experience for me as well, although I put it off for as long as was possible out of fear. The support groups were again littered with bad experiences of being rudely told it wasn't possible and the prevailing wisdom was you might have to try several branches of the same bank before you found a person who knew anything about the company's trans change of name policy. I was worried, as living out in the sticks meant actual branches of my bank were even fewer and further between than in the cities. If my 'local' branch said 'No, what are you even talking about' it was going to be an irritating escapade to sort this out. I wished I didn't have to do this face to face, I wished it was like getting my passport altered, which involved sending off my online application as well as my deed poll and a letter from my GP stating my change would be permanent, for which I'd provided her with an exact template. With my new passport it was easy to change my driving licence online, but the bank need to see you in person and I was bricking it. I picked what I hoped would be a quiet time of day and went in doing my best impression of a confident person. I was in luck, the lady behind the glass did not sneer or make rude comments and I felt immediately relieved that this might actually be simple and painless. However, she had never done this before and it took about an hour, during which I sat in a consultation room, for her and the branch manager to sort their way through it.

You get pretty used to being a nuisance as a trans person, a social anomaly which people do not expect and are unprepared for. One other reason I had kept from changing my bank account over was that it would mean I'd need to inform my work and thus my manager at the leisure centre of my change of details. I'd decided it was just simpler not to come out to my colleagues. I didn't pass, largely because I didn't bind and since it was a customer-facing job, asserting my real gender identity would have led to a tiresome coming out practically every day and to the possibility of everyone in the town knowing I was trans. I wasn't ready for that and I wasn't convinced it would be safe, the spectre of transphobia was always there. Friends were one thing, but strangers were another entirely. But I now had to tell my manager, he was a young guy not long in the job and I liked and trusted him. One quiet night I cornered him in his office and struggled through my tightening throat to inform him of the last thing he had in his mind as the reason I'd asked to speak to him. He took it very calmly, however, as I had hoped he would, not even blinking and appearing to understand and accept with no problem what it is to be trans. Though he did have the vaguely fearful look of someone who didn't particularly know what this was going to mean for workplace practices. We decided it was best if I wrote the email to head office informing of the change to details and also that I did not wish to come out to everyone else just yet. It would remain his knowledge only for over a year.

I got my first appointment at the NHS GIC 14 months after my referral and when that letter hit my door mat I actually rather twistedly thought, *'Wow that was quick! I wasn't expecting it for another four months at least.'* Even though I had been assessed privately and was already on testosterone, I was required to be assessed from scratch again. I expected this and went through the motions, although it did seem a bit of a waste of resources. Five months later I had my second appointment and thus reached the point at which I could begin NHS approved hormone therapy. It was ten months since I'd actually begun testosterone, a move that proved extremely worthwhile because not only was I reaping the amazing benefits of the physical changes brought by it but also because they like you to have been on it for at least six months before referring you for top surgery. It is possible to have surgery without being on hormones, but if you want to be on hormones and have surgery then this is the general timeframe. Then there was the wait for the surgeon I wanted. I could have chosen another surgeon with a shorter wait, but this was arguably the most important decision of my life and I wanted the best results I could get and that meant waiting for who I considered to be the best surgeon.

From the point of getting on that waiting list, the wait was over a year for NHS surgery. Unfortunately, the dysphoria surrounding my chest had not dissipated in the slightest with the onset of hormone therapy and now the juxtaposition between my gloriously deepening voice and growing muscles was causing a new type of dysphoria and social anxiety. I had been told at the GIC it would take around only two years for maximal physical changes to take place, which I thought was rather quick given the slower scale of usual puberty. Just a few months into hormones Mum had asked me, 'Is your voice deeper?', which was her way of saying my voice was deeper. Now the problem was I was passing more often than not and when I did so unexpectedly to customers at work I would then have to spend the rest of the time they were around desperately trying to hide the breasts from them or else out myself. Several times I sat on the high chair at work trying to pretend I couldn't hear groups of tweenagers having a whispered discussion in the water below as to whether I was a man or a woman. Nine out of ten times they opted for man and as much as it made my day I would then have to sit with my arms folded well over my chest in a move that always had me reliving all those uncomfortable summer family walks I'd been forced to go on.

Facial hair was also coming in all over my face and rather more on my arms and torso than I had anticipated given the relative bodily hairlessness of my family. It was at about five months in that I shaved my face for the first time and therein learned the importance of keeping one's mouth closed when shaving one's moustache. Being closeted at work but also hurtling down the right pubertal path caused some hairy moments, literally. Several times I had to dash back into the house to shave after having caught sight of my face in the car mirror when about to set off to work. Despite being on testosterone, nobody at work ever enquired as to why my voice was getting progressively lower and I relied on the capacity people have to selectively ignore things that challenge their view of a situation in order to hide in plain sight. Some noticed my muscles though, which I was working on with the help of a personal trainer, Olly, who had to my surprise been curiously excited about the prospect of training an FTM person as a new experience and once again I was impressed with the level of trans awareness and acceptance there is amongst most people.

Training was important to me as I wanted to get into the best shape possible for top surgery, for which I was now so desperate I had turned my mind to the idea of spending literally all of my money on an expedited private operation. James and I had been fortunate enough to inherit some money from our grandparents and, while he had been able to utilise this to help with a deposit on a house, I knew now where mine was going to have to go, despite my hopes otherwise. It wasn't enough for the operation, though, and I kept the thought of it in my mind night after night as I cleaned human fat off the swimming pool changing room walls and swept masses of hair out of the drains. I needed to save as much as I could so that I would at last be rid of these horrific burdens, mental as well as physical.

Every time I thought about the possibility of being finally rid of them, that it was actually going to happen in my real actual life, and not be any more what it had always been, my deepest but most unobtainable wish, was completely mind-blowing. Each and every time I realised that, it was like being a child on Christmas Eve having those sudden moments of shooting excitement at the remembrance that tomorrow was Christmas Day. So close, I was *so close*… Finally, I had saved enough money and took the plunge to book the surgery. 12 February 2018 was to be hereby known as Freedom Day. In preparation, I took to sorting out my wardrobe and laid out over my bed the collection of t-shirts I had hoarded over the years, some for over ten. As a coping mechanism, I would sometimes cave and buy t-shirts I liked and didn't want to bury under a thick hoodie. But always my chest situation had meant I could do nothing more than stare at them forlornly when I got home and hang them sadly in the back of my wardrobe, hoping one day in some magical future time I'd be able to wear them openly and proudly. I could never give up on that dream, however remote it seemed and would move them with me from student house to student house and hang them in wardrobe after wardrobe as Mum lamented, 'You buy these clothes but you never wear them!' But now their time was coming. How profoundly extraordinary it would be to openly wear only a t-shirt in public again, to enjoy that most simple and most taken for granted of things – to walk around on a hot summer's day, arms casually by my side with not a care in the world. Shooting, tingling excitement.

But that didn't stop me being so nervous before the operation, a feeling most akin to the horrible nausea that builds up in the hours before an important exam, no matter how prepared you feel you are. It was a real moment, as I waited in my room to be taken to theatre, thinking about how I had finally made it to this point. In the car on the way to the hospital, as Dad filled up with fuel, Mum told me, 'You know when you were eight years old you said to me that if you grew breasts then when you were older you would have them chopped off.' *'True story, Mum,'* I thought, *'True story.'*

The hospital was wonderful and the nurse who prepared me was sage-like and kind as I got awkwardly into my backwards gown and walked with her down the corridor to theatre wearing the Harry Potter slippers I'd got for Christmas. I looked down at them as I climbed onto the hospital bed and was greeted on my other side by a nurse who commented on them and then outed herself as possibly the only person alive to have neither read any of the books nor seen any of the films. She wheeled me into theatre as I thought back to those times I'd stood in front of the bathroom mirror wishing I had magic powers so as to melt away the growing lumps and how I'd come to appreciate science as the real 'magic' in the world and how grateful I was to live in a time when it was able to free me from my torture.

That image, of waking up on a hot summer's day and not being filled with a crushing dread at how difficult it would be to navigate through the day with my brain being hammered into the ground by dysphoria, was what kept me going in the hard first few days after surgery. I had never had a serious wound before and the closest I'd previously come to surgery was a root canal – the product of my childish lack of respect for the properties of sugar. The recovery was hard, arguably the hardest thing I've ever had to endure, which was not helped in the slightest by my intense anxiety surrounding matters of health. My fears created in that near-fainting train incident still lingered in the background and had intertwined in the last couple of years with a fear of dying before I'd ever actually properly lived. This manifested in a number of ways that greatly troubled Mum, most notable of which was hypochondria. I had not appreciated the true extent to which my movement would be impaired and the tiredness created by the anaesthetic and the pain. I didn't want to leave the hospital, where the touch of a button brought a nurse within ten seconds – every single one of them the salt of the Earth, I might add. The week between leaving hospital and going back to see the surgeon was the hardest of my life. My chest was wrapped in a tight binder which made me feel strongly as though I was wearing the breast plate from a suit of armour, but with the difficult addition of a tube running out the bottom of each side draining blood and fluid out of the incisions and into two pouches I had to carry around with me.

I sat day after day, filled with painkillers, trying and failing to understand the tactics involved in the Winter Olympic sport of curling and wishing I could snowboard. I thought a lot about puberty blockers during this time. I could not believe that anyone could think it would be a good thing to prevent a trans child from receiving them in favour of making them wait until they were older. This surgery recovery was damn hard and how anyone could think it was a kindness to force a trans boy to grow breasts and then have to go through this surgery was beyond me. I counted the days until I returned to the hospital to have the drains removed and to have my anxiety about whether my chest was OK soothed by my surgeon who was very pleased with the result. It was then that I stood in front of a mirror and, ignoring the anaesthetic bloated stomach, which looked much like a carefully cultivated beer-belly, saw my real chest for the first time in 17 years. It was a curious mix of glorious and disconcerting to see it, almost as if my brain couldn't understand it, so used to being intensely braced for the sadness that threatened to overwhelm me whenever I usually saw my naked torso. *'This is not an overlay from my imagination,'* I thought with utter astonishment. *'This is real, this is me!'*

There was still a long way to go, however. The hardness of the initially recovery period had made it difficult to see the woods for the trees and those carefree summer days still seemed an awful long way off. After the drains were out came the next binder I would have to wear for weeks and the tape I'd have to wear for three months after that. But, gradually, the pain and wound fears subsided and with each passing day the tightness in my torso felt less and less. Finally one day I got up and, without thinking, bent down and casually threw on a shirt I'd deposited on my floordrobe so I could go down and eat before having a wash. But before buttoning it, I straightened up and caught sight of my reflection in the mirror. I knew this shirt well; I had carried it around with me unworn for nine years after all. I stopped scrabbling for buttons and opened it to reveal my beautiful real chest. My face broke into a wide, happy grin and I realised I could do with a shave. I heard a bark outside. It was early, so early the pre-work dog walking was still going on in the streets and my parents, who had come such a long way on the path to understanding and acceptance, were still fast asleep. But I was already up; there was so much to do, so much I had planned for the day. I clocked myself for a moment; so this was what it was like to have a free mind, no dysphoria, no coping mechanism cunning plans, no sadness, no shame. I hardly knew what to do first with my blissfully peaceful mind. There was so much I could focus on now that there was space in my head! Suddenly pensive, I went over to the keepsake drawer and opened it to view the old navy crop top. Some people choose to burn away all the things tied to the horrors of their previous forced life, but I wanted to keep this as a reminder of the years I had struggled and the strength I had had to maintain. If I ever found myself doubting my courage, I knew where to go looking for it. I was never going to get those years back, but neither was I going to let them overshadow my future. I turned and looked again at my reflection in the mirror. As I looked at it with pride, I thought about that old picture I still cherished, taken by Kat on the Isle of Wight just before the dark cloud of puberty descended. I had often curled up with that photo, staring longingly at that child, wishing I could return to that moment. But now I had something better, that child had finally grown up.

EPILOGUE

One day, after I had started testosterone, when I was busy indulging in my new found interest in looking at my own face in the mirror, I caught sight of something I hadn't expected to see at the age of 27: my first wrinkle. Down the centre between my eyes was a small permanent crease line. Where had that come from? I frowned in annoyance and got my answer. Unclenching my eyebrows, I recalled what Dad had always told me as a child about frowning, 'Don't make that face or it'll get stuck like that.' I smiled to myself, he was right after all. I quite liked it though the more I looked at it, for in truth it told a story of what I had been through in my life, what I had survived. Like a natural tattoo, it was a permanent display of the mental, physical and emotional pain I had endured over my first three decades, which had often forced my face into that most unpleasant and consequential of expressions.

I see that line every day when I look in the mirror, as my eyes scan all over my face, *my real face*, I have fought so hard to get. My eyes almost always then drop down to marvel still at the sight of my flat chest, *my real chest*, as it should be. I'm not afraid to grow old now, to see more lines appear slowly around the grooves of my features. For I know these days they are more likely to be caused by the laughter found in a full and happy life. The future is good and bright and clear. Gone is the crushing burden of gender dysphoria, which once had me thinking, as I stared at the statue of Atlas straining to hold up the world that stood in the Uxbridge shopping centre, *'You and me both, buddy.'* My world had been a heavy, lonely and melancholic place, ruled by a necessary survivalist mentality. It has been profoundly cathartic to write out my story in this book; it has helped at last to sweep out the remaining cobwebs of pain and anguish from those years of lying and coping and hiding.

I look around at the Internet these days and see videos about the new generation of trans young people living openly and free at wonderfully young ages and am struck by several emotions all at once. First, sadness, for at 28 I feel I only just missed the boat of gender revolution. I came to know myself at 22 because of the rise in awareness, but just ten years advancement and I could have been spared the tomboy presumption and the agony of false puberty. How difficult it was to learn only a couple of years ago about the existence of the Tavistock and Portman Gender Identity Development Service. It could have been different, after all this service was founded in 1989, the same year that I was born, meaning at no point in my life has there not been a service to help children like me. I just didn't know it because nobody told me. Nobody spoke about gender, nobody was out there as a visible presence in the lives of children and consequently I did not know who or what I was or that there was any support. Although, perhaps it's good I didn't know about the service then for puberty blockers have only been allowed in this country for children under sixteen since 2011 (NHS Choices 2015). To have known about the existence, as I had desperately dreamed, of a medicine that could prevent me being dragged kicking and screaming down the wrong pubertal path, but that which I would have been denied from taking at the critical moment would have destroyed me, I am certain.

From this, the second emotion is fierce, *fierce* protectiveness towards those young trans children finding themselves growing up still within an uncertain world. I have seen a number of misguided adults trying to say trans children shouldn't have puberty blockers before sixteen or even eighteen. It is difficult to stay calm in those moments. They don't know. They just don't know what they are talking about, what horror they see fit to condemn a gender dysphoric child to against worldwide medical advice. One expects bigotry and ignorance of course, but a part of me wishes they had a better grasp of logic. When I was sixteen I had E cup breasts, widened hips and had been menstruating for four years. There was nothing left to block. The current NHS protocol is to offer blockers to those children who have undergone extensive assessment within the service when they are observed to have entered into the first stage of puberty, known as Tanner Stage 2 according to the well-established clinical scale (NHS Choices 2016). Not before as the press would like you to believe. No one is giving blockers to seven-year-olds, there is no point, unless of course they have the condition of precocious puberty in which puberty begins aberrantly early in very young children. This after all was what puberty blockers were originally developed to treat back in the 1970s, meaning there are decades and decades of clinical data on the efficacy and safety of this treatment (Antoniazzi and Zamboni 2004). You will be forgiven for thinking blocking puberty is a new thing or that it was created specifically for trans children. The press and associated misguided people would like you to believe that in their desire to push the notion that pausing puberty is a radical and dangerous medical intervention cooked up by trans activists.

Pausing puberty – that's all it is. It keeps a child stationed at the fork in the road so that they don't have to be dragged kicking and screaming down the wrong path, as I was. It buys them time so that they can reach an intellectual competency in order to make an informed decision upon embarking on any irreversible treatment, which in practice is the taking of hormones, testosterone or oestrogen. In England this step can only be taken once the young person has been assessed further and reached the age of sixteen (NHS Choices 2016). Thus, a trans person does not get anywhere near permanent medical intervention until they are sixteen, which incidentally is also the age at which a person is first deemed capable of deciding to become a parent – arguably the biggest responsibility a person will ever possess. I mention that because there are those pushing for no treatment of any description of trans people until they are eighteen on the grounds that they are somehow still too young to be making important decisions.

These are the people who claim it is wrong to intervene to pause puberty, saying a child of ten or eleven is too young to know what they want or who they are. I disagree and I do so because of scientific evidence. It tells those who bother to research it and learn that appreciation of gender identity develops by the age of five (Ruble *et al.* 2007). Children are perfectly capable of knowing who they are. Ask yourself how old you were when you know what you were and think about how you knew it. It wasn't simply because people were saying so. Cisgender (non-trans) boys for example aren't just blindly swallowing it when their mum calls them a 'good boy', they know who they are and thus so do trans kids. If you are not too young to know you are cis then you are not too young to know you are trans. Actually listening to children is vital. Some people worry about differentiating between those kids who are non-conforming or simply going through 'a phase' of opposition to their assigned gender, they will worry about those kids who might say they are another gender as easily as they may say they are a dog or a cat as a form of play. To that I say gender dysphoria is not a game and that soon becomes apparent to the caregiver of a child who is able to be vocal. Phases pass, dysphoria does not. For example, as a child I did in fact spend a few blissful months tearing around my house on all fours with my fingers bent into paws in the hope of making myself as cheetah-like as possible. But I grew out of it and found other ways to appreciate the majesty of the world's fastest land animal. I never grew out of knowing I was not a girl. Indeed, it was actually part of my dysphoria coping mechanisms – I would rather have spent my days as a male cheetah cub called Speedy than as a human girl called Katie. Listen to the child and the differences between a silly game and a deep-seated inner pain will become as clear to you as the differences between Earth and Mars.

In regard to those who say there should be no medical intervention at all in people under sixteen or eighteen, I speak in the strongest possible terms as someone who has suffered the consequences of such inaction. Not blocking puberty in children with gender dysphoria who indicate its importance to their lives is not a neutral act. It is not a course that does no harm. The choice is not a one-sided decision as to whether to intervene to pause puberty for to not pause puberty is itself just as much a decision, arguably more so as one within extremely severe consequences. Anti-trans individuals or organisations, be they brazen with their bigotry or skilled in the subtle art of 'concern trolling' (masking bigotry inside seemingly helpful 'concerns' about the person's welfare or the impact on others, see also 'hate the sin, love the sinner'), do their best to muddy this water. Because of their efforts you will be forgiven for thinking pausing puberty involves pumping an eleven-year-old child's bloodstream full of powerful hormones with irreversible effects. It does not. They are GnRH (gonadotrophin-releasing hormone) agonists that prevent the pituitary gland from releasing LH (luteinising hormone) and FSH (follicle stimulating hormone), which begin the pubertal changes and bring on the release of testosterone or oestrogen (Kaplowitz and Bloch 2015). In layman's terms, they jam the signal. Stop the jam and the signal gets through just fine. It is simple and it is reversible. But I'll tell you what does involve pumping an eleven-year-old child's bloodstream full of powerful and irreversible hormones: puberty. And that is why not deciding to pause puberty is not a neutral act. When it comes to trans children at this junction, there is no such thing as do something or do nothing. Surely then it is better to intervene medically with the use of blockers than to force the child to be dragged down what is very likely to be the wrong path that distorts their body away from where it should be in ways that are difficult and painful to rectify later on. In what other area of medicine would we, after finding out what is wrong, insist someone suffer terribly with extremely escalated and difficult to reverse symptoms for many further years before we offer them any treatment?

It is here that these people will say that taking blockers puts a child 'on a path' to taking irreversible hormones. They say this because they have no appreciation of the effort that goes into assessing children for blockers. To be shocked that those children accepted after a great deal of assessment onto a plan to use puberty blockers are very likely to then go on to take hormones at the approved time is akin to expressing shock that those who are accepted onto a maths degree course are much more likely than anybody else to become professional mathematicians.

It's generally at this point that they drop all pretence to reveal their true belief, which is that there is no such thing as being transgender and to say that you are makes you at best an object of pity and at worst a disgusting perverted maniac. In any regard you are certainly deemed to have a mental illness. There are these people as there are those who still believe there is no such thing as being gay or there is no such thing as the Earth being round. Such people are currently in that order of prevalence. It is one of the jobs still left to activism to make trans deniers as scarce as round Earth deniers and to be seen in the same light. I make this comparison because it is probably never going to be possible to entirely rid the world of anti-trans bigots, given the way the continued existence of Flat-Earthers has shown how human stupidity is apparently infinite, just as Einstein suggested. But they are few in number and if they want to believe the Earth is flat and hatch a plan to sit in their own rocket and launch themselves to prove it (Belam 2017) then they can knock themselves out. What they do not get is to be in positions of power in which they can influence NASA policy and mission choices.

The same goes for anti-trans people. Just presently they are trying very hard, with varying degrees of subtlety, to influence Government policy regarding trans issues, doing so under the usual guise of championing the rights of women and girls. But they reveal their anti-trans animus immediately by making it clear they pit the rights of cis women and girls against those of trans women and girls in the belief that these groups are in direct opposition. They are of course in no such thing. As is so often pointed out to mostly deaf ears, there are many ways to be a woman, to experience womanhood and one cannot say that the experience of any one woman is necessarily the same as another, there are far too many variables in everyone's lives for that – ethnicity, ability and age to name a few. Thus, being a trans women is just another way of being a woman and just as valid. It's here that they will launch into a diatribe about biology and how possession of a womb or XX chromosomes are some kind of gold standard of womanhood. And there was me thinking an important tenant of feminism was refusing to allow woman to be defined and constrained because of their bodies. There are more ways than being a trans woman to be born without a womb. In terms of chromosomes, I say show me your karyotype and I'll show you mine. Not that any of it matters, given how chromosomes play no part in daily life, but it is fact that nobody knows for sure what their chromosomes are without testing, no matter how sure they think they are. It's sweet in a way how bigots think biology is simple; it always makes me think back to those nights during my degree spent banging my head against the top of a large stack of thick textbooks. Biology and genetics and development are simple until they're not, so they can stop waving about that O-level from 1985 because they're just embarrassing themselves. You can start with Ainsworth (2015) if you're interested. We will not be going down the road that some US lawmakers are seemingly itching to go down in the putting of chromosomes and apparent physicality on a pedestal as the most important determinants of a person's gender (Steinmetz 2016). Are they going to want to start scanning people's cells before bathroom entry? It is important to be careful what you wish for, especially with biology. We know better and we are better.

But they keep trying. The Government's proposal to at long last review and change the Gender Recognition Act (GRA 2004) is causing a huge swell of transphobia from assorted places, in parliamentary parties, in the press and in the public. Whilst, at the time of writing in 2018, Brexit shrouds us all in a cloud of apprehension I, at the time of writing in 2018, am getting tired of worrying about when we can expect this review to happen and exactly what the outcome will be. It should be relatively straightforward as politics goes, given that both Government and Opposition party leaders have stated public support for it (Duffy 2017) as a key recommendation of the Woman and Equalities Committee Transgender Equality report of 2016 (Woman and Equalities Committee 2016). It is not a vote-losing issue and would in fact be beneficial to the Conservative Party, who seem to be haemorrhaging young people's support. The problem is, the longer they drag it out, the more time there is to fill heads will transphobic nonsense. The small but incredibly vocal group of pseudo-feminists, also known as TERFs (trans-exclusionary radical feminists), have been around for many years screaming their same old junk theories into the void and just lately on Twitter. I had the misfortune of running into them there myself without realising it a few months back and began what I thought was an educational conversation. However, as is their custom, I soon noticed they were referring to me as 'he' not because they knew I was a trans man but because they had assumed I was a trans woman. Clearly, they keep to common decency only so far as they know the wider public are definitely looking. You can always tell an anti-trans bigot by the way they deliberately misgender people and in the cunning way in which they use phrases like 'trans-identified male' and the use of 'transgender' as a noun so as to be able to drop the word 'people' from sentences – a common tactic in the dehumanisation of any marginalised group one hopes to prevent others from seeing as fellow human beings.

As I say, in the public domain for the most part they try their best to keep within the cloak of concern trolling so as to maintain some air of respectability and have been aided in this by counting on the sympathies of several major newspapers, and by candidates now mostly either suspended or removed from several parties (see the all-woman's shortlist fiasco). The almost weekly edition of 'Transphobia on Sunday' with added mid-week extras has been running with increased momentum since the GRA reform proposal was announced. As a trans person, waking up on a Sunday in the latter half of 2017 and into 2018 was like waking up on some kind of anti-birthday. *'What transphobia has the press got for me today?'*, I'd wonder. See Wardlaw (2017) for a useful roundup. If you read newspapers you probably have noticed a certain rise in the amount of discussion over trans people and rights. It's not out of any kind of desire for enlightenment, it's because of the GRA review. It's an excellent opportunity for them to whip up a Section 28-style moral panic to further poison the public's minds about trans people, to try and keep us in the shadows and inch closer to what I fear is their ultimate aim, which is not only to prevent the GRA overhaul but to altogether remove the trans protections from the Equality Act (2010). What else is there to expect from a group who don't believe in the existence of trans people?

In order to do this they are concern trolling at an Olympic level and employing the art of pretending one thing is actually something else. This is a very common tactic, with a notable example being the way, during the debates on marriage equality, an argument against was put up as 'there shouldn't be marriage equality because children need a mother and a father.' That is of course not an argument against marriage, but an argument, such as it is, against same-sex adoption laws, which had already passed. But it was used with wild abandon during those debates to merge two hot-button issues together in an attempt to bamboozle people who might be against same-sex parenting into voting against same-sex marriage. Here, in the same way, proposed changes to the GRA are being conflated with a twisted rendition of issues pertaining to trans rights that are already a feature of the Equality Act in an attempt to confuse people over what the GRA proposals actually mean. The GRA changes will simply mean a trans person will be able to obtain a corrected birth certificate without having to subject themselves to an insulting medicalised process. This is important in marriage and in the ability to change your record at the tax office. Currently a trans person must submit a large quantity of personal information, including detailed medical and psychiatric reports, despite medical treatment not being a requirement of the GRA, to a unseen panel of people whose say over your ability to fully live your own identity is absolute. It is insulting and degrading and I, for one, have zero interest in subjecting myself to it. Why should I have to yield such a decision to anyone else? The only person who gets to make those decisions is me. At any rate I still don't even qualify to apply, given they make you wait two years from the time you legally change your name. This is despite having changed my passport (both name and gender marker) a year ago as well as my bank, NHS records and driving licence. I did all those things by self-declaration, aided by my deed poll and a simple letter from my GP stating the change is to be permanent. The GRA changes are merely to bring correcting the birth certificate in line with this. It is quite odd indeed to have only one piece of documentation held off to one side when arguably more important documentation, at least from a day-to-day standpoint, have been subject to self-declaration for years. The self-identification procedure for birth certificate is working blissfully in Ireland among several other countries. It is not, as the anti-trans brigade would have you believe, a procedure so easy as to be akin to buying something from Amazon, as if there is some kind of website featuring a button that says 'change your legal gender with one click' and then another that says 'change it back again with one click'. In Ireland a person must complete a form and then have it witnessed by a solicitor or a notary public (Department of Employment Affairs and Social Protection 2016). It is a serious undertaking.

They are trying to frame this procedure as one open to abuse. Unsurprisingly they do so with no evidence (Brooks 2018). But to spread this fear they have wrapped it into concern trolling about the effects on woman and girls (which to them means cis women and girls) and conflated it with rights already present from the Equality Act, such as the right to use the public facilities to which you identify. As I described in Chapter 6, trans people have the right to go where they identify and at any rate there are no particular laws about who can actually go where. Yet this would appear to be news to those proclaiming how adopting the Irish system would, in the UK, lead to rapists having an easier method to gain access to women and girls by proclaiming to be trans women. But why? First, why would something happen in the UK when it had not happened in Ireland? What is it about the UK that makes us at such a severe risk when Ireland is fine? Second, why would changing your birth certificate make it easier to enter women's facilities? Do you need a birth certificate for these reasons? No, you don't. A lot of people aren't even in possession of the knowledge of where theirs can be found. I've only got a certified copy of my incorrect one after the original went astray years ago. In addition, as I mentioned in Chapter 6, such criminal-minded men in practice don't look for any kind of excuse to aid them in their behaviour. But assuming, in some parallel universe, that they were looking for an excuse, is that likely to be by dressing up as a women when you are so filled with hatred and disdain for women that you think nothing of assaulting them? Such men wouldn't dream to 'lower' themselves. Again, as I said before, surely the simplest excuse for such an attacker to act upon, if they were to be gripped to look for one, would be to slap on a fake name badge, grab a broom and pretend to be the cleaning attendant. Meanwhile, criminal acts inside public facilities are just as illegal as they have always been and will always stay.

Once that has been explained they switch to what they believe is their trump card – the issues pertaining to sport, women's refuges and prison. These are, however, nothing of the sort. The Equality Act makes clear the conditions upon which it may be necessary to take into consideration the trans status of an individual. That is why sporting bodies like the International Olympic Committee have their own set of standards (International Olympic Committee 2015) and why being trans even with a corrected birth certificate does not automatically mean a prisoner, such as a violent trans woman, would be housed with other women in a women's estate (National Offender Management Service 2016). Women's refuges too are coming out and setting the record straight upon where they stand on the demand by anti-trans campaigners that trans women should not be allowed in (never mind the fact trans women face extreme levels of violence). In Scotland where GRA reform consultations have already taken place, women's rights charities have come together to make it clear that trans women are welcome and that if anti-trans campaigners think refuges do not have years of experience and protocols in place in order to safeguard all the women in their care then they are sorely mistaken (Engender 2018).

I've been talking entirely about trans women again. Anti-trans campaigners rarely talk about anything else. Trans men are still an inconvenient footnote, inconvenient because we often serve to throw a spanner into their carefully constructed concern trolling. If trans women should have to use men's facilities then trans men should have to use women's facilities. Oh dear. If trans women shouldn't be allowed onto all-women's shortlists without a corrected birth certificate then trans men should be allowed onto them without a corrected birth certificate. Oh dear again. The last time I went into a women's toilet, a lady who saw me coming stopped dead, clapped her hand over her mouth and shrieked into her palm. It was disconcerting and awkward all around as I hurried out after her as she went to check the sign on the door. Incidentally I was only in there due to being gripped by the public bathroom fear that infests almost half of trans people according to the latest Stonewall Trans Report (Stonewall 2018).

However, anti-trans campaigners aren't entirely blind to trans men. They've paid attention just enough to overflow with warped misogyny to decide we are simply lost lesbians. They espouse how, unlike those calculating trans women, trans men aren't even capable of making their own decision – we're nothing but silly women who have been swept along in a 'social contagion' telling us it's somehow easier or more desirous to be trans men than to be lesbians. I almost choked on the mouthful of mini-eggs I was eating to help me through my top surgery recovery when I saw in their gold-standard, extra-glossy con-cern trolling attempt at a legitimate trans guidance for schools document (Transgender Trend 2017) that they believe in poor research suggesting 95–100 percent of trans boys who transition in adolescence are really just lesbians. I find that interesting in a morbidly amusing sort of way given that I am one of a considerable number of gay trans men who spent his whole adolescence being falsely presumed a lesbian. I think also of my best friend, Kat, who actually is a lesbian and who also expresses gender freely in her own way. You cannot coerce someone to be what they are not. For the whole of my life, the entire world has told me to be cis and it has not worked. In reality and in my experience, just like cis people, trans men and trans masculine people exist across the full spectrum of sexualities. The perception the anti-trans campaigners have is a greatly exaggerated response to the fact some straight trans guys had previously identified themselves as lesbians when it was too dangerous and difficult to live their actual authentic selves.

Trust me, the world is not about to experience a lesbian shortage because a few straight trans guys gain the ability to live as they truly are. But they talk as though trans men are hiding in the online bushes, as it were, ready to kidnap and indoctrinate another unsuspecting young lesbian who wonders away from looking at cat videos, as if being trans is some cool new fun way to be that will make you instantly popular, never mind that bullying of trans kids in school is the norm (Stonewall 2017). They've even come up with a pseudo-scientific diagnosis for it: 'rapid onset gender dysphoria' (ROGD). As a former academic nothing makes me angrier than brazen attempts at attaching scientific legitimacy to bigotry. This term has been traced in the academic literature to nothing more than a poster abstract and more recently a terribly poor research paper (Littman 2018), detailing the poorly constructed conclusions of the responses from a survey of selected online havens of transphobia (for full details and a comprehensive shredding of this research see Tannehill 2018 and Serano 2018). Anyone with more than three brain cells can see that 'ROGD' is simply the refusal a parent has to believe their child is trans when they don't think they saw any signs of it before they came out. But the thing about being trans in a home and society where you worry about the reception you will receive is that it makes you supress who you are until you can take it no more. It's no wonder that 'ROGD' as a believed-in 'scientific' diagnosis exists solely within the confines of websites in which transphobic parents and individuals set up camp.

Far from making a young person popular, the Stonewall 2017 School Report found 45 percent of trans young people have attempted suicide, a statistic which should be written in huge bold letters on the front of every major publication. Were you aware of that? Ask yourself why you might not have been. There is hope, however, as depressing as it was to see the transphobic schools guidance that advocated soft conversion therapy, it was good to see, among other things, the *Times Educational Supplement* (TES) article (Jarmin 2018) advertised, on the front page, no less, about how schools can go about being better able to meet the needs of their trans students as many are trying to do.

I discuss these things here with some hesitation as to give time to them is to create the possibility of giving them even a tiny slither of credibility. But they are out there and on balance I felt it was important to make sure that if you, the reader, come across them you will know them for what they really are. It is perhaps the only thing we can do, given the lack of power in the 'powerful trans lobby', if we cannot stop the transphobic news headlines we can at least arm people to be able to recognise truly what they are seeing. I for one believe the GRA reforms will go through fine and perhaps by the time you read this it will already be history. But I write out the transphobic and deliberately misleading arguments that were placed against it here because I do not believe those who spread them should be allowed to have that cast into history and forgotten within the passage of time.

In the end it is clear that at the heart of this tiresome crusade against trans people is simply hatred. We disgust these campaigners and that is the bottom line. Some try to hide that fact, many don't. But we've had these kinds of conversations before and now even the press have managed to grasp that being gay is not a choice and children cannot be influenced to become gay, and the only people still really seriously clinging to that are extremist religious organisations. Being trans is an innate characteristic that can't be changed. It's not a hard concept. When I think about this I think of my own family of which there are two trans members, my sister and myself. But I hardly knew her growing up; we were bound almost solely by our shared father. We grew up with different mothers in different decades in different locations with different siblings in a different sibling order. This of course is just anecdotal, but the conclusions of the Endocrine Society are not and they state:

> Considerable scientific evidence has emerged demonstrating a durable biological element underlying gender identity. Individuals may make choices due to other factors in their lives, but there do not seem to be external forces that genuinely cause individuals to change gender identity. (Endocrine Society 2017)

However, it is interesting but as ultimately unimportant to know exactly why some people are trans as it is unimportant why some people are gay. What is important is that we exist and insist upon doing so with full equality. Trans people have no interest in 'debating' with people who within ten minutes or less burst out of their containment and show the true depth of their transphobia. If there are any issues that need to be debated then it will be done so situated on the fundamental understanding that trans men are men, trans women are women and non-binary people exist. If this is lacking then no debate can proceed. It's as simple as that. Being homophobic in the press will now derail your career, as MP Jared O'Mara found out (Elgot 2017). What was OK even a few years ago is not OK now. I look at all those transphobic tweets and statements being published, even as I write, by people with designs upon or established political careers and hope they know the Internet never forgets. The removal of some of the most virulent transphobes in their ranks by Labour after their appalling hatred towards trans women as seen in their petitions against trans women on all-women shortlists and bullying of a nineteen-year-old trans girl who dared to stand as women's officer (Butterworth 2018; Glass 2018) is testament to the fact that the lessons learned in previous fights haven't been completely ignored.

But there is so much more to be done. In contrast to being some all-powerful force, trans people have no representation in parliament or really anywhere else. During my surgery recovery I had the great fortune of reading *Trans Britain: Our Journey from the Shadows* (Burns 2018) and learned how it is that we've got to where we are and in so doing what else we also need to achieve. I'm very aware of the fact that I live in a time where the need for activism is still in the acute stages and I find myself gripped with the desire to contribute to that effort as much as I can. From this one thing that's clear to me is that most of the transphobic onslaught is against trans women. That is one of the reasons I decided to answer the call for more trans men and trans masculine voices in literature, for it is in the awareness of trans men and trans masculine people that the ridiculous transphobia is further seen for what it really is. That and the hatred being directed at trans children. On a personal level, it is my great fear that even now some trans boys are being told that there is no distinction between them and 'tomboys', as I was told, and that they are being forced to turn away from the help and support they need the most. My life is immeasurably better now that I am finally able to live openly and freely as my real self and, with that freedom, I will fight with every fibre of my being to prevent any more children having to deal with what I had to deal with. That's a promise.

RESOURCES

WEBSITES

Be: Trans Support and Development in the North (www.be-north.org.uk): Organisation based in Newcastle supporting trans people in the North.

FTM London (www.ftmlondon.net): Support for trans men and trans masculine people in London.

Gendered Intelligence (www.genderedintelligence.co.uk): Support for young trans people aged 8–25, delivering trans youth programmes, support for parents and carers, professional development and trans awareness training for all sectors.

Mermaids (www.mermaidsuk.org.uk): Support for young trans children/teens and their families.

My Genderation (www.mygenderation.com): Films about trans people, made by trans people, for everyone.

Northumberland Pride (www.northumberlandpride.org.uk): Organisation for annual pride parade and regular community engagement and support events, including a trans network.

TMSA-UK – Trans Masculine Support and Advice UK (www.tmsauk.org): National support for trans men and trans masculine youth and adults.

BOOKS

Atkinson, C.J. (2016) *Can I Tell You about Gender Diversity?* London: Jessica Kingsley Publishers.

Barkin, J. (2017) *He's Always Been My Son: A Mother's Story about Raising Her Transgender Son.* London: Jessica Kingsley Publishers.

Barnes, E. and Carlile, A. (2018) *How to Transform Your School into an LGBT+ Friendly Place: A Practical Guide for Nursery, Primary and Secondary Teachers.* London: Jessica Kingsley Publishers.

Bertie, A. (2017) *Trans Mission: My Quest to a Beard.* London: Wren and Rook.

Iantaffi, A. and Barker, M.J. (2017) *How to Understand Your Gender: A Practical Guide for Exploring Who You Are.* London: Jessica Kingsley Publishers.

Kergil, S. (2017) *Before I Had the Words: On Being a Transgender Young Adult.* New York: Skyhorse Publishing.

Kermode, J. (2018) *Transgender Employees in the Workplace: A Guide for Employers.* London: Jessica Kingsley Publishers.

Kiss, C. (2017) *A New Man.* Leicester: Matador.

Savage, S. and Fisher, F. (2017) *Are You a Boy or Are You a Girl?* London: Jessica Kingsley Publishers.

Waites, M. (2017) *Supporting Young Transgender Men: A Guide for Professionals.* London: Jessica Kingsley Publishers.

Whittington, H. (2016) *Raising Ryland: Our Story of Parenting a Transgender Child with No Strings Attached.* New York: William Morrow Paperbacks.

GLOSSARY

Cisgender Term used to describe a person whose gender assigned at birth is in accordance with their gender identity.

Gender dysphoria The distress caused by the disparity between the gender assigned at birth and the true gender identity.

Gender identity A person's own innate inner sense of their gender.

FTM Female to male.

Non-binary Someone who does not define as man or woman. Having a gender identity that is outside of this gender binary. They may define as somewhere in between, both or neither.

Trans Short form of 'transgender'.

Trans feminine Someone who was assigned male at birth but whose gender identity is towards the female end of the gender spectrum (see also non-binary).

Transgender Umbrella term used to describe those whose gender identity is not the same as that which they were assigned as birth.

Transition The process of aligning one's outward self with one's gender identity. Transition means different things to different people and may include some or all of the following: social changes – for example in name, pronouns and dress, physical changes including hormonal treatment and surgery.

Trans man Someone who was assigned female at birth but whose gender identity is at the male end of the gender spectrum.

Trans masculine Someone who was assigned female at birth but whose gender identity is towards the male end of the gender spectrum (see also non-binary).

Trans woman Someone who was assigned male at birth but whose gender identity is at the female end of the gender spectrum.

REFERENCES

Ainsworth, C. (2015) 'Sex redefined.' *Nature 518*, 289–291.

Antoniazzi, F. and Zamboni, G. (2004) 'Central precocious puberty: Current treatment options.' *Pediatric Drugs 6*, 4, 211–231.

Ball, R. and Miller, J. (2017) *The Gender Agenda*. London: Jessica Kingsley Publishers.

Belam, M. (2017) 'Self-taught rocket scientist plans launch to test flat Earth theory.' *The Guardian*, 22 November. Accessed on 10/06/18 at www.theguardian.com/us-news/2017/nov/22/self-taught-rocket-scientist-plans-launch-to-test-flat-earth-theory

Boulton, T. (2014) 'The surprisingly recent time period when boys wore pink, girls wore blue, and both wore dresses.' *Today I Found Out*, 17 October. Accessed on 10/06/18 at www.todayifoundout.com/index.php/2014/10/pink-used-common-color-boys-blue-girls

Brooks, L. (2018) 'A monumental change: How Ireland transformed transgender rights.' *The Guardian*, 15 January. Accessed on 10/06/18 at www.theguardian.com/society/2018/jan/15/monumental-change-ireland-transformed-transgender-rights

Buschbaum, B. (2010) *Blue Eyes Remain Blue: My Story*. Frankfurt: Fischer e-books.

Burns, C. (ed.) (2018) *Trans Britain: Our Journey from the Shadows*. London: Unbound.

Butterworth, B. (2018) 'Activist who launched anti-trans crowdfund campaign suspended by Labour.' *Pink News*, 26 January. Accessed on 10/06/18 at www.pinknews.co.uk/2018/01/26/activist-who-launched-anti-trans-crowdfund-campaign-suspended-by-labour

Chapman, B. (2017) 'Clarks sparks sexism row with girls shoe called "Dolly Babe" and boys shoe called "Leader".' *The Independent*, 14 August. Accessed on 10/06/18 at www.independent.co.uk/news/business/news/clarks-shoes-sexism-dolly-babe-girls-leader-boys-gender-identity-a7892441.html

Christensen, R. (2016) 'Why NC's first GOP governor in a generation lost.' *The News and Observer*, 8 December. Accessed on 10/06/18 at www.newsobserver.com/news/politics-government/politics-columns-blogs/rob-christensen/article119693873.html

Department of Employment and Social Protection (Ireland) (2016) *Gender Recognition Certificate*. Accessed on 10/06/18 at www.welfare.ie/en/Pages/GRC1.aspx

De Vaal, D. (2018) 'PUB ATTACK Mum's horrific injuries after jealous women "smashed her head against pub toilet SINK" in rage over boyfriend.' *The Sun*, 27 February. Accessed on 10/06/18 at www.thesun.co.uk/news/5685498/mum-injuries-jealous-woman-smashed-head-pub-toilet-sink-boyfriend

Duffy, N. (2016) 'Labour MP Caroline Flint claims trans-friendly toilets are dangerous for women.' *Pink News*, 1 December. Accessed on 10/06/18 at www.pinknews.co.uk/2016/12/01/labour-mp-caroline-flint-claims-trans-friendly-toilets-are-dangerous-for-women

Duffy, N. (2017) 'Jeremy Corbyn praises Theresa May for pushing forward with transgender rights reforms.' *Pink News*, 27 October. Accessed on 10/06/18 at www.pinknews.co.uk/2017/10/27/jeremy-corbyn-praises-theresa-may-for-pushing-forward-with-transgender-rights-reforms

Elgot, J. (2017) 'Labour MP quits equality committee over homophobic posts.' *The Guardian*, 23 October. Accessed on 10/06/18 at www.theguardian.com/politics/2017/oct/23/labour-mp-jared-omara-sheffield-hallam-sorry-girls-aloud-orgy

Endocrine Society (2017) 'Transgender health: An Endocrine Society position statement.' Accessed on 13/06/18 at www.endocrine.org/advocacy/priorities-and-positions/transgender-health

Equality Act (2010) London: HMSO.

Engender (2018) 'Frequently asked questions: Women's equality and the Gender Recognition Act.' Accessed on 10/06/18 at www.engender.org.uk/news/blog/frequently-asked-questions-womens-equality-and-the-gender-recognition-act

Falk, B. (2014) 'How *The Little Mermaid* saved Disney.' Yahoo Movies UK. Accessed on 13/06/18 at https://uk.movies.yahoo.com/how-the-little-mermaid-saved-disney-103214773706.html

Fine, C. (2010) *Delusions of Gender*. London: Icon Books.

Gender Recognition Act (2004) London: HMSO.

GLAAD Media Reference Guide – Transgender (2018) *Glossary of Terms – Transgender*. GLAAD. Accessed on 10/06/18 at www.glaad.org/reference/transgender

Glass, J. (2018) 'Anti-trans activist suspended from Labour Party after posting transphobic memes.' *Pink News*, 23 January. Accessed on 10/06/18 at www.pinknews.co.uk/2018/01/23/anti-trans-activists-suspended-from-labour-party-posting-transphobic-memes

Godfrey, C. (2016) 'How the British Empire's gay rights legacy is still killing people to this day.' *The Independent*, 1 February. Accessed on 10/06/18 at www.independent.co.uk/news/world/africa/freedom-of-expression-the-fight-for-lgbt-rights-across-africa-a6834781.html

Graham, D.A. (2016) The business backlash to North Carolina's LGBT law. *The Atlantic*, 25 March. Accessed on 10/06/18 at www.theatlantic.com/politics/archive/2016/03/the-backlash-to-north-carolinas-lgbt-non-discrimination-ban/475500

Hartley-Parkinson, R. (2016) 'Girl used McDonald's toilets and got kicked out after staff thought she was male.' *Metro News*, 7 April. Accessed on 10/06/18 at https://metro.co.uk/2016/04/07/girl-used-mcdonalds-toilets-and-got-kicked-out-after-staff-thought-she-was-male-5800905

Heath, T. (2015) 'The backlash against discrimination and the GOP's "Indiana" problem.' *HuffPost*, 4 February. Accessed on 10/06/18 at https://www.huffingtonpost.com/terrance-heath/the-backlash-against-discrimination-and-the-gops-indiana-problem_b_6987324.html?guccounter=1

Human Fertilisation and Embryology Authority (2018) 'Egg freezing.' Accessed on 10/06/18 at www.hfea.gov.uk/treatments/fertility-preservation/egg-freezing

International Olympic Committee (2015) 'IOC Consensus Meeting on sex reassignment and hyperandrogenism.' Accessed on 10/06/18 at https://stillmed.olympic.org/Documents/Commissions_PDFfiles/Medical_commission/2015-11_ioc_consensus_meeting_on_sex_reassignment_and_hyperandrogenism-en.pdf

Jarmin, L. (2018) 'How schools can support transgender children.' *Times Educational Supplement*, 23 February. Accessed on 10/06/18 at www.tes.com/news/tes-magazine/tes-magazine/how-schools-can-support-transgender-children

Jarvis, C. and Campbell, C. (2017) 'HB2 off the books as Gov. Roy Cooper signs compromise into law.' *The Charlotte Observer*, 30 March. Accessed on 10/06/18 at www.charlotteobserver.com/news/politics-government/article141658044.html

Kaplowitz, P. and Bloch, C. (2015) 'Evaluation and referral of children with signs of early puberty.' *Pediatrics 137*, 1. Accessed on 13/06/18 at http://pediatrics.aappublications.org/content/early/2015/12/11/peds.2015-3732

Kemp, G. (1977) *The Turbulent Term of Tyke Tiler*. London: Faber & Faber.

Kopan, T. and Scott, E. (2016) 'North Carolina governor signs controversial transgender bill.' *CNN*, 24 March. Accessed on 10/06/18 at www.cnn.com/2016/03/23/politics/north-carolina-gender-bathrooms-bill/index.html

Let Clothes Be Clothes (2018) *Let Clothes Be Clothes*. Accessed on 10/06/18 at www.letclothesbeclothes.uk

Let Toys Be Toys (2018) *Let Toys Be Toys for Girls and Boys*. Accessed on 10/06/18 at www.lettoysbetoys.org.uk

Littman, L. (2018) 'Rapid-onset gender dysphoria in adolescents and young adults: A study of parental reports.' *PLOS ONE 13*, 8. Accessed on 11/09/18 at http://doi.org/10.1371/journal.pone.0202330

McGaughy, L. (2017) 'Texas Senate OKs bathroom bill with minor changes.' *Dallas News*, 25 July. Accessed on 10/06/18 at www.dallasnews.com/news/texas-legislature/2017/07/25/follow-live-texas-senate-debates-called-bathroom-bill

Molloy, P. (2015) 'Here's what it'll look like if trans people aren't allowed to use the right bathroom.' *Upworthy*, 31 March. Accessed on 10/06/18 at www.upworthy.com/heres-what-itll-look-like-if-trans-people-arent-allowed-to-use-the-right-bathroom

National Offender Management Service (2016) *The Care and Management of Transgender Offenders*. London. Ministry of Justice.

NHS Choices (2015) 'My trans daughter.' Accessed on 13/06/18 at https://modalitypartnership.nhs.uk/self-help/livewell/topics/transhealth/transrealstorymother

NHS Choices (2016) 'Gender dysphoria.' Accessed on 10/06/18 at www.nhs.uk/conditions/gender-dysphoria/treatment/#treatment-for-children-and-young-people

National Conference of State Legislatures (2017) 'Bathroom bill legislative tracking.' Accessed on 10/06/18 at www.ncsl.org/research/education/-bathroom-bill-legislative-tracking635951130.aspx

Richardson, B. (2016) 'Woman wrongly accused of being transgender is kicked out of Walmart bathroom.' *Washington Times*, 17 May. Accessed on 10/06/18 at www.washingtontimes.com/news/2016/may/17/woman-accused-being-transgender-kicked-out-walmart

Ruble, D.N., Taylor, L.J., Cyphers, L., Greulich, F.K., Lurye, L.E and Shrout, P.E. (2007) 'The role of gender constancy in early gender development.' *Child Development 78*, 4, 1121–1136.

Serano, J. (2018) 'Everything You Need to Know About Rapid Onset Gender Dysphoria.' *Medium*, 22 August. Accessed on 11/09/18 at https://medium. com/@juliaserano/everything-you-need-to-know-about-rapid-onset-gender-dysphoria-1940b8afdeba

Steinmetz, K. (2015) 'The transgender tipping point.' *TIME*, 29 May. Accessed on 10/06/18 at www.time.com/135480/transgender-tipping-point

Steinmetz, K (2016) 'Gender is not just chromosomes and genitals.' *TIME*, 23 February. Accessed on 10/06/18 at www.time.com/4231379/gender-south-dakota-bathroom-bill

Stonewall (2017) *School Report*. Accessed on 10/06/18 at www.stonewall.org.uk/school-report-2017

Stonewall (2018) *LGBT in Britain – Trans Report*. Accessed on 10/06/18 at www. stonewall.org.uk/lgbt-britain-trans-report

Strudwick, P. (2014) 'Nearly half of young transgender people have attempted suicide – UK survey.' *The Guardian*, 19 November. Accessed on 10/06/18 at www.theguardian.com/society/2014/nov/19/young-transgender-suicide-attempts-survey

Tannehill, B. (2018) '"Rapid onset gender dysphoria" is biased junk science.' *Advocate*, 20 February. Accessed on 10/06/18 at www.advocate.com/commentary/2018/2/20/rapid-onset-gender-dysphoria-biased-junk-science

Transgender Trend (2017) 'Supporting gender non-conforming and trans-identified students in schools.' Accessed on 13/06/18 at www.transgendertrend.com/schools-resources

Wardlaw, S. (2017) 'When will the Sunday Times stop its stream of anti-trans invective?' *Huffington Post*, 22 November. Accessed on 10/06/18 at www. huffingtonpost.co.uk/entry/when-will-the-sunday-times-stop-its-stream-of-anti-trans-invective_uk_5a142e46e4b05ec0ae84458d

Woman and Equalities Committee (2016) *Transgender Equality*. London: House of Commons.

World Health Organization (2018) 'Gender, equality and human rights.' Accessed on 13/06/18 at www.who.int/gender-equity-rights/understanding/gender-definition/en

World Professional Association for Transgender Health (2018) *Standards of Care Version 7*. Accessed on 10/06/18 at www.wpath.org/media/cms/Documents/Web%20Transfer/SOC/Standards%20of%20Care%20V7%20-%202011%20WPATH.pdf